Foundation Expre Blend 4 with Silverlight

Victor Gaudioso

friendsof

DESIGNER TO DESIGNER™

an Apress® company

Foundation Expression Blend 4 with Silverlight

Copyright © 2010 by Victor Gaudioso

ISBN-13 (pbk): 978-1-4302-2973-5

ISBN-13 (electronic): 978-1-4302-2974-2

Printed and bound in the United States of America 9 8 7 6 5 4 3 2 1

Distributed to the book trade worldwide by Springer Science+Business Media LLC., 233 Spring Street, 6th Floor, New York, NY 10013. Phone 1-800-SPRINGER, fax (201) 348-4505, e-mail orders-ny@springer-sbm.com, or visit www.springeronline.com.

For information on translations, please e-mail rights@apress.com or visit www.apress.com.

Apress and friends of ED books may be purchased in bulk for academic, corporate, or promotional use. eBook versions and licenses are also available for most titles. For more information, reference our Special Bulk Sales– eBook Licensing web page at www.apress.com/info/bulksales.

The source code for this book is freely available to readers at www.friendsofed.com in the Downloads section.

Credits

President and Publisher:
Paul Manning

Lead Editor:
Ben Renow-Clarke

Technical Reviewers:
Joe McBride

Editorial Board:
Clay Andres, Steve Anglin, Mark Beckner, Ewan Buckingham, Gary Cornell, Jonathan Gennick, Jonathan Hassell, Michelle Lowman, Matthew Moodie, Duncan Parkes, Jeffrey Pepper, Frank Pohlmann, Douglas Pundick, Ben Renow-Clarke, Dominic Shakeshaft, Matt Wade, Tom Welsh

Coordinating Editor:
Tracy Brown

Copy Editor:
Corbin Collins

Compositor:
Bronkella Publishing LLC

Indexer:
BIM Indexing & Proofreading Services

Artist:
April Milne

Cover Designer:
Anna Ishchenko

I would like to dedicate this book to my family: my courageous and protecting father Ralph; my dedicated and loving mother Elfie; my strong, loving and beautiful wife Shay; my vigilant and wise uncle Joseph; my moral and sweet eldest daughter Brianna; my tough and noble daughter Tristan; and finally, my ever-cautious and fun-loving son Luke. I love you all and derive strength from each of your special and wonderful attributes mentioned here.

Contents at a Glance

Contents

About the Author

Victor Gaudioso, a Microsoft Most Valuable Professional (MVP) and Microsoft Solutions Advocate, is an independent Windows Presentation Foundation/ Silverlight/Windows 7 Mobile/Surface developer, instructor (classroom/video tutorials/written articles), published author, and public speaker.

Victor has more than ten years of experience in the web and software development industries, and has worked with large Fortune 500 companies such as Microsoft, Universal, Warner Bros., Disney, Mattel, and Paramount Pictures. Victor is currently a Silverlight/Windows Presentation Foundation User Experience (UX) evangelist with TechPath, based in Southern California.

In his spare time, Victor continues to write books under the friends of ED flagship Foundation series in hopes of presenting the powerful new Microsoft technologies of Windows Presentation Foundation, Silverlight, and most recently Windows Phone 7 to developers and designers around the globe. Victor produces free Silverlight video tutorials on his personal blog at www.windowspresentationfoundation.com. Victor also speaks all over the world on Silverlight; most recently at the Microsoft Store in Los Angeles, RIAPalooza in Chicago, and a two-day Silverlight boot camp in Dallas. Victor also co-founded the first Los Angeles Silverlight User Group (LASLUG) with Microsoft.

About the Cover Image Designer

 **Corné van Dooren** designed the front cover image for this book. Having been given a brief by friends of ED to create a new design for the Foundation series, he was inspired to create this new setup combining technology and organic forms.

With a colorful background as an avid cartoonist, Corné discovered the infinite world of multimedia at the age of 17—a journey of discovery that hasn't stopped since. His mantra has always been: "The only limit to multimedia is the imagination," a mantra that is keeping him moving forward constantly.

After enjoying success after success over the past years—working for many international clients, as well as being featured in multimedia magazines, testing software, and working on many other friends of ED books—Corné decided it was time to take another step in his career by launching his own company, *Project 79*, in March 2005.

You can see more of his work and contact him through www.cornevandooren.com or www.project79.com.

If you like his work, be sure to check out his chapter in *New Masters of Photoshop: Volume 2* (friends of ED, 2004).

Acknowledgments

I would like to acknowledge the amazing team I have here at Apress/friends of ED; Ben Renow-Clarke, my long-time friend and editor, whom I desperately rely on to make me sound like I can hold an intelligent conversation on something *other* than technology! Joe McBride, my technical editor who kept my words true and my samples working. My sweet and spirited project manager Tracy Brown, who made sure I got my work done on time even if I had to write on a plane on the way back from Chicago (hint hint), Corbin Collins, my quick-witted copy editor whose questions confuse me and who is confused by mine, and all of the other folk behind the scenes in the production, marketing, and editorial departments who have helped to bring this book together and get it into your hands

Introduction

Welcome to *Foundation Expression Blend 4 with Silverlight*! I am very excited about this, my third book, as I have been able to take all the lessons learned from my first two books and make a book that I think really can take the reader from a beginner in Silverlight to someone who is ready to enter the job market as a junior Silverlight developer. After you have completed this book, you will have ten or so Silverlight projects that you can add to your professional portfolio and build upon in your own work. Further, you will have an all-around understanding of how Silverlight works, from the improved designer/developer workflow, to content controls, to custom `UserControls`, to `Behaviors`, and even the all-powerful `MediaElement`. Follow along as I take you from setting up the Silverlight development environment to creating your own Rich Internet Applications (RIAs) complete with video, Animations, and dazzling graphics. And if at any time you get stuck or lost, I invite you to shoot me an e-mail at my personal address: `wpfauthor@gmail.com`. Teaching Silverlight is not something I do for money, it is my passion; if you have the same passion to learn it as I have to teach it, I promise you that I will do all I can to facilitate your becoming a knowledgeable Silverlight developer. So roll up your sleeves, and let's dive into Blend 4 and Silverlight!

Who this Book Is For

Throughout my career, I have purchased many technological publications just to realize that I was not part of the target audience for that particular book. In order to help potential readers avoid this situation, I will outline exactly who this book is for. This book is for you if you know the basics of Object-Oriented Programming (OOP) and have some programming experience in languages such as JavaScript, ActionScript, C++, Visual Basic, Java, or C, but have not used Silverlight. If you understand even just a little about OOP, you can benefit from this book and start to develop in Silverlight; however, if you do not have any experience in any of these languages, I suggest you buy a beginner's guide on C# first. *Beginning C# 2008: From Novice to Professional, Second Edition*, by Christian Gross (Apress, 2008), is a good book and will give you far more information than you will need to make good use of the title in your hands. An extra added skill would be experience with XML (Extensible Markup Language), as it is what a large part of Silverlight is based upon, including XAML (Extensible Application Markup Language). However, this isn't essential, as in this book I assume you know as little as possible, and I start off with the basics before leading you through more advanced tutorials.

What this Book Will Teach You

The following is a list of exactly what this book will teach you so that you know what you will be able to accomplish in Silverlight and Blend once you have completed the book. You will

- Understand the typical Silverlight/Blend/Visual Studio workflow for creating Silverlight applications
- Understand the Blend 4 IDE—what tools are available and how to use them properly
- Understand XAML and C# basics, as well as some advanced C# constructs such as a `CLRInstance` of a `DataFactory` and a very popular user interface design pattern called Model-View-ViewModel (MVVM)
- Know the basic Silverlight content element controls

- Understand the very powerful Silverlight `MediaElement` and how to use it to create video and audio for your applications
- Learn how to create reusable styles and control templates
- Learn how to raise events and EventHandlers
- Learn about Behaviors: how to use them and create them
- Learn how to create an interactive prototype of a web application called a SketchFlow
- Understand the difference between Timelines and Storyboards, and learn how to use Timelines to create complex Storyboard Animations
- Learn about the new features of Silverlight 4, including the Webcam and COM APIs

What Are Silverlight/Blend 4, C#, and XAML?

Silverlight has a large number of framework elements and controls, including `Button`, `Grid`, and `MediaElement`. These are all written in XAML, which is an XML-based markup language. XAML also enables you to create Storyboard Animations. The user interface controls can be controlled partially in XAML using Storyboards, but for the most part they are controlled with C#. This type of structure is very similar to the relationship between HTML and JavaScript, as HTML displays the content, whereas JavaScript adds functionality and interactivity, such as mouse-over effects. Conversely, user interface controls can be created in C#, but are most often created in XAML. XAML can also display assets such as images, audio, and video. C# is a very robust Object-Oriented Programming language developed by Microsoft, and is part of the .NET 4.0 Framework. I like to think of XAML as the pretty exterior of a cool car, and C# as the powerful engine under the hood. So, the typical way that Silverlight creates and displays content goes like this:

1. XAML describes how the controls, images, video, and other assets are shown.

2. C# gives these assets their functionality.

3. The compiler then puts the XAML user interface and functionality together into an executable (EXE) file for a Silverlight desktop or web application.

4. The browser or desktop then displays the application.

The real power of Silverlight is the robustness of C# and the capability of using XAML to create the interface.

Using Visual Studio and Blend

C# is usually created and edited in Visual Studio 2010, and XAML can be edited in both Blend and Visual Studio 2010. Since Blend 3, though, you have the ability to create and edit C# in Blend as well as Visual Studio 2010, and this ability has been enhanced in Blend 4. However, you may still want to edit or create your C# code in Visual Studio, because Visual Studio has tools to assist in writing code, such as Intellisense (discussed later in the book).

Blend, on the other hand, is a new instrument that allows you to create and display Silverlight assets such as controls and images in code or visually. The Selection, Brush Transform, and various shape tools are just a few of the features that Blend offers the developer. I go into these and other tools in Chapter 2, and you will master these development tools in later chapters.

What Silverlight Is and How It Differs from WPF

Silverlight, formerly known as Windows Presentation Foundation Everywhere (WPF/E), is a cross-platform version of WPF. Basically, it is a subset of WPF that can run on a Mac or a PC. WPF can only run on Windows 7, Windows Vista, or Windows XP with .NET 3.0 or later installed (Windows XP ships with .NET 2.0). There are other differences, but most important is that WPF can make use of 3D objects, whereas Silverlight can do some faking of 3D, but it's not true 3D. This is because WPF can make use of the host machine's graphics card, and Silverlight cannot, as it is difficult to port 3D hardware acceleration across different platforms. The final difference is that Silverlight integrates right into an HTML page by using the Silverlight browser plug-in, whereas WPF needs to be inserted into an iframe to mix with HTML content. It is worth noting that now Silverlight can also run Out Of Browser (OOB).

Online Resources

Throughout this book, I point you to online Silverlight examples I have created, as well as code snippets and video tutorials. Currently I have some 50 or so Silverlight video tutorials that can all be found on the following blog post: `www.windowspresentationfoundation.com/?p=587`. At the end of each chapter I often point you to a specific video tutorial that will help broaden your understanding of the subject matter we just went over.

Layout conventions

To keep this book as clear and easy to follow as possible, the following text conventions are used throughout:

- Important words or concepts are normally highlighted on the first appearance in *italics*.
- Code is presented in `fixed-width font`, as are the names of most objects, controls, properties, and classes.

`New or changed code is presented in bold fixed-width font.`

- Menu commands are written in the form **Menu ➤ Submenu ➤ Submenu**.
- Where I want to draw your attention to something, I've highlighted it like this:

> *Ahem, don't say I didn't warn you.*

Chapter 1

Setting Up the Silverlight Development Environment

What this chapter covers:

*   Downloading and installing the tools that allow you to develop Silverlight applications
*   Creating your first Silverlight application
*   Installing Blend 4

Installing Silverlight

Start by opening a web browser and navigating to `http://silverlight.net/getstarted/`. On the right side of the page you will see the Install Silverlight Runtime box. On the left side of the page, you will see a Start Learning Silverlight section. This contains videos, blogs, and tutorials that you will find helpful to return to and click through when you have some free time later. Particularly I encourage you to take advantage of the very good "how to" videos by Microsoft greats Tim Heuer, Adam Kinney, and Jesse Liberty. I myself took advantage of these videos when first starting with Silverlight 4 in November 2007 when it was still known as WPF/E (short for Windows Presentation Foundation Everywhere). That being said, let's move on and start to install the tools we need to begin developing in Silverlight.

Downloading and Installing Visual Studio 2010

The first thing you need to do is to install Visual Studio 2010, as you cannot develop for newer versions of Silverlight using Visual Studio 2008. I find that the new Microsoft Web Platform Installer (the big green button) can actually be more confusing than just manually downloading the required tools, so I'm going to step you through the old-fashioned way to make sure that we're all on the same page. Immediately below the big green button, you will see a link to Visual Studio 2010. Click that link to be taken to the Visual

Studio 2010 download page. For the purposes of this book I suggest you download and install the trial version of Visual Studio 2010 Professional. I recommend that you use the Web Installer rather than downloading the full 2GB ISO file. If you find that you want to continue developing Silverlight applications, then I suggest you purchase Visual Studio 2010. However, if you would like to install and use the free version, called Microsoft Visual Web Developer 2010 Express (available from http://www.microsoft.com/express/web) you may, as it will be sufficient for this book. Just know that it is a free, less robust version of Visual Studio 2010, but it will still enable you to develop Silverlight 4 applications. If you decide to start off with Visual Web Developer, you can always go back and purchase Visual Studio 2010 at a later time.

After you decide which version is right for you, click the appropriate link and follow the instructions to install either Visual Studio 2010 or Visual Web Developer Express 2010. Once you have done that you can move along to the next section.

Installing the Silverlight 4 Tools for Visual Studio 2010

Locate the URL on the Silverlight.net Get Started page for the Silverlight 4 Tools for Visual Studio 2010 — it should be at the end of the block of text containing the first Visual Studio 2010 link that you clicked. This will install the developer runtime for Silverlight 4, the Visual Studio 2010 Project Templates that allow you to create Silverlight 4 applications in Visual Studio 2010, and the Silverlight 4 Software Development Kit (SDK). This is the very minimum you need to be able to develop Silverlight applications. However, we are still missing one piece of software that I consider essential to Silverlight development, and that is Blend! Go on to the next section and install Expression Blend.

> *Oftentimes the links for these products will move around the page. I tend to press Ctrl+F in Internet Explorer and search for the product by name.*

Installing Expression Blend 4

Scroll down the Get Started page, and under the heading Expand Your Silverlight Toolset, click the link that says Microsoft Expression Blend 4. This will download and install the latest version of Blend for developing Silverlight applications.

Now that you have Visual Studio 2010 or Visual Web Developer Express 2010, the Silverlight 4 Tools for Visual Studio 2010, and Expression Blend 4, you are ready to go ahead and start developing Silverlight applications. Now you can move ahead and create your very first Silverlight application to make sure you got everything installed properly.

Creating Your Very First Silverlight Application

Now that you have all the required tools installed, you can create your very first Silverlight application. To do that, follow the steps below:

1. Open Visual Studio 2010.

2. Click **File ➤ New ➤ Project.**

3. In the Installed Templates, select Silverlight.

4. Make sure **Silverlight Application Visual C#** is selected.

5. Name the project MyFirstSL4App.

6. Make a mental note of where the **Location** of the application is being saved (mine is `C:\Projects 2009\SL4\`).

7. Make sure that "**Create directory for solution**" is selected.

8. Click **OK** (see Figure 1-1).

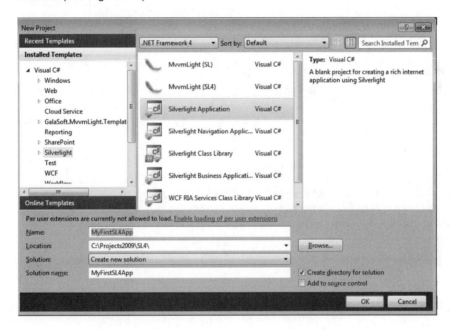

Figure 1-1. Use these settings for your first Silverlight 4 application.

The **New Silverlight Application** dialog box will appear. Uncheck the "Host the Silverlight application in a new Web site" and click OK, as I am doing in Figure 1-2.

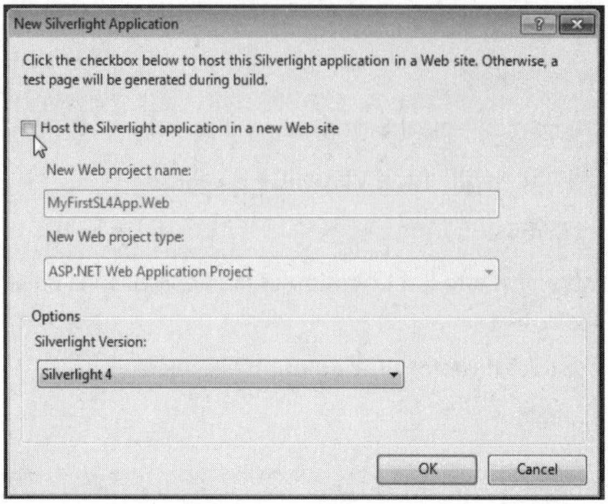

Figure 1-2. Uncheck the "Host the Silverlight application in a new Web site" check box.

You will then see that Visual Studio 2010 creates a new project for you and opens a page called MainPage.xaml. You will learn more about XAML later, but for now just know that this is markup language that builds the User Interface (UI) of what people see when they first run your application. The code should look like this:

```
<UserControl x:Class="MyFirstSL4App.MainPage"
    xmlns="http://schemas.microsoft.com/winfx/2006/xaml/presentation"
    xmlns:x="http://schemas.microsoft.com/winfx/2006/xaml"
    xmlns:d="http://schemas.microsoft.com/expression/blend/2008"
    xmlns:mc="http://schemas.openxmlformats.org/markup-compatibility/2006"
    mc:Ignorable="d"
    d:DesignHeight="300" d:DesignWidth="400">

    <Grid x:Name="LayoutRoot" Background="White">

    </Grid>
</UserControl>
```

You need to edit this XAML so that users of your application will actually see something. You are going to add a Button control that reads Click Me. To do that, edit your code so that it looks exactly like what I have below (new code is in bold):

```
<UserControl x:Class="MyFirstSL4App.MainPage"
    xmlns="http://schemas.microsoft.com/winfx/2006/xaml/presentation"
    xmlns:x="http://schemas.microsoft.com/winfx/2006/xaml"
    xmlns:d="http://schemas.microsoft.com/expression/blend/2008"
    xmlns:mc="http://schemas.openxmlformats.org/markup-compatibility/2006"
    mc:Ignorable="d"
    d:DesignHeight="300" d:DesignWidth="400">
```

```
<Grid x:Name="LayoutRoot" Background="White">

    <Button
        x:Name="MyButton"
        Height="25"
        Width="100"
        Content="Click Me" />

</Grid>
</UserControl>
```

Now press F5 to compile and run the application, and you should see a browser open up and look like what I have in Figure 1-3.

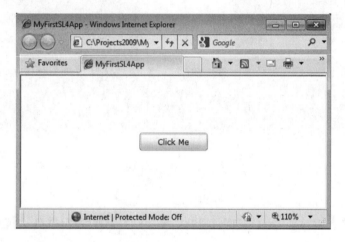

Figure 1-3. Your running application should look like this.

If you do in fact see what I have in Figure 1-3, then congratulations! You have successfully installed the Silverlight 4 development environment. But we still need to make certain that Expression Blend has been installed correctly.

To do that:

1. Open Expression Blend.

2. If you see the Welcome Screen, click **Open Project.**

3. If you do not see the Welcome Screen, click **File ➤ Open Project/Solution.**

4. Navigate to where you saved your application and double-click the .sln (Solution) file.

If you right-click MainPage.xaml *in Visual Studio 2010 Solution Explorer and left-click* **Open** *in Expression Blend, Visual Studio 2010 will open Blend and load your project, thus skipping the previous steps 1-4.*

You should then see your MainPage.xaml right inside of Blend, as I do in Figure 1-4.

Figure 1-4. Your project should look like this in Expression Blend.

Giving Your First Silverlight 4 Application Some Functionality

At this point you have completely installed the Silverlight development environment. But as an additional bonus, I think it would be fun for me to show you how quick and easy it is to add functionality in Silverlight. To do that, go back to Visual Studio 2010 and look at MainPage.xaml. Place your cursor somewhere on the code, right-click, and left-click **View Code,** as I am doing in Figure 1-5.

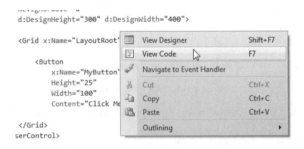

Figure 1-5. View the code-behind for MainPage.xaml.

You can also open the code-behind page for any XAML page by double-clicking it in the Visual Studio Solution Explorer (but more on that later).

Now you are viewing the code-behind file for `MainPage.xaml`. If this all seems quite strange to you, don't worry, it should—and I will explain it all in detail later. This is just a quick guide to show you how to quickly add functionality to your Silverlight 4 applications.

1. Place your cursor directly after the line of code that reads `InitializeComponent();` and press the Enter key to give you an empty line which you can add code to.

Note: You may need to go to Project ➤ Stop Debugging if the project was still running.

2. Start to type **MyButton**, which is the `x:Name` of the `Button`.

3. When the autocomplete feature known as Intellisense shows you `MyButton`, press the Enter key, as I do in Figure 1-6.

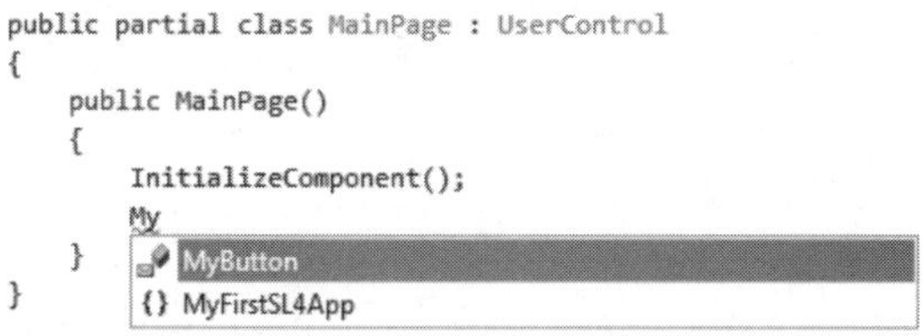

```
public partial class MainPage : UserControl
{
    public MainPage()
    {
        InitializeComponent();
        My
    }            MyButton
}            {} MyFirstSL4App
```

Figure 1-6. When Intellisense shows you `MyButton`, press Enter.

4. Next, type a period followed by the word **Click**, and when Intellisense shows you the word *Click,* press Enter again (see Figure 1-7).

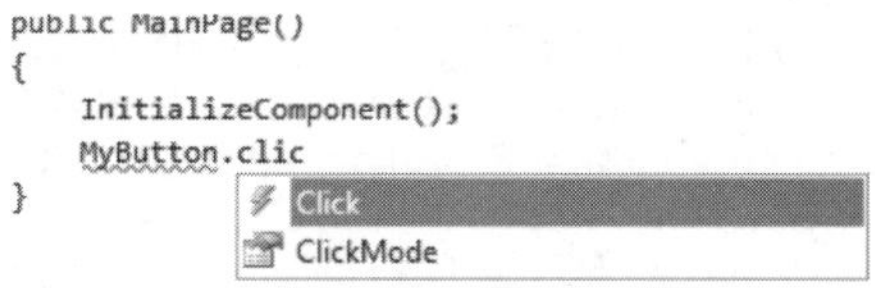

```
public MainPage()
{
    InitializeComponent();
    MyButton.clic
}            Click
            ClickMode
```

Figure 1-7. Press Enter when Intellisense shows you the word *Click*.

5. Next type **+=** and press the Tab key twice. Visual Studio will then raise the `Click` event and create an `EventHandler` that will fire when the user clicks `MyButton`. See the following code:

```
public MainPage()
    {
```

```
        InitializeComponent();
        MyButton.Click += new RoutedEventHandler(MyButton_Click);
    }

    void MyButton_Click(object sender, RoutedEventArgs e)
    {
        throw new NotImplementedException();
    }
```

Now you can erase the default line of code that reads throw new NotImplementedException(); and replace that with your own code that shows a MessageBox that reads "You Clicked!" See the new code in bold:

```
    void MyButton_Click(object sender, RoutedEventArgs e)
    {
        MessageBox.Show("You Clicked!");
    }
```

Now press the F5 key once again to run the application, and when it starts, click the Button. You should then see a MessageBox with a message that reads "You Clicked!" as shown in Figure 1-8.

Figure 1-8. A MessageBox now appears when you click the Button.

Summary

In this chapter you learned how to set up the Silverlight development environment by installing Visual Studio 2010 or Visual Web Developer Express 2010, the Silverlight 4 Tools for Visual Studio 2010, and Expression Blend 4. You then created your first Silverlight application and added a simple Button control to it. You then viewed your new Silverlight application in Blend 4, and finally you added code in Visual Studio that made a MessageBox appear when the Button was clicked. Let's move on and learn all about the Blend IDE.

Chapter 2

The Blend Integrated Development Environment

What this chapter covers:

- The Blend 4 toolbar
- The Objects and Timeline panel
- The Project panel
- The Properties panel
- The Resources panel
- The 3D objects that can be created in Blend 4

Now that you have your development environment set up and have had a taste of how fun and easy it is to create a cool-looking and interactive Silverlight application, we can take a step back, get to the basics, and discuss some of the major features of the Blend 4 integrated development environment (IDE). As we proceed, I will explain each major feature and then task you with little exercises to help you to familiarize yourself with these tools and features. Some of these tools and features I will discuss briefly here and in more depth in later chapters. Before we get started, I want to provide you with a quick list of features brand new to Blend 4.

New Features in Blend 4

Microsoft has come a long way since Blend 3 and has added some very cool new features. Here is a list of features that are brand new to Blend 4:

- Intellisense for XAML editing
- The ability to edit C# and Visual Basic code-behind files (no more having to jump into Visual Studio for quick code edits)
- A new Effects tab in the Asset Library
- The ability to create XML-based sample data
- The ability to import Adobe Illustrator (AI) files
- Project template support
- A new Behaviors tab in the Asset Library that allows designer to drag snippets of code to the Timeline
- Improved object selection in the workspace
- A Brush Transform tool that is now separated into two tools
- Easier positioning of objects on the Objects and Timeline panel

> *Christian Schormann has a great post on the new features of Blend 4 at* `http://electricbeach.org/?p=438`.

The Blend 4 Toolbar

If you are familiar with popular design/development products such as Adobe Photoshop, Flash, or Illustrator, the Blend 4 toolbar will be nothing new to you, as Microsoft has apparently attempted to make its toolbar functionally match that of the Adobe suite of design products. This, in my humble opinion, was a very smart move on the part of Microsoft, as it makes transition from an Adobe product to this new product quite easy. If, however, you are not familiar with the toolbar concept, this section will serve as a good introduction. The toolbar provides a set of tools that allow you to create and edit user interface (UI) content that the users of your Silverlight applications can interact with. The Blend 4 toolbar is located on the left side of the Blend 4 IDE, as shown in Figure 2-1.

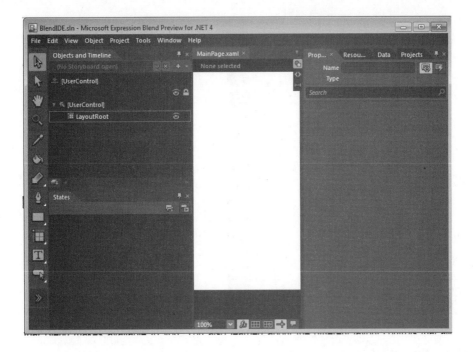

Figure 2-1. The Blend IDE

Figure 2-2 shows an isolated view of the toolbar. I cover some of the tools in more depth than others in this chapter, because I discuss some of the others in greater depth in later chapters. To get started, go ahead and create a new Silverlight project:

1. Open Blend 4.

2. Click File ➤ New Project.

3. Select Silverlight 4 Application.

4. Name the project ExploringBlend.

5. Click OK.

Figure 2-2. The Blend 4 toolbar

The Selection Tool

The Selection tool is the tool to use when you want to select objects (such as a MediaElement or an Image control) that the user of your Silverlight 4 applications will interact with) in the workspace or artboard (known as the *stage* in Flash). This tool allows you to select objects to change their properties, such as modifying their size or shape or changing their opacity or color (you will see how to do all of this later). This is probably the most used tool in all of Blend, so you should become very familiar with its location on the toolbar.

Most of the tools on the toolbar can be selected by using keyboard shortcuts. For example, to select the Selection tool, press the V key. You can see the keyboard shortcut in the tooltip.

The Direct Selection Tool

The Direct Selection tool, shown in Figure 2-3, is a tool that allows you to see and edit the different nodes that make up a custom shape known as a *path* (drawn using the Pen or Pencil tool). If you are not familiar with vector-drawing tools such as Illustrator, I probably just lost you. Because I don't want to lose you, I will jump ahead a little and show you how to use the Pen tool to create paths.

Figure 2-3. The Direct Selection tool

The Pen/Pencil Tools

The Pen/Pencil tools (shown in Figure 2-4) allow you to create custom shapes or paths in Silverlight. By default, you will see the Pen tool in the Blend 4 toolbar. To get to the Pencil tool, you can click and hold or right-click the Pen tool until you see the option appear for the Pencil tool. The Pen tool basically allows you to create a series of points that can be manipulated with the Direct Selection tool. In order to demonstrate this, I will show you how to use the Pen tool to create a path.

Figure 2-4. The Pen tool

1. Select the Pen tool from the Blend 4 toolbar.

2. Click to make a series of points.

3. Click the first point to close the shape.

The Pen tool icon has features that help you understand the action that is about to be performed by the tool. For example, if you have created a series of points (see Figure 2-5), and you mouse over the first point, the Pen tool cursor shows a circle icon, indicating that if you click, you will close the path. Also, once you have created a path and mouse over a line on the path, a plus icon appears next to the Pen tool cursor, indicating that you are about to add a new point. Finally, if you mouse over a point in the path, you will see a minus icon appear next to the Pen tool cursor; this indicates that if you click, you will remove the point.

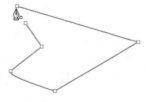

Figure 2-5. Use the Pen tool to create points. Click the first point to close the shape.

You have just created a custom path. Now you can select the Direct Selection tool and modify those points. You can also click and drag on a line segment of the path to move it.

4. To move a point, place the cursor directly over it, click once to select it, and then drag it. If you want to add a Bezier curve to a point, hold down the Alt key and then click and drag a point, as shown in Figure 2-6.

5. If you Alt-click a Bezier curve point, it will convert it back to an angle point.

6. Finally, dragging the handles on a Bezier curve will move them together, changing the shape of the curve. Alt-dragging a handle will reshape that side of the curve independently. Use this technique to create complex curved shapes.

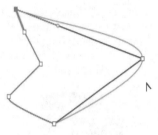

Figure 2-6. You can use the Direct Selection tool to modify your shape.

The Pencil tool allows you to create a shape by clicking and drawing in the workspace as you would on a piece of paper (see Figure 2-7).

Figure 2-7. Using the Pencil tool, you can create shapes by drawing like you would on a piece of paper.

The Pen and Pencil tools in conjunction with the Direct Selection tool are very handy for creating shapes that are not symmetrical, as opposed to simple Ellipses and Rectangles.

The Pan Tool

You should now have a better idea of paths and what the Direct Selection tool does, so let's jump back up the toolbar and carry on from where we left off. The Pan tool, shown in Figure 2-8, allows you to navigate around the workspace. This is very handy for large applications. When you select this tool, your cursor turns into a hand icon. If you click and drag your mouse, you can move your workspace. Manually selecting this tool, however, is impractical, because you can get the same result by holding down the spacebar and clicking and dragging your mouse. But there is something else that this tool useful for: double-clicking it snaps into view the item that is currently selected in the workspace or the Objects and Timeline panel. Sometimes I find myself so far off of the workspace that I don't know where it has gone; at these times, I can just double-click the Pan tool and voilà, I have the object that I am working on right in the center of my view—very handy.

Figure 2-8. The Pan tool

The Zoom Tool

The Zoom tool, shown in Figure 2-9, allows you to click the workspace to zoom in. You can also click and drag out the area you want to zoom in on. Further, if you hold down the Alt key and click, you zoom out. Finally, if you double-click the Zoom tool, you will be shown your workspace at 100% with no zoom at all. I find this tool very handy for working with design details, such as complex buttons with many gradients.

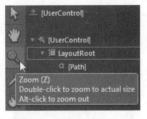

Figure 2-9. The Zoom tool

The Eyedropper Tool

The Eyedropper tool, shown in Figure 2-10, is a very handy tool for selecting colors. The Eyedropper tool will select any color that is directly underneath it, whether it be a color of a vector shape or a bitmap image. I rarely use the Eyedropper tool from the toolbar, because the same tool can be found on the Brushes palette, which is much handier to use. I will discuss this more in later chapters, but for now just be aware that it exists.

Figure 2-10. The Eyedropper tool

The Paint Bucket Tool

The Paint Bucket tool, shown in Figure 2-11, allows you to select an object, and then when you click this tool Blend copies the object's properties, such as the fill color, stroke fill and thickness, opacity, and so on. You can click another object to apply these attributes.

Figure 2-11. The Paint Bucket tool

The Brush Transform and Gradient Tools

The Brush Transform and Gradient tools, shown in Figure 2-12, are two of my personal favorites because they are so powerful. These tools allow you to manipulate an object's gradient.

A color gradient specifies a range of position-dependent colors, generally as an alternative to specifying a single color.

Figure 2-12. The Gradient and Brush Transform tools

The Gradient Tool

To demonstrate these tools, the following exercise will show you how to create a `Rectangle` with a gradient and then use the Brush Transform and Gradient tools to manipulate its gradient.

   1.   Select the Rectangle tool, as shown in Figure 2-13.

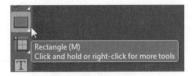

Figure 2-13. Selecting the Rectangle tool from the toolbar.

> **2.** Draw a `Rectangle` in the workspace, as shown in Figure 2-14.

Figure 2-14. Drawing a `Rectangle` in the workspace

> **3.** Activate the Selection tool (by pressing the V key) and click the `Rectangle` to select it.
>
> **4.** In the Brushes section of the Properties panel, click the Fill property, as shown in Figure 2-15.

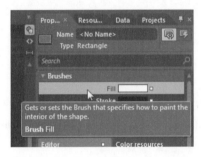

Figure 2-15. Click the Fill property in the Brushes section of the Properties panel.

> **5.** With the Fill property selected, click the Gradient brush button, as shown in Figure 2-16.

Figure 2-16. Click the Gradient brush button.

Notice that your `Rectangle` now has a black-to-white color gradient, as shown in Figure 2-17.

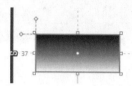

Figure 2-17. Your `Rectangle` now has a gradient that runs from top to bottom.

But say you want to change the gradient's direction. Well, as you might have guessed, you would use the Gradient tool. Do that now.

   6. Click the Gradient tool (shown previously in Figure 2-12).

Notice that your `Rectangle` now has an arrow over it running in the same direction as your gradient (starting at the left and pointing right), as you see in Figure 2-18. You can now use this arrow to manipulate your gradient.

Figure 2-18. The gradient arrow

   7. Place your cursor over the arrow until it turns into a hand. When it does, click and drag your mouse to change the size of the gradient.

   8. Next, move your cursor around the tip of the arrow until it turns into a curved, two-headed arrow; you can now click and hold the mouse to rotate your gradient from left to right, as in Figure 2-19.

Figure 2-19. When your cursor turns into a double-headed arrow, you can then rotate your gradient.

When rotating your gradient using the Gradient tool, you can hold down the Shift key to constrain the angles so that it is easier to get a perfect up-to-down gradient.

Notice there are two circles on the Brush Transform arrow. You can use those to reposition the color stops.

The Brush Transform Tool

You can select the Brush Transform tool by clicking and holding the Gradient tool until the Brush Transform tool appears. When it does, select it. Basically, this tool allows you to transform the Gradient brush, whereas the Gradient tool allows you to manipulate the Gradient brush's properties, such as start and stop points.

We get into gradients in much more depth in later chapters, but this provides the gist of the Gradient and Brush Transform tools. With that, you can move forward.

The Shape Tools: Rectangle, Ellipse, and Line

There are three shape tools. The one that shows by default is the Rectangle tool (see Figure 2-20). If you click and hold the Rectangle tool or right-click it, you will see the icons for the Ellipse and Line tools, which you can then select. Because you have already seen how the Rectangle tool works, let's move on to the other shape tools.

1. Click and hold the Rectangle tool, and when you see the option for the Ellipse tool, select it.

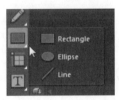

Figure 2-20. The Rectangle shape tool

2. With the Ellipse tool selected, draw an Ellipse in the workspace, as shown in Figure 2-21.

If you hold down the Shift key while drawing a shape (specifically a Rectangle or Ellipse), your shape will be perfectly symmetrical. Also, if you hold down the Alt key, the shape will be drawn from the center rather than the corner.

Figure 2-21. Draw an Ellipse in the workspace using the Ellipse shape tool.

Notice how Blend drew out the Ellipse with the same gradient that you used on the Rectangle earlier. This is a pretty cool feature and can save some time when making objects that are meant to look exactly alike.

Now try out the Line tool:

1. Click and hold the Ellipse tool on the toolbar until the Line tool becomes visible and select it.

2. Now draw a `Line` in the workspace, as in Figure 2-22.

Figure 2-22. Using the Line shape tool to draw a `Line` in the workspace.

If you hold down the Shift key while drawing a `Line`, its angle will be constrained so that it is easier to make a `Line` that is perfectly vertical or horizontal.

The shape tools, as you will see in later chapters, allow you to make very cool objects, such as custom buttons.

Layout Controls

Next, we'll look at the layout controls (shown in Figure 2-23). The default layout control shown when Blend first starts is the Grid. That is because the Grid is by far the most common layout control. In fact, when you create a new Silverlight project, the default layout control that is placed in your workspace is a Grid named `LayoutRoot`. Basically, layout controls are the controls that handle the size and positioning of elements inside of them in a Silverlight application; that is, they are the containers that house your Silverlight objects.

Figure 2-23. If you click and hold the Grid tool on the toolbar, all six layout controls appear.

There are many different layout controls, and they are all used at different times to accomplish different goals, because they each display their content differently. I will go into these controls in depth later on in the book, but for now just be aware that there are six: the Grid, the Canvas, the StackPanel, the ScrollViewer, the Border, and finally the Viewbox, newly added to Silverlight 4. Again, don't worry about what these are and what they do now, because in Chapter 4 I really break them down for you and work through them with exercises.

Text Controls and Text Input Controls

The next tool on the toolbar is the TextBlock tool. If you click and hold this tool, other controls will appear (see Figure 2-24). These are controls that allow you to add text to your applications, as well as text input controls such as a TextBox (a text input field) and a PasswordBox. I discuss these controls in depth later in the book.

Figure 2-24. If you click and hold the TextBlock tool, the other text and text input controls will appear.

Input Controls

The next tool on the toolbar is the Button tool. If you hold down this tool, you will see the other input controls available to you (see Figure 2-25).

Figure 2-25. If you click and hold the Button tool, the other input controls will appear.

These controls are essential because they allow your application to interact with the user. Probably the most common of these input controls is the Button control. If you have done any web development, most of these controls will already be familiar to you. We use most of these controls later on in the book.

The Asset Library Last Used tool

The next tool on the Blend 4 toolbar is the Asset Library Last Used tool. This is a handy little feature that will turn into the last control you have used from the Asset Library. Say, for example, you select the CheckBox tool from the Asset Library to create a check box. The Asset Library Last Used tool will turn into a CheckBox control. What is the Asset Library, you ask? Find out in the next section.

The Asset Library

The next button you will find on the toolbar is a very handy one called the Asset Library. This is a collection of every control available to you in Silverlight (see Figure 2-26).

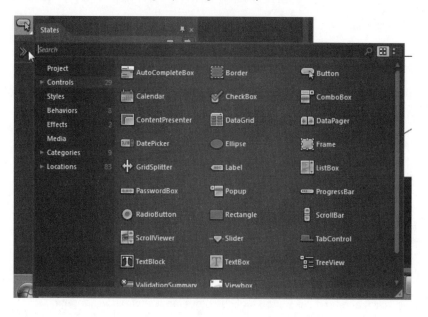

Figure 2-26. The last tool on the Blend toolbar is the Asset Library.

This tool is great for a few reasons. First, it has a search feature that filters out the controls you see. For example, if you type **B** in the search field, all controls that have the letter B in them will appear. If you continue to type the word **Button**, all controls with the word *Button* in them will appear. Currently, there are seven controls with the word Button in them . . . I know that not because I am a genius, but because I tried the search I just mentioned while writing this chapter. Which brings up a good point: often we Silverlight developers forget the names of controls. When we do, the Asset Library is a great place to come to browse through them.

The other reason this is a great tool is because if you make a custom UserControl (we do this in a later chapter), it will show up here under the Custom Controls tab. This makes it easy to implement the custom UserControl that you have made. But for now, you are just going to have to take my word for it, until you get to the custom UserControl tutorial in Chapter 12.

There are so many controls in the Asset Library that it would be impractical and beyond the scope of this book to discuss them all. In fact, someone could write an entire book on all of these controls.

The Objects and Timeline Panel

Now that you are familiar with the toolbar, let's move on to the Objects and Timeline panel of the Interaction panel, located on the left side of the Blend IDE, just to the right of the toolbar, as shown in Figure 2-27.

Figure 2-27. The Objects and Timeline panel is located just to the left of the toolbar in the Blend IDE.

If you place an object in your artboard—say, a TabControl—it will show up here as an object because it now becomes part of your Visual Tree. The *Visual Tree* is a list of any objects in your application that show the hierarchy of the controls, much like a family tree shows ancestry. As you can see in Figure 2-27, the Visual Tree consists of a UserControl that contains a Grid named LayoutRoot that contains three Paths and one Ellipse (none of which have been named). That is my Visual Tree, and if I want to select an object—say, the Ellipse—I can just click it here in the Objects and Timeline panel. Often I prefer to select items here because it can be difficult to select an item on the artboard when there are a lot of things going on. For example, say I want to select a Button I have on the artboard, but it's being covered by a StackPanel. It would be very tricky to select the Button without moving items around. In this case, it would be much easier to simply select the Button from the Objects and Timeline panel.

Another thing you should know about this panel are the little eyeball icons for each object in the Visual Tree (again, shown in Figure 2-27). If you were to click the eyeball icon of the LayoutRoot layer, your LayoutRoot Grid would become invisible on the artboard, and the eyeball icon would be replaced by a small blank circle icon. To reveal the item again, just click the blank circle icon, and it will reappear. Also, if there are any objects in that object (as in the case of the LayoutRoot Grid), they and their eyeball icons would be invisible as well. This is because they are children of the LayoutRoot Grid (when an object contains other objects, those objects are called *children*). Keep in mind it hasn't been deleted, it's just hidden. And it is only hidden in the IDE, so if you were to run the application, you would see the LayoutRoot Grid again. If you actually wanted to make it invisible to the user, you would have to change its visibility in the Properties panel—but we will get to that a little later.

If you look again at Figure 2-27, you will see that the LayoutRoot Grid object has a little circle icon next to its eyeball icon. If you click the circle icon, it will change into a padlock icon, effectively locking the object and all of its children. This is helpful because when you get an object designed and positioned perfectly, you can lock it so that nothing accidentally changes that object while you are working on other objects.

I have now covered the basics of the objects part of the Objects and Timeline panel, but I have yet to address the Timeline aspect of it. I do so in Chapter 5, which covers Storyboards and animation, as that's where you'll actually put the Timeline feature to use.

The Project Panel

The Project panel (see Figure 2-28) shows you all the assets that make up your application.

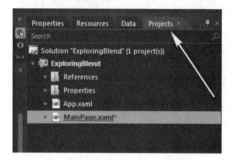

Figure 2-28. The Project panel shows all the application's resources.

Interestingly, the Projects panel used to be located on the right side of the IDE. In the more recent versions of Blend it is now located on the left side, next to the Objects and Timeline panel. Because I have been using Blend from the very beginning (when it was called Sparkle) I am used to it being on the right side of the IDE, so that is where I move it to. This brings up another interesting point: all panels in Blend are configurable and can be moved around.

The first thing you see is the name of your project solution. The project solution name in Figure 2-28 is ExploringBlend. Below that is a directory called References. This folder holds references to other DLLs that make the application work. You don't need to worry about that directory for the purposes of this book. But, just so you know, the References folder allows you to add references to other Silverlight projects and have all of the resources available in those projects available to your new project.

Below that is a directory called Properties. I won't go into details about this folder, as it's not necessary for the purposes of this chapter. Next, you see App.xaml, which is a file that holds resources for your application, such as any Styles you create. We talk more about Styles in Chapter 12.

Now you finally come to MainPage.xaml. This is the file that you have been working with when creating shapes. I talk about XAML and C# in depth in the next chapter, but it's worth mentioning here that XAML is the user interface (UI) layer. Visual objects are most often contained here, but they can also be added via code-behind files. Notice there is an arrow next to this file. If you click the arrow icon, it will expand and you will see MainPage.xaml.cs. This is called a *code-behind page*. Most every XAML page has a code-behind page. This code-behind page is written in C#. Code-behind files can be written in C# or Visual Basic in Silverlight 2 and newer projects (Silverlight 1.0 code-behind pages are written in JavaScript). Code-behind pages can now be edited in Blend, starting with version 3, but I still recommend you edit them in Visual Studio. But again, I talk in depth about this in the next chapter.

The Project panel is important because it allows you to easily navigate to any file you want by double-clicking it. Also, you can add items such as videos, music, or images to a project solution in the Project panel. Blend then makes a copy of whatever item you select and places it in the project in the folder you specify. To put an asset into a new folder you've created, follow these steps:

1. Right-click that new folder.

2. Click Add Existing Item.

3. Navigate to an item—say, an image on your hard drive—and double-click it.

A new feature that was added to Blend 3 and newer allows you to actually drag and drop images from your hard drive right into the Project panel.

The Properties Panel

The Properties panel, shown in Figure 2-29, is where you set the properties for controls in your workspace. It has sections, also known as *buckets*, that help to make it easier to navigate. For example, the Brushes bucket describes how objects are shown (Fill Color, Stroke, and so on), and the Layout bucket describes how objects are laid out in the application (Height, Width, Column, Row, and so forth). You can get from the Project panel to the Properties panel by clicking the tab that reads Properties.

Figure 2-29. The Properties panel

The Properties panel is important, and you will use it often, so now is a good time to start some hands-on work with Blend to demonstrate its use.

The Brushes bucket

We've already taken a brief look at the Brushes bucket of the Properties panel, but let's take a closer look at it now and set up a very simple project that you'll use to view the effects of some of the other panels.

1. Create a new project in Blend and call it PropertiesPanel.

2. Select the Rectangle tool and draw a Rectangle in the workspace. Make it any size you want, as you will change it later.

3. Make certain that the Rectangle is selected.

4. Find the Brushes bucket of the Properties panel. If it is collapsed, click the arrow icon next to the word *Brushes* to expand it—do so now so that you have something that looks like Figure 2-30.

Figure 2-30. The Brushes section of the Properties panel.

First, take a look at the Fill property. Notice that this property is currently set to a solid color (see Figure 2-30).

5. Change the color from white to another color. You can do this a few different ways:

   • You can just click the color palette, and the color will change to whatever color you click (number 1 in Figure 2-31).

   • You can adjust the RGBA values individually (number 2 in Figure 2-31).

   • You can change the color by setting the hexadecimal value (number 3 in Figure 2-31).

   • You can change the color value by using the Eyedropper (number 4 in Figure 2-31). The Eyedropper will pick up any color that is underneath it. This goes for your workspace or the Blend application as well.

   • You can change the color by making use of a color resource (number 5 in Figure 2-31). You will create a color resource and apply it to another object a little later in this section.

Figure 2-31. Numbers 1 through 5 indicate the different ways you can change the solid fill of an object.

You can also choose a gradient for your object by selecting the Gradient brush option. Change your `Rectangle`'s fill to a gradient now by clicking the Gradient brush icon, as I am doing in Figure 2-32. Now let's take a look at gradients in a little more detail.

Figure 2-32. Change your rectangle to a gradient fill.

Once you choose a gradient fill, your object will by default have a white-to-black gradient across it. This can be changed much like it is changed in popular design programs such as Adobe Flash and Photoshop. To change one of the gradient colors, follow these steps:

1. Select the color handle for the gradient color you want to change (as shown by the arrow in Figure 2-33) and then change the color by any method described in the previous exercise.

2. Drag the color slider (just right of the color palette) to pick a hue and then select a suitable color from the color palette (number 1 in Figure 2-31).

Figure 2-33. Changing one of the gradient color stops that make up your gradient

To add more color handles, and therefore more colors to the gradient, simply click in the gradient bar, and a new handle will appear below where you clicked. To remove a handle, click it and drag it down off of the gradient bar.

This is a good time to talk about Color Resources. Say you have a gradient or even a color that appears in many different places in your application. As you may know, designers are very particular about maintaining their designs, and any deviation from the developer can cause problems. Because of this, developers in the past had to be meticulous and re-create the gradient or color for every object. But now you can create a color or gradient once and then turn it into a Color Resource so it can be applied to any object. But it goes much further than just Color Resources. Any property can be saved as a Resource (for example, a `Fill`, the source of a `MediaElement`, the angle of an object—almost anything). Other objects can then use these Resources. If the Resource changes, all the objects using that Resource will automatically be updated throughout the project.

Back to the gradient example; assume your new gradient is exactly to the designer specifications. You can now turn that `Fill` of your `Rectangle` into a Color Resource. Let's do that now.

Creating the Color Resource

1. Click the Advanced icon next to the Fill property (it looks like a little white square (see Figure 2-34).

Figure 2-34. Click the Advanced icon next to the Fill property.

2. In the Advanced menu click Convert to New Resource.

3. When the Create Color Resource dialog box appears, give the resource a name of
BlackToWhiteGradient (don't click OK yet), as I am doing in Figure 2-35.

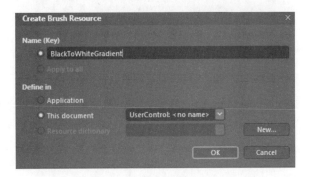

Figure 2-35. Name the new resource BlackToWhiteGradient.

4. Now click the New... button as I am doing in Figure 2-36.

Figure 2-36. Click the New button.

5. When the New Item dialog appears, make sure Resource Dictionary is selected . Leave the
default name and click OK, as I am doing in Figure 2-37.

Figure 2-37. The New Item dialog box.

6.   Once you click OK, you will again see the Create Color Resource dialog box—but now the Resource Dictionary option is enabled and checked. You can now Click OK to create the new Resource Dictionary and add the `BlackToWhiteGradient` Color Resource to it, as I am doing in Figure 2-38.

Figure 2-38. You now can click OK to create a new Resource Dictionary with the `BlackToWhiteGradient` in it.

Using the New BlackToWhite Color Resource

Now that you have made a new Color Resource in a new Resource Dictionary, it is time to show you how to make use of it. Let's do that now:

1.   Select the `Rectangle` on the toolbar.

2. Draw a new `Rectangle` out on the artboard.

3. Your new `Rectangle` might have a default black and white gradient because it was the last color we used. So to change it, select the Fill property for the new rectangle and click "Solid color brush," as I am doing in Figure 2-39.

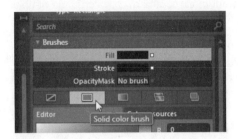

Figure 2-39. Change the new `Rectangle`'s fill to a Solid color brush.

4. Now to change the fill to the resource, click the Advanced icon next to the Fill property.

5. Click Local Resource ➤ BlackToWhiteGradient, as I am doing in Figure 2-40.

Figure 2-40. Use the Advanced icon to change the fill to use the `BlackToWhiteGradient` Color Resource from the Resource Dictionary we created earlier.

Now that you have successfully created a Color Resource in a Resource Dictionary and applied it to another object. we can move along and learn more about OpacityMasks.

Using OpacityMasks to Create a Reflection Effect

You have the option of editing the alpha of either one of the colors in a gradient or the entire color in a solid fill. The slider for this is right under the RGBA sliders in the Brushes section of the Properties panel. This is useful, but what if you want more control over which parts of object can be seen through? In such cases, you can use an OpacityMask (shown in Figure 2-41). An OpacityMask allows you to apply different opacity levels to different parts of an element (as opposed to simple opacity, which is applied to an entire element in an all-or-nothing manner).

Figure 2-41. An OpacityMask allows you to apply various opacity levels to different parts of an object.

For example, you can use an OpacityMask if you want an object to fade from opaque on one side to transparent on the other, as in a reflection. The following exercise shows you how create a reflection effect using OpacityMasks:

1. Select the Rectangle tool from the toolbar and draw a new one out on the artboard. Make it roughly 200 by 200 display units with a solid black fill.

2. Press Control+C to copy your new rectangle and Control+V to paste in one just like it.

3. Move the new Rectangle so it is just below the original one; this will be the reflection Rectangle. You should have something like what I have in Figure 2-42.

Figure 2-42. You should have two Rectangles, one on top of the other.

4. With the bottom rectangle selected, click OpacityMask so it is highlighted.

5. Now click Gradient brush, as I do in Figure 2-43.

Figure 2-43. Give your OpacityMask a Gradient brush fill.

Here it is important to understand that the colors you select are irrelevant in an OpacityMask. The only important part of a brush in an OpacityMask is its transparency. The value of alpha is calculated, but the values for red, green, and blue are ignored.

6. Click one of the color stops for the Gradient brush of the OpacityMask

7. Set the alpha of one that color stop to 0%, as shown in Figure 2-44A.

8. Now reverse the gradients by clicking "Reverse gradient stops," as I am doing in Figure 2-44B.

Note: The alpha sets how much you can see through an object. An alpha of 100% means you cannot see through the object at all.

Figure 2-44. A: Set the alpha of one of the gradient colors to 0%. B: Reverse the gradient stops.

Now you should have something that looks like a reflection effect and something like what I have in Figure 2-45.

Figure 2-45. Your project should now look like this.

Let's go through the other options in the Brushes bucket of the Properties panel very quickly:

- The BorderBrush option allows you to set the border color of an object.
- The Foreground option allows you to set the color of text in the foreground. This is most commonly used for text controls.
- You can choose to give any one of these no color at all by clicking the No Brush option. The No Brush button is shown by the arrow in Figure 2-46.

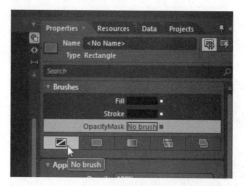

Figure 2-46. The Background, BorderBrush, Foreground, and OpacityMask settings can have the No Brush option applied.

Now that we've explored the Brushes section, let's briefly go over a few other sections in the Properties panel.

The Appearance Bucket

The Appearance bucket of the Properties panel, shown in Figure 2-47, controls how the object will appear. Click the little arrow at the bottom of the Appearance bucket to see all the properties that can be set. You can set an object's opacity and visibility and give it bitmap effects. Let's look at that now.

Figure 2-47. The Appearance bucket of the Properties panel

This short exercise will show you how to give the `Ellipse` you made earlier a bitmap effect.

1. Select the `Ellipse` in the workspace.

2. In the Appearance bucket, look for the Effect property and click the New Effect button, as I am doing in Figure 2-48.

Figure 2-48. Adding a bitmap effect.

3. When the Select Object dialog box appears, select DropShadowEffect, and click OK as shown in Figure 2-49.

Figure 2-49. Select DropShadowEffect.

Now you will see that your `Ellipse` has a drop shadow effect (see Figure 2-50).

Figure 2-50. The Ellipse with a drop shadow bitmap effect.

Also notice that in the Appearance bucket, a bitmap effect (DropShadow) properties section appears. This allows you to control the properties of your newly created drop shadow. You can collapse this section using the collapsible arrow button, as shown in Figure 2-51.

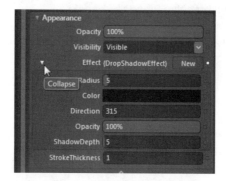

Figure 2-51. The properties section for your new drop shadow effect.

The Layout Bucket

Moving along, you come next to the Layout bucket of the Properties panel, as shown in Figure 2-52. This section allows you to set how the object is laid out in the workspace. You can

- Set an object's height and width to a specific number, or let Blend do it for you by setting one or both to Auto.
- Set the row and column of an object that resides in a Grid.
- Set the row span and column span if the object is in a Grid. These options allow you to span rows across columns and columns across rows, much like HTML tables.
- Set the horizontal and vertical alignment of an object.
- Set the margin of an object, which describes in numbers how far an object is from the top, bottom, left, and right of its parent object (Grid, StackPanel, and so forth).

- Set the *z-index* of an object—that is, whether it is on top of or under other objects. (A higher z-index places the object higher in the stack. For example, an object with a z-index of 1 will appear in front of an object with a z-index of 0.)
- Set advanced properties by clicking the collapse arrow at the bottom of the section.
- Set advanced properties such as whether an object has horizontal or vertical scrollbars.

There are other advanced layout properties, but I won't go into them at this time.

Figure 2-52. The Layout section of the Properties panel.

The Common Properties Bucket

The Common Properties bucket of the Properties panel, shown in Figure 2-53, contains properties common to all UI elements or controls. Here you can set properties such as

- What cursor (mouse pointer) an object will display when the mouse is over it (by specifying a value in the Cursor field).
- Whether the object can detect hits (by enabling the IsHitTestVisible option).
- Whether the object will display a tooltip and what it will read (by specifying text in the ToolTip field).

Figure 2-53. The Common Properties section of the Properties panel

One thing I want to cover in more depth is the `Cursor` property. In Silverlight, no control by default shows the hand cursor when you mouse over it—not even the `Button` control. However, the hand cursor creates a very good call to action for users; when they see the hand cursor, they know that they can click the object and something will happen. So, for any clickable object in my applications, I always set the `Cursor` property to `Hand`. You can set different cursor options (such as the arrow and the stylus, which are quite useful when creating interfaces), so I suggest you investigate them.

The Text Bucket

The Text bucket of the Properties panel, shown in Figure 2-54, only appears when controls that have text are selected. This bucket has properties for font, paragraph, line indent, and lists. These settings are all pretty self-explanatory, and I encourage you to play around with them.

Figure 2-54. The Text bucket of the Properties panel.

The Transform Bucket

The Transform bucket of the Properties panel, shown in Figure 2-55, allows you to transform objects. You can perform transformations (rotate, skew, and so on) here, or directly on the object, like you did when you rotated your `Rectangle`. I usually like to make my transformations directly on the object in the workspace. However, this panel is useful for making exact transformations, or for making sure that a group of objects are transformed in the same way.

There are two types of transformations that you should be aware of: the render transform and the layout transform. The layout transform is applied before an object is positioned, and the render transform is applied after an object is positioned. What is the difference, you ask? Say you have three `Rectangles` laid out in the workspace. The first one is at the top, the second one starts at the bottom of the first one, and the third one starts at the bottom of the second one. If you applied a layout transform to the middle one that rotated it 90 degrees so that it was laying on its side, and then ran the application, the top `Rectangle` would move up to accommodate the rotated second one, and the third one would likewise move down. That is because the second one was transformed before anything was drawn or rendered. However, if you performed a render transform to rotate the second `Rectangle` 90 degrees and then ran the application, the second `Rectangle` would end up on top of the first and third `Rectangles`, because they were laid out before the second one was transformed.

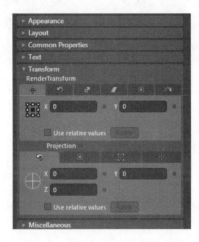

Figure 2-55. The Transform section of the Properties panel.

The Miscellaneous Bucket

The Miscellaneous bucket of the Properties panel (see Figure 2-56) contains any properties that don't fit into the previously described buckets.

Figure 2-56. The Miscellaneous bucket of the Properties panel.

Search

The final section I will go over for the Properties panel is the Search section feature, shown in Figure 2-57. This is a very handy and time-saving feature that I use regularly. Because the Properties panel is very large and has many properties for any given control, it is sometimes difficult to remember where exactly a property is located. Say, for example, you want to change the Cursor property, but you can't remember where it is located in the Properties panel. You can just start to type the word **cursor** into the search field, and Blend will locate it for you.

Figure 2-57. The Search section of the Properties panel.

The Resources Panel

The Resources panel, shown in Figure 2-58, contains a list of all Resources of your application. Remember the ResourceDictionary1.xaml file you created? It shows up in this list, and inside of it, the Brush1 Resource color gradient you created is shown. You can use the Resources panel to actually apply the resources, which you'll do now by following these steps:

1. Select the Rectangle tool and create a Rectangle in the workspace.

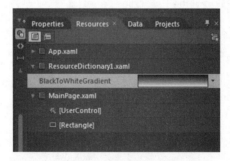

Figure 2-58. The Resources panel, which contains all Resources available to your project, including the Resource Dictionary you created earlier.

2. On the Resources panel, click the ResourceDictionary1 arrow so that the BlackToWhiteGradient gradient is shown, as in Figure 2-58.

3. Click and drag BlackToWhiteGradient to your new Rectangle in the workspace and let go.

4. Blend will now ask you what property you want to apply Brush1 to; click Fill (see Figure 2-59).

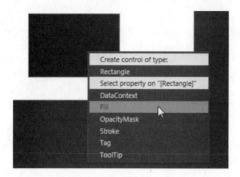

Figure 2-59. After droping the BlackToWhiteGradient gradient onto your new `Rectangle`, click Fill.

The BlackToWhiteGradient gradient will now be applied to your `Rectangle`.

Blend Development Views and Workspaces

Previously, Blend had two different development views. With the release of Blend 4 there are now three. At some point, you as a developer will have to work in all three, so you need to be familiar with each. I discuss them briefly here and in depth in later chapters.

Design View

Blend's real power is its Design view. You can get to Design view by clicking the Design button, as shown in Figure 2-60. Visual Studio 2010 also has a Design view, but it is not nearly as powerful as Blend's, which can visually represent complex applications.

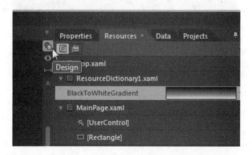

Figure 2-60. You can access Design view by clicking the Design button.

Design view allows you to basically do what you have been doing in these exercises—that is, drawing controls in the workspace visually instead of with code. What you may or may not know is that Blend is actually creating the code for you in the XAML. You could (and at one time had to) write the XAML code manually, but that becomes cumbersome and takes quite a bit of time. Further there are some XAML objects that would be impossible to code by hand. An example would be a complex path.

Another advantage of Design view is that you can easily tweak UI controls and see the effects immediately. Remember a while back when you were making your rectangle reflection, and it looked all wrong until you adjusted the stroke with the Brush Transform tool? You were able to do that visually and keep tweaking it until it looked the way you wanted it to look. Imagine now if you wanted to tweak that gradient in the code. To better illustrate this point, let me show you the code that Blend created for you due to your adjustments:

```
<Rectangle.OpacityMask>
 <LinearGradientBrush EndPoint="0.487,0.236" StartPoint="0.487,1.387">
  <GradientStop Color="#FF000000" Offset="0"/>
  <GradientStop Color="#00FFFFFF" Offset="1"/>
 </LinearGradientBrush>
</Rectangle.OpacityMask>
```

See what I mean? That would have been much more difficult if you had to come to this exact code by trial and error. This provides a good segue into the next development view: XAML view.

XAML View

XAML view can be turned on by clicking the XAML button, as shown in Figure 2-61. This view reveals the code that is generated by Design view. You can add UI controls in XAML view, but it's better to add them using Visual Studio, for a couple of reasons. First, Visual Studio has collapsible code. That is, you can collapse a huge chunk of code so that it is not visible, save for a couple of lines. This allows you to ignore large blocks of XAML and focus on the block you are currently working on. Another good reason is that Visual Studio will format your XAML markup for you. This is very helpful in that it makes XAML more readable and just makes your markup cleaner in general.

Figure 2-61. You can access XAML view by clicking the XAML button.

Split View

Split view is a feature in Blend that allows you to view half of the screen in Design view and half in XAML view. If you have ever played around with Adobe Dreamweaver, this concept should be nothing new to you. I think it is a real blast to draw out a control—say, a Rectangle—in the workspace, and then instantly see the XAML be created.

You can split the screen horizontally by clicking View ➤ Split View Orientation ➤ Split View Horizontally.

Workspaces

Now that you know about views, it's important to understand what workspaces are. The Blend IDE provides you with two distinct workspaces: the Design workspace and the Animation workspace. In each of the two workspaces, the Blend IDE will change to allow you to focus on different aspects of development, namely design and animation.

The Design Workspace

The Design workspace focuses on the Visual Tree of your application. Some panels are not visible in this workspace (for example, the Timeline panel). This allows the developer more room to see the application, and thus makes it easier to design. By default, Blend opens in the Design workspace. If you are in the Animation workspace (see the next section), you can click Window ➤ Workspaces ➤ Design to get back to the Design workspace. Conversely, if you are in the Design workspace, you can click Window ➤ Workspaces ➤ Animation to get to the Animation workspace.

You can view the Timeline and Interaction panels in the Design workspace, but they are docked to the right and are very narrow, and thus not very easy to work with.

The Animation Workspace

The Animation workspace is a place where you can create storyboard animations in the Objects and Timeline panel, and create EventTriggers in the Interaction panel. Both of these panels are docked along the bottom of the IDE, which gives you to more vertical space to work with. This lends itself very well to creating storyboards, as it allows you to see more of the Timeline.

In the following exercise, you'll create an animation that will run when your page is loaded:

1. Delete everything from the workspace except your `Rectangle` and its reflection.

2. Select the `Rectangle`, hold down the Shift key, and click the reflection to select both `Rectangles`.

3. Select Object ➤ Group Into ➤ StackPanel, as shown in Figure 2-62.

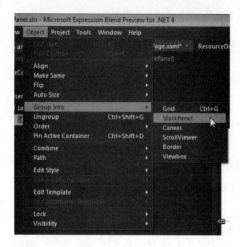

Figure 2-62. Group your `Rectangles` into a StackPanel.

4. Give your new StackPanel the name `ReflectionSP`, as shown in Figure 2-63.

Figure 2-63. Name your new StackPanel `ReflectionSP`.

5. Center your new StackPanel in the workspace and move it just below the workspace so that when the application starts, it won't be visible, as shown in Figure 2-64.

Figure 2-64. Place the `Rectangle` and its reflection in the `ReflectionSP` StackPanel.

6. Press F6 to view the Animation workspace.

7. With the StackPanel selected, click the New Storyboard button, as shown in Figure 2-65.

Figure 2-65. Click the New Storyboard button.

8. When the Create Storyboard Resource dialog box appears, leave the default name and click OK. A new Timeline will appear, as shown in Figure 2-66, allowing you to create a new storyboard Resource.

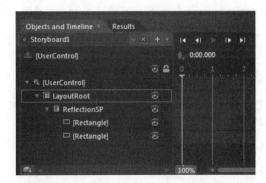

Figure 2-66. A new Timeline appears.

9. Move the playhead out to 1 second, as shown in Figure 2-67.

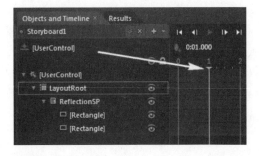

Figure 2-67. Move the playhead out.

10. Move the StackPanel to the center of the workspace.

11. Click the Close Storyboard button, as shown in Figure 2-68.

Figure 2-68. Close the storyboard.

12. Press F6 to go back to the Design workspace.

13. Now we need to move to Visual Studio to wire up the functionality. In the Project panel, right-click the Solution and left-click Edit in Visual Studio, as shown in Figure 2-69.

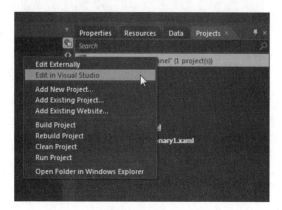

Figure 2-69. Edit the application in Visual Studio 2010.

14. When Visual Studio 2010 opens, look at the application in the Solution Explorer.

15. Click the little arrow next to MainPage.xaml to view the code-behind page MainPage.xaml.cs, as I have done in Figure 2-70.

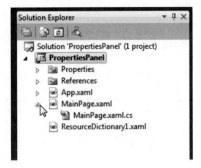

Figure 2-70. The application in Visual Studio 2010's Solution Explorer.

16. Double-click the `MainPage.xaml.cs`.

17. Place your mouse pointer under the `InitializeComponent();` call and press Enter to create a new line, as in Figure 2-71.

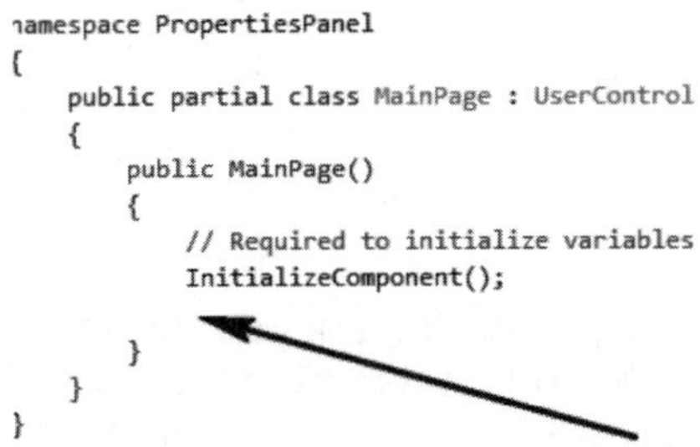

```
namespace PropertiesPanel
{
    public partial class MainPage : UserControl
    {
        public MainPage()
        {
            // Required to initialize variables
            InitializeComponent();

        }
    }
}
```

Figure 2-71. Create an empty line in the code-behind file.

18. Next start to type **Loaded** and when Intellisense shows you the Loaded Event press Enter, as I am about to do in Figure 2-72.

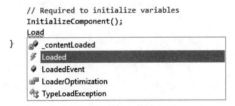

Figure 2-72. Intellisense in action

19. After the word *Loaded* type **+=** and press the Tab key twice. Visual Studio will raise the Loaded Event and create an `EventHandler` for it. See my code here:

```
namespace PropertiesPanel
{
    public partial class MainPage : UserControl
    {
        public MainPage()
        {
            // Required to initialize variables
            InitializeComponent();
        Loaded += new RoutedEventHandler(MainPage_Loaded);
        }

        void MainPage_Loaded(object sender, RoutedEventArgs e)
        {
          throw new NotImplementedException();
        }
        }
}
```

20. Now all you have to do is remove the default "throw..." code and tell `Storyboard1` to begin:

```
void MainPage_Loaded(object sender, RoutedEventArgs e)
    {
        Storyboard1.Begin();
    }
```

Press F5 to compile and run the application and watch your StackPanel slide into place. You can even view it here online: `http://windowspresentationfoundation.com/SL4Book/Ch2/`. You can also download my source code for this project from the book's page at `http://www.friendsofed.com`, or here: `http://windowspresentationfoundation.com/SL4Book/Ch2/PropertiesPanel.zip`.

Easy, right? We will get into more complex animations later in the book, but for now you should be comfortable with the basics of both the Design and Animation workspaces.

On my personal blog I have a five-part free video series on the Blend IDE that will help strengthen your knowledge of the Blend IDE:

Part 1: The Blend Toolbar: `http://tinyurl.com/yh48uh8`

Part 2: Layout Controls and User Input Controls: `http://tinyurl.com/yblcjyk`

Part 3: The Properties, Projects and Data panels: `http://tinyurl.com/ykvcdkk`

Part 4: The Objects & Timeline and States panels: `http://tinyurl.com/y8ztcds`

Part 5: Blend's Animation Workspace—Everything you need to know to create Storyboard Animations: `http://wp.me/pxXri-56`

Summary

In this chapter, you learned all about the Blend 4 IDE and how to make use of the toolbar and all the tools that Blend makes available to you. You also learned about the different layout controls that allow you to house controls in the workspace. Finally, you learned about the Design and Animation workspaces. In the next chapter, I will cover XAML and C# in greater detail.

Chapter 3

C#, XAML, and Object-Oriented Programming

What this chapter covers:

- C# and the .NET Framework
- The basics of XAML

In this chapter, I am give an overview of the programming languages C# and XAML (Extensible Application Markup Language). I will give you a little bit of background on the origins of each language and then explain in more detail how they interact to create Silverlight applications. Finally, I have you create a new Silverlight application, and you do a little bit of basic Object-Oriented Programming (OOP). So with that, let's get started and discuss the very robust language known as C# (pronounced *see-sharp*).

C# and the .NET Framework

C# is a very robust OOP language developed by Microsoft based on the C++ syntax. C# is designed to use the tools in the .NET Framework efficiently. The .NET Framework is a series of technologies and products also developed by Microsoft. It has continued to evolve, beginning with the .NET 1.0 release in 2002, and continuing on with 1.1 and 2.0, and most recently 3.0, 3.5, and most recently version 4. The .NET Framework is shipped as part of the Microsoft Windows OS. It was created to be an easy-to-use programming solution to many common programming needs including, but not limited to, web application development (.aspx and the older .asp pages), database connectivity, network communications, user interface (UI) components, and numeric algorithms. The .NET Framework allows for programmers to use methods of its class library in conjunction with their own code to create robust applications—in this case, Silverlight applications.

The .NET CLR

The .NET common language runtime (CLR) ships as part of the .NET Framework. It is an important part of the .NET Framework and worth giving a quick mention. The CLR is a *virtual machine*—similar to Adobe's Flash Player—that interprets code and translates it into a language that the computer can understand. The main purpose of this layer of abstraction between the programmer and the computer is to simplify management of memory, exceptions, threads, garbage collection, and security. The second purpose of the CLR is to allow the developer to write code in any CLR-supported language and know that it will execute the same way once compiled. This allows for Silverlight applications to be developed in C#, as well as Visual Basic, JScript, JavaScript, Python, Ruby, and other languages (although C# and Visual Basic are by far the most common).

In case you don't know, *exception handling* is a programming mechanism whose job it is to handle exceptional occurrences, also known as *errors*, in a programming routine of an application. In the .NET environment of Visual Studio 2010, every time an exception is thrown (that is, there is an error in your code), the development environment records debugging information known as *stack* and *heap* values. This debugging information is then given to you so that you can tell exactly what the exception thrown was. The debugging values can seem at times to be very cryptic and not at all intuitive regarding what the error was.

> *I find it useful to take exception errors and do a web search on them, because chances are very good that any problem you run into has been encountered by another programmer in the past. Also, the MSDN forums are a great place to post questions about exceptions.*

You may not be familiar with memory management. *Memory management* is simply the act of managing computer memory by allocating chunks of a computer's memory to programs that are running.

For our purposes, this is an adequate description of the .NET CLR.

Why C#?

C# is a very popular OOP development language in both online and offline development communities. What makes OOP so special, you ask? OOP uses *objects* to create applications. An example of an object would be a built-in Silverlight `Button` control (you will learn more about this control and many others as you work your way through the book). Objects are important because they have several characteristics, which I discuss in the rest of this section.

Encapsulation

Any complex software system may have hundreds or even thousands of individual "moving parts"—each one with its particular responsibilities. *Encapsulation* is a principle that states that each part is responsible for itself and its duties, and knows as little as possible about the other parts. This leads to stabler, easier-to-understand code because making a change to one part is less likely to affect the rest of the system.

Classes

In OOP, objects get their instructions, or details of how they will function, from classes. Classes include two very important things: *properties* and *methods* (collectively known as class members). If objects are like nouns, the "things" in an application, properties are the adjectives that describe objects, like their color or position. Properties can be built in or custom made. Using a sample Silverlight "Hello World" application as an example, `MainPage.xaml` has a code-behind page called `MainPage.xaml.cs`. This page has in it a class called `MainPage`. `MainPage` has built-in properties such as a `Background` property. You can create your own custom properties in a class. The following code is the entire code for `MainPage.xaml.cs`. I have modified it so that it creates a Boolean (true or false variable) called `thisBookRocks`, sets it to `true`, and then prints out the result in the **Output** window from Visual Studio 2010, as shown in Figure 3-1.

```csharp
using System;
using System.Windows;
using System.Windows.Controls;
using System.Windows.Documents;
using System.Windows.Ink;
using System.Windows.Input;
using System.Windows.Media;
using System.Windows.Media.Animation;
using System.Windows.Shapes;
using System.Diagnostics;

namespace HelloWorldSample
{
    public partial class MainPage : UserControl
    {
        Boolean thisBookRocks = true;

        public MainPage()
        {
            // Required to initialize variables
            InitializeComponent();
            Debug.WriteLine("thisBookRocks = " + thisBookRocks.ToString());

        }
    }
}
```

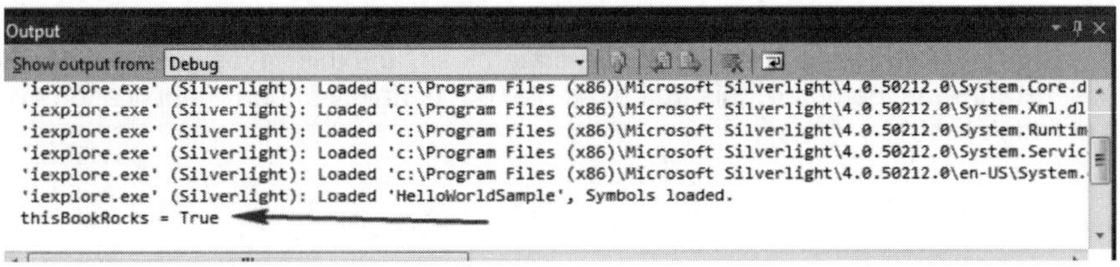

Figure 3-1. The Output window in Visual Studio shows the value of the `thisBookRocks` Boolean variable.

Methods are an object's verbs—the things an object can do. Classes come with a built-in method called a *constructor*. A constructor is a method that is named the same as the class and will run every time the object is *instantiated* (that is, every time the object is placed on the workspace or artboard, either physically or by code). You can see the constructor in the following code as well; it is called `MainPage`. If you are new to classes, properties, methods, and constructors, fear not—I show you how to work with them in great detail later on in the book.

The final thing I would like to mention about classes is that, as with custom properties and methods, there can be custom classes. For example, you can use a built-in .NET class called the `Button` class to create a button in your Silverlight application. You could, however, also make a custom class called `MyCoolButtonClass`. A good question for you to be asking might be "If I build this new custom button class, would I have to build into it all of the functionality of the .NET built-in `Button` class in order for them to act the same?" That's a good question, and the simple answer is yes, but .NET has provided a very good solution to this in the form of *inheritance*. So, if you want your new custom `MyCoolButtonClass` to act the same way as a .NET `Button` control, all you have to do is make your custom class *inherit* all the methods and properties of the .NET `Button` class. That way, you can just add features to it, or even override (change) the features it currently has to make it your own. Inheritance is one of the key characteristics of OOP, so I look at it next.

> *Blend's artboard is where your user interface (UI) elements are placed—what will be seen when the user runs your applications.*

Inheritance

Inheritance actually belongs to classes, but I want to give it its own section because it is a very important part of OOP. A class can be a child of another class and have child classes of its own. Basically, a class "inherits" all the traits of its parent. Here's a classic example that I see in nearly every OOP book: imagine you have a class called `Fruit`. `Fruit` is the parent class or superclass. `Fruit` has some child classes— say, `Apple`, `Orange`, and `Peach`. All three subclasses `Apple`, `Orange`, and `Peach` inherit from their parent class `Fruit`. So they all know they are a fruit and have all the traits of the `Fruit` class (in other words, they are edible containers for the seed of a plant).

So what is the advantage of inheritance? Imagine if you didn't have inheritance. In the preceding example, you would have to tell `Apple`, `Orange`, and `Peach` via code that they are all edible containers for the seed of a plant. That would mean you would have to write the code three times, once for each class. That is a big waste of time, and most importantly, it's prone to errors, because if you type a block of code once, you have one chance of getting it wrong; type it three times, you have three chances of getting it wrong. With inheritance, your classes can all share the code of a superclass, and this saves you a lot of time because it generates fewer errors—maybe not for this fruit example, but certainly for large applications with hundreds of thousands of lines of code.

Modularity

OOP encompasses the concept of modularity, which was first presented by Information & Systems Institute, Inc., at the National Symposium on Modular Programming in 1968. *Modularity* basically means that large applications should be built-in modules that each have their own specific purpose. Further, these modules act independently within the application. The advantage to this type of programming is that modules can be reused in other applications or duplicated and used more than once in the same application. Another big advantage to this type of programming is that if you change the functionality of one module, you will not affect the functionality of any other module, as they have the ability to function independently of one another. Silverlight takes full advantage of this concept with classes and `UserControls`, which I cover in depth later in this book.

Maintainability

Because OOP makes use of objects in its applications, and because these objects use classes that are built to be modular, the code is much easier to maintain than that of a traditional, procedural application. Say, for instance, you have a class called `Foo`. `Foo` has some complex functionality (exactly what is not important for this example). `Foo` has total encapsulation and is completely modular. So, if you go in and change `Foo` to give it some additional functionality, you know that you will not break the application, because no other object needs `Foo` in order to do its job. In procedural programming (non-OOP languages such as C, whereby the code is read line by line from top to bottom), it was very common for changes in one line of code in your application to cause some other part of your code to fail, because it was dependent on the line of code you changed, and thus the application would break.

I think that is a pretty adequate outline of why OOP is worth using. But I have yet to finish telling you why C# is a great programming language. Let's continue.

Automatic Garbage Collection

Automatic garbage collection is basically memory management. And it does exactly what the name implies: it takes out the garbage for you. (I wish I had one of these in real life—just ask my wife, Shay). Okay, let's break it down: objects take up memory when they are instantiated (another fancy name for "created"). Eventually, some instantiated objects will no longer be necessary. The garbage collector automatically finds and disposes of them, freeing precious memory. You can imagine how powerful this is in an application with hundreds (or even hundreds of thousands) of objects. It is worth noting here that some languages, such as C++, don't have automatic collection of garbage, so the programmer has to manually manage his/her garbage, and this can get quite cumbersome and have devastating performance effects if not done or not done properly.

Language Integrated Query

Language Integrated Query (LINQ) was introduced in .NET 4.0 and it allows for context-sensitive keywords such as `from`, `select`, and `where`. This allows the programmer to use similar syntax for managing databases, data collections, and even XML (Extensible Markup Language).

XML documentation

C# now allows programmers to embed XML comments right into their source files by putting `///` before any line of code. C# then treats that code as XML, and can even export it to a separate XML file. This is very handy when you have many developers working on the same application, and documentation is needed to explain to the next developer how to make use of the source file.

C# possesses many more powerful features, but for the scope of this book, I think I have adequately discussed some of the major ones. After all, this is a hands-on book, and I don't want to bore you with theory, but rather I'm brushing over this stuff so you can get to some real development. I think at this point it would be beneficial to go over XAML.

XAML

XAML is an XML-based declarative language developed by Microsoft. XAML is basically, as I described before, the UI language of Silverlight that defines objects and their properties. I say that XAML in its basic form describes how the application looks, but it can do much more than that. The number one advantage of XAML is its speed and efficiency—often, a single line of XAML can represent dozens of lines of equivalent C#. Further, with only a few lines of XAML, any Silverlight object can be hooked up to C# code-behind classes that can contain complex functionality. It is also worth mentioning that anything that can be done in XAML can also be done in C#, though usually the C++ requires many more lines of code.

XAML objects are written in XML-based form and describe how the user sees the object or framework element, by setting properties in the XML. A typical XAML control looks like this:

```
<Button
  x:Name="spinBtn"
  HorizontalAlignment="Right"
  Margin="0,0,19.8,42.5"
  VerticalAlignment="Bottom"
  Width="186.25"
  Height="80"
  Background="Blue"
  Foreground="White"
  Content="Spin"/>
```

The preceding code creates a `Button` control. The `Button` is able to be referenced by C# code because it has an `x:Name` property set to `spinBtn`.

As you can see, it also has other properties, such as the following:

- `HorizontalAlignment`: Controls how the `Button` will be aligned in the application
- `Margin`: Determines where in the parent grid the control will be placed
- `VerticalAlignment`: Controls how the `Button` will be aligned in the application
- `Width`: Sets the width of the `Button`
- `Height`: Sets the height of the `Button`
- `Background`: Sets the background color of the `Button`
- `Foreground`: Sets the color of the content (text) of the `Button`
- `Content`: Controls what the text on the `Button` will be

Following is the C# code that would create the exact same `Button`:

```
Button button = new Button();
button.Name = "spinBtn";
button.HorizontalAlignment = HorizontalAlignment.Right;
button.Margin = new Thickness(0, 0, 19.8, 42.5);
button.Width = 186.25;
button.Height = 80;
button.Background = new SolidColorBrush
  (Color.FromArgb(255, 0, 0, 255));
button.Foreground = new SolidColorBrush
  (Color.FromArgb(255, 255, 255, 255));
button.Content = "Spin";
LayoutRoot.Children.Add(button);
```

As you can see, it is a bit more work in that you have to first create an object called `button` of the `Button` type. You then have to set each margin separately for `Top`, `Left`, `Bottom`, and `Right`. Finally, you then have to add the object as a child of the `LayoutRoot` (a `Grid` control in most cases).

XAML is great because it helps to separate the design of the application from the C# development. This allows for faster development by increasing the efficiency between designers and developers, as discussed in Chapter 2. To reiterate, this is done by separating the design layer (XAML) from the logic layer (C#).

Another advantage to Silverlight is its native support of vector graphics in addition to standard bitmap graphics. What is the difference, you ask? *Vector* graphics are created with mathematical coordinates and have no actual pixels like bitmaps do. This allows you to scale a vector graphic to any size and still retain perfect clarity of the graphic. If you scale up a bitmap, the quality of it reduces significantly, and it will *pixelate* (become blocky).

XAML has one very awesome functionality feature called *binding*. That means that an object can have one of its properties "bound" to the properties of another. For example, you can bind the property of a `Rectangle`'s `Width` to the value of a `Slider`. This will be discussed later on in greater depth. Therefore, when you slide the slider up, the `Button` grows in size, and when you slide it down, the `Button` size decreases. Binding is very powerful, and I think you will understand that when we get into it later in Chapter 9.

It is important to note that any object can be created in the C# code-behind file and added to the workspace. Also, binding can be done in C# as well because an XAML file and its C# code-behind file are both partial classes, connected to each other with the `InitializeComponent` method run in the code-behind's constructor method. They are different parts of the same object, whether it is a `Button`, `UserControl`, or any other class; as such, at different times it may be more appropriate to write code for that object in the XAML file or the C# code-behind file.

XAML also allows you to define resources for the application. *Resources* can include Silverlight objects such as `Storyboard`, `ControlTemplate`, and `DataSource`. I go over these in depth later on as well.

Although XAML is very powerful, there is not much more to say about it on a background level, so at this point it will be better for you to learn about XAML through hands-on exercises, which is what you will start to do in the following chapters.

A Simple OOP Project

This book is primarily about Blend 4, but it is also very much about Silverlight, and Silverlight makes use of OOP. That being the case, it would be good to go over some basic OOP principles and constructs in a hands-on manner. In this section, you learn about the following:

- Creating custom classes
- Instantiating objects
- Adding properties to objects
- Encapsulating fields
- Superclasses
- Inheritance
- Extending classes
- Abstract classes
- Abstract methods
- Overriding methods
- Interfaces
- Extracting interfaces
- Enums

So let's get to it. First, carry out the following steps:

1. Open Visual Studio.

2. Click **File ➤ New Project**.

3. Select **Silverlight** as the project type.

4. Select **Silverlight Application** as the template.

5. Name the project OOP, as shown in Figure 3-2.

6. Click **OK**.

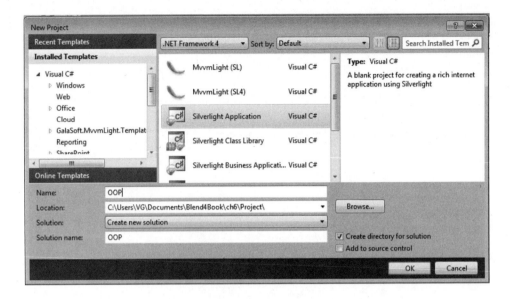

Figure 3-2. Create a new Silverlight application called OOP.

7. When the **New Silverlight Application** dialog box appears, uncheck "**Host the Silverlight application in a new Web site**," as shown in Figure 3-3, and then click **OK**.

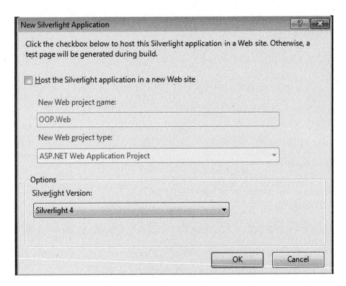

Figure 3-3. Uncheck the "Host the Silverlight application in a new Web site" check box.

The first thing you are going to do is create an object. In keeping with the preceding discussion on OOP, you will call this object `Fruit`. You'll then add some common features that all fruits share. That is, all fruits are edible containers for a seed. So, let's create our `Fruit` object now:

1. In Visual Studio's Solution Explorer, right-click the **OOP** project.

2. Click **Add ➤ Class**, as shown in Figure 3-4.

Figure 3-4. Add a new class.

3. When the **Add New Item** dialog box appears, name the new class `Fruit`, and click **Add**.

Now you can start adding your properties. You will make two Boolean properties—`IsEdible` and `HasSeed`—and set them both to `true`.

4. Inside the class, type `private bool _IsEdible = true`, as shown in Figure 3-5.

```
namespace OOP
{
    public class Fruit
    {
        private bool _IsEdible = true;
    }
}
```

Figure 3-5. The `_IsEdible` class

5. Next, right-click the new property, click **Refactor ➤ Encapsulate Field**, and then click **OK**.

6. When the **Encapsulate Field** dialog box shows up, uncheck **Preview Reference Changes** and click **OK**.

What this does is turn your private variable into a public variable, and it also creates getters and setters for it, as shown in the following code:

```
namespace OOP
{
```

```
    public class Fruit
    {
        private bool _IsEdible = true;
        public bool IsEdible
        {
            get { return _IsEdible; }
            set { _IsEdible = value; }
        }
    }
}
```

A requirement of our fruit is that it is always edible, and therefore no other object can ever set the IsEdible property to false. To fix this, what you do is remove the setter. Then other objects will be able to read the IsEdible property, but not set it. So, now your code should look like this:

```
namespace OOP
{
    public class Fruit
    {
        private bool _IsEdible = true;
        public bool IsEdible
        {
            get { return _IsEdible; }
        }
    }
}
```

Now that you have your Fruit superclass, you need to create a child for it. Let's create the Apple class.

7. Follow the same steps as you did previously to create a new class, but name this one Apple.

8. When the new class's code appears, enter " : Fruit" after the class declaration of public class Apple, as shown here:

```
namespace OOP
{
    public class Apple : Fruit
    {

    }
}
```

This means that the Apple class extends the Fruit class, and thus is one of its children. And as you know from the discussion on inheritance, Apple will inherit everything that Fruit contains, namely IsEdible. You can prove this by going to MainPage.xaml.cs and instantiating (creating) an instance of Apple.

9. In MainPage.xaml.cs, instantiate an Apple object called apple (all lowercase) under the InitializeComponent(); line, as shown here:

```
namespace OOP
{
    public partial class MainPage : UserControl
    {
        public MainPage()
        {
            InitializeComponent();
            Apple apple = new Apple();
        }
    }
}
```

Now you can write some code that proves that Apple really is a child of Fruit.

10. Write a conditional statement that will tell you if the Apple class's IsEdible property is true, as shown here:

```
namespace OOP
{
    public partial class MainPage : UserControl
    {
        public MainPage()
        {
            InitializeComponent();
            Apple apple = new Apple();
            if (apple.IsEdible == true)
            {
                MessageBox.Show("apple IsEdible is True");
            }

        }
    }
}
```

11. You could actually stop here, because when you typed **apple** and then a period, Intellisense showed you that one of the properties of apple is IsEdible. Since you have not even written any code in Apple, there is no way it could have this property if it weren't a child of Fruit. But to be complete, press F5 to compile and run the application, and you will see the message box shown in Figure 3-6.

Figure 3-6. The message box showing the value of IsEdible

12. Now let's create a new class called `Orange`. Follow the preceding steps to create the `Orange` class, and make it extend `Fruit`. Your code should look like the following:

```
namespace OOP
{
    public class Orange: Fruit
    {

    }
}
```

13. Now go back to `MainPage.xaml.cs` and instantiate an instance of the `Orange` class, as shown here:

```
namespace OOP
{
    public partial class MainPage : UserControl
    {
        public MainPage()
        {
            InitializeComponent();
            Apple apple = new Apple();
            if (apple.IsEdible == true)
            {
                MessageBox.Show("apple IsEdible is True");
            }
            Orange orange = new Orange();
        }
    }
}
```

Now, you know full well that the new `Orange` object is going to have an `IsEdible` property, and that property is set to `true`, so let's do something a little more fun. What I want to do is to have each `Fruit` have its own color. I could easily go into the superclass and make a public string variable called `color` and set it to, say, `Green`. I would also put a setter on it so each fruit could either accept the default color of green, change its color property itself, or have some other object change it. But say I want to set the default color in the `Fruit` superclass to `Empty` or `None`, and I want to demand that the children of this class define a color for themselves. I could use something called an *interface* to do exactly that. Let's do that now:

1. Go into the `Fruit` class and change it to an abstract class. This means that `Fruit` will never be instantiated itself; only its children will be instantiated. I explain why this is done in a moment. First, enter the following code:

```
namespace OOP
{
    public abstract class Fruit
    {
```

```
        private bool _IsEdible = true;
        public bool IsEdible
        {
            get { return _IsEdible; }
        }
    }
}
}
```

2. The next thing you need to do is declare a public abstract method called `SetMyColor` in `Fruit`:

```
namespace OOP
{
    public abstract class Fruit
    {
        private bool _IsEdible = true;
        public bool IsEdible
        {
            get { return _IsEdible; }
        }

        public abstract void SetMyColor();
    }
}
```

Notice how `SetMyColor` has no curly brackets after it. This is because the method will never be fired from here. Instead, the children of `Fruit` are going to be forced to implement this method, and they will need to have curly brackets. Let's extract the interface for this method now:

3. Right-click `SetMyColor` and click **Refactor ➤ Extract Interface**, as shown in Figure 3-7.

Figure 3-7. Extract the interface from `SetMyColor`.

4. When the **Extract Interface** dialog box appears, change the interface name to IColor, check the SetMyColor method, and click **OK**, as shown in Figure 3-8.

Figure 3-8. Set the properties for the new interface.

Notice that Visual Studio creates a new interface file for us called IColor.cs. This file has only one method in it, called—yep, you guessed it—SetMyColor (see the following code):

```
namespace OOP
{
    interface IColor
    {
        void SetMyColor();
    }
}
```

Now here is the fun part. Press Control+Shift+B to compile the Silverlight application, and notice you get two build errors saying that Orange and Apple do not implement Fruit.SetMyColor. This is exactly what we had hoped for because it means that Orange and Apple are now required to implement SetMyColor, but they have not done so. Let's have them implement SetMyColor now:

5. Open Orange.cs, place your cursor over Fruit, and click.

6. Press Control+. (period), and Intellisense will ask you if you want to implement the abstract class Fruit (see Figure 3-9).

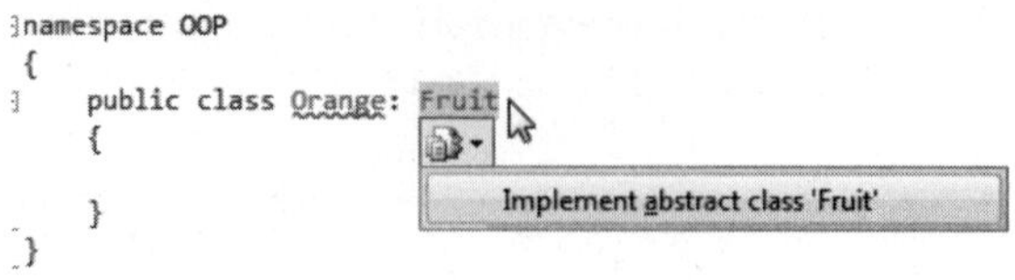

```
]namespace OOP
  {
]    public class Orange: Fruit
     {

     }
._}
```

Figure 3-9. Intellisense wants to implement the abstract class for you.

7. Press the Enter key and notice from the following code that Visual Studio actually implemented the override for SetMyColor (and notice to that it *does* have curly brackets).

```
namespace OOP
{
    public class Orange: Fruit
    {

        public override void SetMyColor()
        {
            throw new NotImplementedException();
        }
    }
}
```

So now go ahead and open Apple.cs and do the same thing. Once you have done that, you need a property for Color for both Apple and Orange. But wait, didn't I say that if they have anything in common, it should be part of the superclass? Yes, I did. So if you create a MyColor property in Fruit, then both Apple and Orange will automatically inherit it. But what if the children want to make their color property something impossible, like turquoise? (As far as I know, there is no such fruit with this color.) You could implement something called an *enum* (an enumerable list) of allowed colors. Then the children would only be able to select from that select group of colors. Let's implement this now:

8. Open Fruit.

9. Create a public enum called FruitColor:

```
namespace OOP
{
    public abstract class Fruit : OOP.IColor
    {
        private bool _IsEdible = true;
        public bool IsEdible
        {
            get { return _IsEdible; }
        }

        public enum FruitColor
        {
```

```
            None,
            Green,
            Red,
            Yellow
        }


        public abstract void SetMyColor();
    }
}
```

10. Now you need to create a private variable called `_MyFruitColor` and set it to `FruitColor.None`:

```
namespace OOP
{
    public abstract class Fruit : OOP.IColor
    {
        private bool _IsEdible = true;
        public bool IsEdible
        {
            get { return _IsEdible; }
        }

        private FruitColor _MyFruitColor = FruitColor.None;

        public enum FruitColor
        {
            None,
            Green,
            Red,
            Yellow
        }


        public abstract void SetMyColor();
    }
}
```

11. Now right-click `_MyFruitColor` and click **Refactor ➤ Encapsulate Field**.

12. Press the Enter key twice, and you should see something like the following:

```
namespace OOP
{
    public abstract class Fruit : OOP.IColor
    {
        private bool _IsEdible = true;
```

```
        public bool IsEdible
        {
            get { return _IsEdible; }
        }

        private FruitColor _MyFruitColor = FruitColor.None;
        public FruitColor MyFruitColor
        {
            get { return _MyFruitColor; }
            set { _MyFruitColor = value; }
        }

        public enum FruitColor
        {
            None,
            Green,
            Red,
            Yellow
        }


        public abstract void SetMyColor();
    }
}
```

13. Now you can go into both `Apple` and `Orange`'s `SetMyColor` override method and set their color.

Apple:

```
namespace OOP
{
    public class Apple : Fruit
    {

        public override void SetMyColor()
        {
            MyFruitColor = FruitColor.Green;
        }
    }
}
```

Orange:

```
namespace OOP
{
    public class Orange: Fruit
    {
```

```
        public override void SetMyColor()
        {
            MyFruitColor = FruitColor.Red;
        }
    }
}
```

14. Now you can go back to `MainPage.xaml.cs` and code your message box to show what color each fruit is:

```
namespace OOP
{
    public partial class MainPage : UserControl
    {
        public MainPage()
        {
            InitializeComponent();
            Apple apple = new Apple();
            Orange orange = new Orange();

            MessageBox.Show
("apple | IsEdible: " + apple.IsEdible + " Color: "
+ apple.MyFruitColor + " orange | IsEdible: "
+ orange.IsEdible + " Color: "
+ orange.MyFruitColor);

        }
    }
}
```

15. Press F5 to run this, and you should see the message box shown in Figure 3-10.

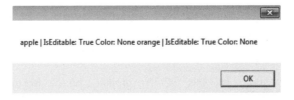

Figure 3-10. The message box is showing the properties for apple and orange.

Wait a minute. Didn't we set those properties in the `SetMyColor` override methods? Yes, actually we did. But think about an abstract method requirement: the child classes are mandated to implement the methods, *not* to actually fire them. In order for them to fire them, you need to tell each class to do so. This is accomplished with the following code:

```
namespace OOP
```

```
{
    public partial class MainPage : UserControl
    {
        public MainPage()
        {
            InitializeComponent();

            Apple apple = new Apple();
            apple.SetMyColor();

            Orange orange = new Orange();
            orange.SetMyColor();


            MessageBox.Show
("apple | IsEdible: " + apple.IsEdible + " Color: "
+ apple.MyFruitColor + " orange | IsEdible: "
+ orange.IsEdible + " Color: "
+ orange.MyFruitColor);

        }
    }
}
```

16. Now press F5 to run the application again, and you should see the message box shown in Figure 3-11.

Figure 3-11. You now see the correct values for each object's color property.

You can download a copy of this OOP project here: `http://windowspresentation foundation.com/Blend4Book/OOP.zip`.

Summary

In this chapter, you learned about C# and the .NET Framework. I went over some advantages of using C# and delved into the basics of classes and OOP and some advantages of both. I also covered the basics of XAML—what it is, what it can do—and talked about some powerful features such as data binding. Finally, I took you through a hands-on tutorial on how to do some basic tasks in OOP. In the next chapter, I talk about the layout controls that allow you to place content into your Silverlight applications.

Chapter 4

Layout Controls: Including the New Silverlight 4 Controls: Viewbox, RichTextBox, FlowDirection Property, and Improved Data Binding

As discussed in the previous chapter, *layout controls* (or *layout elements* as they are sometimes called) are a very important part of Silverlight, allowing you to arrange your content in your applications. Here I go over the most popular ones and the properties that make them unique. Then I over some new controls that have been added in Silverlight 4.

The Grid

Undoubtedly the most popular and most used Silverlight layout element is the Grid. In fact, when you first create a new Silverlight application, Visual Studio 2010 automatically puts in a Grid layout element for you. You can see the code here:

```
<UserControl x:Class="LayoutControlsProject.MainPage"
    xmlns="http://schemas.microsoft.com/winfx/2006/xaml/presentation"
    xmlns:x="http://schemas.microsoft.com/winfx/2006/xaml"
    xmlns:d="http://schemas.microsoft.com/expression/blend/2008"
    xmlns:mc="http://schemas.openxmlformats.org/markup-compatibility/2006"
    mc:Ignorable="d"
    d:DesignHeight="300" d:DesignWidth="400">
    <Grid x:Name="LayoutRoot" Background="White">

    </Grid>
```

```
</UserControl>
```

This does not mean that you can't add other layout elements; in fact, layout elements are meant to have other layout elements placed inside of them. Which one you choose depends on how you want to display your content. A Grid is very much like an HTML table, in that you can define Rows and Columns and then place content inside those Rows and Columns. This is a good time to create a new Silverlight Application project in Blend 4. To do that, first open Blend, create a new Silverlight Application project, and call it LayoutControlsProject, as shown in Figure 4-1. Click **OK**.

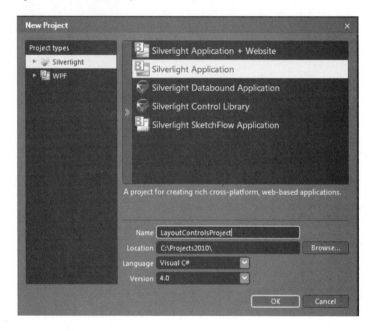

Figure 4-1. Creating a new Silverlight application in Blend 4.

Notice in the XAML that Blend has created a Grid by default.

Notice around your main Grid there is a blue bar at the top and on the left. These are where you add RowDefinitions and ColumnDefinitions. When you place your cursor over the top bar, a yellow line is drawn from the top of your Grid to the bottom. If you click the blue bar, the line becomes blue and does not go away when you move your mouse off it, because you have just created a new ColumnDefinition (see Figure 4-2).

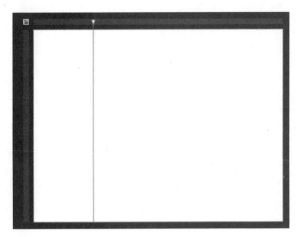

Figure 4-2. Creating Columns visually in Blend 4.

If you place your mouse cursor on the blue bar to the left, you will see that it too draws a yellow line, but this line is horizontal. If you click the blue bar, the yellow line becomes blue and permanent, and a Row is created, as shown in Figure 4-3.

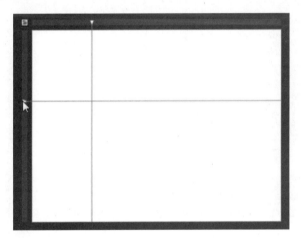

Figure 4-3. Creating Rows visually in Blend.

If you switch over to XAML view or just look at the XAML in Split view, you'll see that Blend has created ColumnDefinitions and RowDefinitions. You can see the code here:

```
<Grid.RowDefinitions>
  <RowDefinition Height="0.37*"/>
  <RowDefinition Height="0.63*"/>
</Grid.RowDefinitions>
```

```
<Grid.ColumnDefinitions>
  <ColumnDefinition Width="0.24*"/>
  <ColumnDefinition Width="0.76*"/>
</Grid.ColumnDefinitions>
```

Notice that the Columns and Rows have Height and Width values. If you hard-code the Height and Width values, it means that your Grid cannot scale to accommodate for content placed inside it. For this reason, it is good practice to *not* hard-code these values, and instead take full advantage of the way Silverlight's powerful layout engine can position objects automatically. Blend has placed Height and Width values in for you because your Grid is in Canvas Layout mode as opposed to Grid Layout mode. The Blend team created Canvas Layout mode to make it easier for designers not experienced with layout panels to get started. Fortunately for you, you are getting started with me, and I am going to teach you about the slightly more complex Grid Layout mode. At the very top left of the Grid, you can see a little button that if clicked will change the Grid's mode to Grid Layout mode, as shown in Figure 4-4.

A freshly installed Blend will default to Grid Layout mode. However, if your last project had a Layout mode of Canvas, your new projects will default to this.

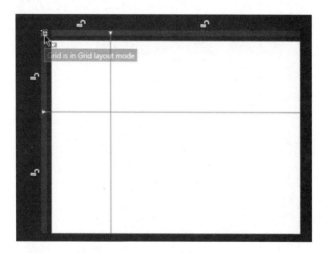

Figure 4-4. The main Grid in Grid Layout mode.

Now you will see little lock icons appear where the blue Row and Column lines are. These little lock icons allow you to lock the height of a Row or the width of a Column; click one of the lock icons so that it turns to a "locked" State. If you look at the XAML code, you will see that the RowDefinitions and ColumnDefinitions still have Height and Width values with an asterisk after them. If the Row or Column's lock icon is not locked, these values can change depending on the size of the content that they display or by the size of the application window. If you lock one of the icons by clicking it, the asterisk disappears and the lock icon appears locked. Now, if the content dynamically changes or the size of the application window changes, the locked Column or Row will not change.

Now that you have Rows and Columns, what can you do with them? Well, you can add controls into the Grid and then specify in the XAML what Row and Column they should be in. Here's how:

1. Select the **TextBlock** tool from the toolbar.

2. Draw a TextBlock on the workspace.

3. Set the text to be Row **0** Column **0**.

Now if you look at the XAML, you will see something that looks like this:

```
<TextBlock Margin="23,37,21.072,51.112" Text="Row 0 Column 0"
TextWrapping="Wrap"/>
```

You can see that the control does not specify what Row or Column it's in. If you don't specify a Column or Row, Blend will automatically place your content into Row 0 and Column 0. So, now you'll alter the code to hard-code the TextBlock to be in Row 0 and Column 0.

4. Change your code so that it resembles the following:

```
<TextBlock Margin="23,37,21,51" Text="Row 0 column 0"
TextWrapping="Wrap" Grid.Column="0" Grid.Row="0"/>
```

5. Now copy this XAML and paste it four times, changing the values for the text as well as the Grid.Column and Grid.Row so that your code looks like this:

```
<TextBlock Margin="23,37,21,51" Text="Row 0 Column 0"
TextWrapping="Wrap" Grid.Column="0" Grid.Row="0"/>
<TextBlock Margin="23,37,21,51" Text="Row 0 Column 1"
 TextWrapping="Wrap" Grid.Column="1" Grid.Row="0"/>
<TextBlock Margin="23,37,21,51" Text="Row 1 Column 0"
TextWrapping="Wrap" Grid.Column="0" Grid.Row="1"/>
<TextBlock Margin="23,37,21,51" Text="Row 1 Column 1"
TextWrapping="Wrap" Grid.Column="1" Grid.Row="1"/>
```

6. Click the **Design** tab in Blend; you will see that your TextBlocks all place themselves into their correct Rows and Columns. Your project should look like Figure 4-5.

Note that the Rows *and* Columns *start with a value of* 0, *not* 1.

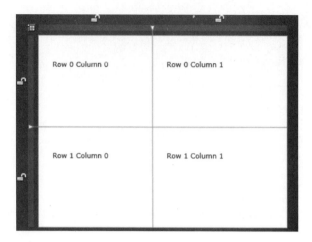

Figure 4-5. TextBlocks in different Grid Rows and Columns.

Another interesting thing about the Grid is that it positions its content using margins. Basically, *margins* determine distance from the boundaries of the Grid, or the boundaries of the Grid cell if the element is inside a Grid cell.

Say, for example, you have a Rectangle control inside a Grid, and its VerticalAlignment is set to Top and its HorizontalAlignment is set to Left. If you give the Rectangle control a Margin property of "10,10,0,0", the Rectangle will be 10 pixels from the left and 10 pixels from the top, as the values for Margin set the left, top, right, and bottom distances in that order. Conversely, if you set the Rectangle's HorizontalAlignment to Right, and its VerticalAlignment to Bottom, and then give it a Margin property of "0,0,10,10", the Rectangle control will be 10 pixels from the right and 10 pixels from the bottom.

The Canvas

The next layout element I want to talk about is the Canvas. This is one of my personal favorites because it allows the user to specify *absolute positioning of its children*. The Canvas will never change the position of child elements in it, and I find this very useful. To see how the Canvas works, you have to make some changes to the project:

1. In Blend, change the XAML so that MainPage is now 600×600 (to give you some breathing room).

2. Change each of the TextBlocks to have a Width of 150 and a Height of 20.

3. Move each of the TextBlocks up to the top left of its cell.

Your project should look something like Figure 4-6.

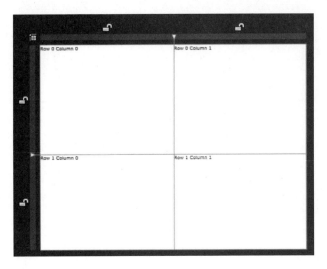

Figure 4-6. The TextBlocks are now in the top left of different cells of the parent Grid.

4. Click and hold down the **Grid** tool on the toolbar until the other layout element options become visible and select the **Canvas** layout element.

5. In the **Row 0 Column 1** cell, draw a Canvas. With the **Selection** tool, click the new **Canvas** in the **Objects and Timeline** panel so that it has a blue line around it indicating it is selected.

Now you can add some content to your Canvas because when a layout control has a blue line around it, anything drawn in the workspace will go into it. Add some content now by following these steps:

1. Select the **Ellipse** tool from the toolbar.

2. Hold down Shift and draw an Ellipse in the **Row 0 Column 1** cell.

3. With the new Ellipse selected, change the Fill to a gradient in the **Brushes** section of the **Properties** panel.

4. Change the gradient to a radial gradient and adjust the colors and gradient with the **Brush Transform** tool until you have something like what you see in Figure 4-7.

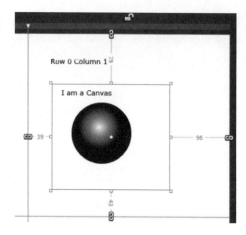

Figure 4-7. A `TextBlock` and `Ellipse` in a Canvas in your main Grid.

   5. Select the **TextBlock** tool from the toolbar.

   6. Draw out a `TextBlock` in your new Canvas.

   7. Change the text to read *I am a Canvas*.

If you look at the XAML, you will see the new Canvas inside your main Grid, and inside the Canvas you will see the `Ellipse` and the `TextBlock`. The interesting thing to see here is that similar to the Grid, the Canvas will give the elements a default position if one is not explicitly set. However unlike the Grid you don't have to create Rows/Columns, and the position in the canvas is fixed (it cannot be altered by horizontal or vertical alignment). The properties such as `Grid.Row`, `Canvas.Left`, and `Canvas.Top` are examples of `AttachedProperties`.

An `AttachedProperty` is a property that is exposed by one element and can be set by another element. In the preceding example, the `AttachedProperty` of `Canvas.Left` is exposed by the parent Canvas and can be set by the child (in the preceding case, the `Rectangle`).

In the preceding example child elements are setting `AttachedPropertys` on their parent elements. It should be noted that a parent/child relationship is not required for one element to set `AttachedPropertys` on another element.

Let's now move on to another very useful layout element called the StackPanel.

The StackPanel

A StackPanel is another layout element, and its claim to fame is that it will position content inside of it for you in a stacking manner (horizontally or vertically). This is different from the Grid or Canvas, which rely on the developer to set the relative or absolute positioning of child objects. Here you'll create a StackPanel and see exactly how it does this:

1. Select the **StackPanel** tool from the toolbar.

2. In **Row 1 Column 0**, draw out a StackPanel.

3. Select the **Ellipse** tool again from the toolbar.

4. Draw three Ellipses with fixed Heights and Widths and no margins in the newly created StackPanel. Here's the resulting XAML that Blend created:

```
<StackPanel HorizontalAlignment="Left" Margin="101,39,0,139" Width="195">
    <Ellipse Fill="#FFF4F4F5" Height="65" Stroke="Black" HorizontalAlignment="Left"
Width="83"/>
    <Ellipse Fill="#FFF4F4F5" Height="68" Stroke="Black" Width="100"
HorizontalAlignment="Left"/>
    <Ellipse Fill="#FFF4F4F5" Height="95" Stroke="Black" HorizontalAlignment="Left"
Width="104"/>
</StackPanel>
```

Notice that the StackPanel arranges your three Ellipses vertically inside of it (see Figure 4-8).

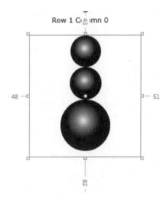

Figure 4-8. A StackPanel will position its child content horizontally or vertically.

You can override the way the StackPanel stacks its content by changing values in the XAML or by changing the Orientation property from **Vertical** to **Horizontal** in the **Layout** section of the **Properties** panel. Do that now, and you will see that the StackPanel changes from displaying its content from vertically to horizontally, as shown in Figure 4-9.

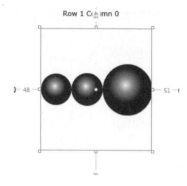

Row 1 Column 0

Figure 4-9. A StackPanel can position its child content automatically.

I set each `Ellipse` *to have a* `HorizontalAlignment` *of* `Center`. *If I hadn't done this, they would have been aligned to the left by default.*

Let's keep going and explore the next layout element in Silverlight, the Border.

The Border

The Border is a very simple layout element that allows you to draw a `Stroke` around another element and then give it a `Background` or an actual border. The Border layout element can only have one child element, and that content can be either left, right, top, bottom, or center aligned. These properties can be set manually in the XAML, or in Blend in the **Layout** section of the **Properties** panel. Try making a Border element now:

1. Select the **Border** tool from the toolbar.

2. In **Row 0 Column 1**, draw a Border.

3. Copy the `Ellipse` inslde your Canvas into the new Border.

4. Change the **HorizontalAlignment** property in the **Layout** section of the **Properties** panel to see how the child object is affected.

5. Change the **VerticalAlignment** property in the **Layout** section of the **Properties** panel to see how the child object is affected.

6. Change the Background of the border to a gradient in the **Brushes** section of the **Properties** panel.

7. Use the **Brush Transform** tool to adjust the gradient to go from top to bottom.

8. Select the **BorderBrush** property in the **Brushes** section of the **Properties** panel and select a solid color; I chose green.

9. In the **Appearance** section of the **Properties** panel, give the Border a **BorderThickness** of 3 for the left and right and 1 for the top and bottom.

Your Border should look something like that shown in Figure 4-10.

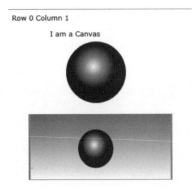

Figure 4-10. The Border content control allows you to draw a stroke and background around an element.

Item Controls

Oftentimes in Silverlight we have collections of data that need to be displayed. For example, we could have a collection of strings (a string of characters such as "Hello," "World," and "Silverlight." To better demonstrate this, I'll show you how to do the following:

- Create a new Silverlight project called ListBoxSample.
- Create sample data in Blend.
- Populate the sample data.
- Add a ListBox item control to the project.
- Bind the ListBox to the sample data.

With that, let's forge ahead and create the new Silverlight project:

1. In Blend, create a new project by clicking **File ➤ New Project**.

2. Select **Silverlight Application**.

3. Name the project ListBoxSample.

4. Click **OK**.

5. Click the **Data** tab and click the **Create Sample Data** button, as shown in Figure 4-11.

Figure 4-11. Add sample data to the project.

    6. Click **New Sample Data**.

    7. When the **New Sample Data** dialog box pops up, give the data source a name of `LBDataSource` and then click **OK**, as shown in Figure 4-12.

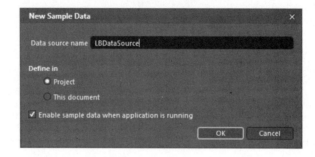

Figure 4-12. Name the data source `LBDataSource`.

    8. On the **Data** tab, click the little arrow next to **LBDataSource** and then click **Collection**.

    9. Click the **Edit sample values** button, as shown in Figure 4-13.

Figure 4-13. Edit the sample data.

    10. When the **Edit Sample Values** dialog box appears, change the number of records to 4, as shown in Figure 4-14.

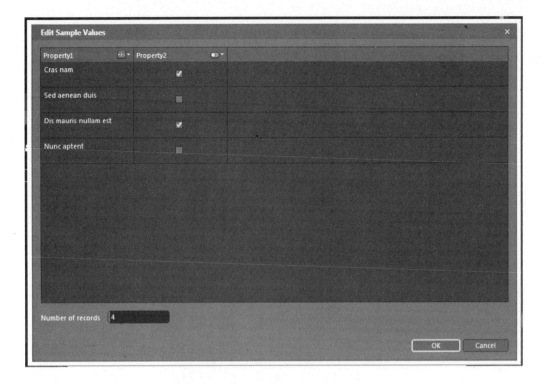

Figure 4-14. Change the number of records to 4.

> **11.** Now double-click each sample value for `Property1`, change them to *Hello*, *World*, *Silverlight*, and *Rocks*, as shown in Figure 4-15, and then click **OK**.

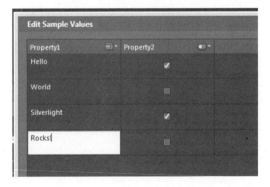

Figure 4-15. Change the value of the sample data.

At this point, you have a collection of `strings`. Now all you need to do is bind this collection to an item control. Luckily, Blend has made this very easy to do. Let's do it now:

1. On the **Data** tab, make sure the arrow next to the **LBDataSource** is turned down; click and hold **Collection** and start to drag it, as shown in Figure 4-16.

Figure 4-16. Click-hold and drag Collection.

2. Drag the collection to the **Objects and Timeline** panel and drop it onto LayoutRoot, as shown in Figure 4-17.

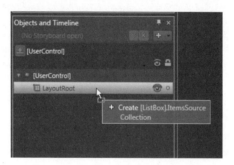

Figure 4-17. Add the collection to LayoutRoot.

Notice how when you drag it over the LayoutRoot in the **Objects and Timeline** panel, you get a message telling you that Blend is going to add a ListBox with an ItemsSource set to your collection. Also notice that when you drop the collection onto the LayoutRoot, it automatically creates a ListBox in the workspace and sets its ItemsSource to your collection. You should have what is shown in Figure 4-18.

Figure 4-18. A ListBox with an ItemsSource of the LBDataSource collection.

At this point, you should adequately understand item controls. So, with that, let's move ahead and discuss the final controls that we'll explore in this chapter: input controls.

Input Controls

Software applications by default are developed to interact with their users. HTML applications, for example, have user input controls such as text fields, buttons, radio buttons, and check boxes, just to name a few. Silverlight is no different in that it, too, has user input controls that have the ability to gather information from the user. In fact, all the HTML controls that I just named are included in Silverlight. You may recall that I mentioned in the preceding section that a `ListBox` is an item control. Interestingly, a `ListBox` is also an input control as well. If you were to run the `ListBox` application you created in the last section, you would notice that you can click any of the items (**Hello**, **World**, and so on) and they would become highlighted. The code-behind could then react to your selection, thus making it an input control. So, let's make a new sample Silverlight application called `InputControlProject` and make some input controls.

1.   In Blend, create a new Silverlight application called `InputControlProject`.

2.   On the toolbar, hold down the **Button** tool until you see a list of the other input controls, as shown in Figure 4-19.

Figure 4-19. A list of all the Silverlight input controls.

3.   Start by adding the most common of all input controls, the `Button` control.

4.   Once you have selected the `Button` control, draw a `Button` in the workspace, as shown in Figure 4-20.

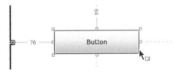

Figure 4-20. A `Button` control

Repeat this process for the CheckBox, RadioButton, and Slider controls, so that you have something that looks like Figure 4-21.

Figure 4-21. Button, CheckBox, RadioButton, and Slider controls

Now you have made four user input controls that can react to user interaction. We are going to be seeing a lot more of these and other input controls as we progress through the book, so we won't wire them up at this stage. Just know that these are a few of the built-in Silverlight input controls and that they can alter the application when interacted with.

New Silverlight 4 Controls

The recent release of Silverlight 4 saw a host of new controls, such as the Viewbox, the RichTextBox, the improved DataGrid, and even a new property for controls called FlowDirection. In this section I discuss each as well as do some hands-on experimentation.

The Viewbox

The Viewbox is a very cool tool that has existed for a long time in Silverlight's big brother Windows Presentation Foundation (WPF) and is a very handy content control. Why, you ask? The Viewbox, like the Border, can contain only one child element, which is usually another content control that can hold many child elements. The difference is that when a Viewbox is scaled, its child elements scale or shrink and grow with the Viewbox. This is not true for other content controls and makes the Viewbox very handy in certain situations. To help you understand this control a little better, go ahead and create a new project in Blend called NewSL4Stuff, as I am doing in Figure 4-22.

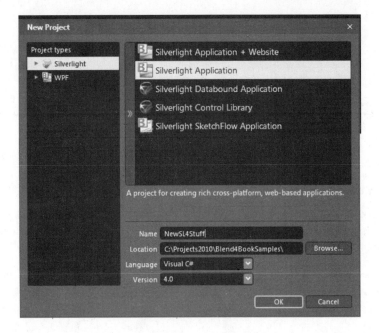

Figure 4-22. Create a new Silverlight project called NewSL4Stuff.

1. From the toolbar hold down the Content Control button until you see the other Content controls appear and click the Viewbox control, as I am doing in Figure 4-23.

Figure 4-23. Select the Viewbox control.

2. Draw a Viewbox on the artboard, as I have done in Figure 4-24.

Figure 4-24. Draw a `Viewbox` about 200×200.

    3.   Now select the Ellipse tool and make certain the `Viewbox` is selected (highlighted) in the **Objects and Timeline** panel and draw an `Ellipse` inside the `Viewbox`, as I have done in Figure 4-25.

Figure 4-25. Draw an `Ellipse` inside the `Viewbox`.

Notice that when you were drawing the `Ellipse` it was trying to snap to the edges of your `Viewbox`. This is because a `Viewbox`'s child element will try to fill up as much of the `Viewbox` as possible. Now use your selection tool and grab the top left corner of the `Viewbox` and make it bigger. Notice how its child element gets bigger as well. Now make the `Viewbox` smaller and see how its child element gets smaller too. This example is a very simple exercise, but what if you were to make the child element a Grid or Canvas and put a lot of child elements inside of it—would everything scale? Yes it would. Say, for example, you need to design a very complex icon. You can, and should use the Zoom tool. Even with the artboard at full zoom, it is difficult to do very small icons. What you could do is design it at a larger size and scale it down by placing it into a `ViewBox`. Give it a try and then we can move on and talk about the `RichTextBox`.

The RichTextBox Control

The `RichTextBox` allows you as a Silverlight 4 developer to display editable documents in a very rich way, almost like a PDF. In a `RichTextBox` you can not only have paragraphs with bold, underline, and italics but you can have other non-text items such as `Buttons`, `Hyperlinks`, `Images`, and much more. This is very handy when developing a newspaper-like application with lots of images, links, and text.

To create a `RichTextBox` click the XAML button in Blend and paste the following code inside the parent Grid named `LayoutRoot`:

```
<RichTextBox
            TextWrapping="Wrap"
            IsReadOnly="False">
        <Paragraph>
            This is a default paragraph.



        </Paragraph>
        <Paragraph>
            <Hyperlink
                NavigateUri="http://www.google.com"
                TargetName="">Google.com</Hyperlink>
        </Paragraph>
        <Paragraph>
            <Run
                Text="I love developing in Silverlight 4!" />
            <Run >Silverlight 4 is improved</Run>
        </Paragraph>
        <Paragraph
                            FontSize="22"
            TextAlignment="Right"
                            Foreground="Red">
                            This is a paragraph with underlined, 22 font,
 right-aligned red text
                            and a
                             <InlineUIContainer>
            <Rectangle
                Fill="Blue"
                Width="100"
                Height="22" />
        </InlineUIContainer>
                            Rectangle
                            </Paragraph>

                            <Paragraph
                            FontSize="12"
                            Foreground="Blue">
                            This paragraph is default aligned and has a
                             <InlineUIContainer>
            <Button Height="20" Width="100" Content="CLick Here"></Button>

                             </InlineUIContainer>
                             Button in it!
                             </Paragraph>
```

```
</RichTextBox>
```

You should see something like what I have in Figure 4-26.

This is a default paragraph.
Google.com
I love developing in Silverlight 4! Silverlight 4 is improved

This is a paragraph with underlined, 22 font, right-aligned red text and a ▮▮▮▮▮ Rectangle

This paragraph is default aligned and has a [CLick Here] Button in it!

Figure 4-26. A RichTextBox.

Notice that the RichTextBox declaration has an IsReadOnly property that is set to False. This means that when you are running this application you can edit the RichTextBox. Notice that when you run it in edit mode you cannot interact with the Buttons or Hyperlinks. Set IsReadOnly to True and you will be able to interact with those elements. Set the IsReadOnly property to True and then run the application and click on the Google link. Notice how it takes you to Google. Very cool! You may also code against the inline elements such as Buttons or even change the RichTextBox in code-behind.

Flow Direction

The FlowDirection property now gives you support for bi-directional support for both Text and Content controls. This is very helpful for developing controls that contain items with text written in languages such as Arabic. To show you this, let's switch over to our Silverlight project and create a real-world example of when we would use FlowDirection.

> *You will not find this property in Blend's Properties panel because the Blend designer does not support RTL (Right-To-Left) FlowDirection, and for this reason the Blend team has chosen not to show it. So, if you change the FlowDirection and don't see it snap to RTL in Blend, don't think you are crazy—you will see it when your application runs.*

1. From the toolbar hold down the Content Control tool, and when StackPanel is shown click it, as I am doing in Figure 4-27.

Figure 4-27. Select the StackPanel tool from the toolbar.

2. Draw a StackPanel on the artboard and give it a black background, as I have done in Figure 4-28.

Figure 4-28. Draw a StackPanel.

3. Select the new StackPanel and double-click the TextBlock tool to add a TextBlock inside the StackPanel; give it a foreground color of white. Do this again so you have two TextBlocks, as I have in Figure 4-29.

Figure 4-29. You should now have two TextBlocks in your StackPanel.

4. Now double-click the first TextBlock to edit the Text and type **in Silverlight Rocks!**

5. Double-click the second TextBlock to edit the Text and paste in **Silverlight!** (the Arabic equivalent of Silverlight Rocks!) Your StackPanel should look like what I have in Figure 4-30.

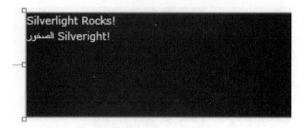

Figure 4-30. Your StackPanel should now look like this.

Although this looks quite cool, it is quite incorrect because Arabic is written and read from right to left—not left to right, as English is. We can correct this by giving the second TextBlock a FlowDirection of RightToLeft. See my code:

```
<TextBlock FlowDirection="RightToLeft" TextWrapping="Wrap" Text=
"          Silveright!" Foreground="White"/>
```

You should have what I have in Figure 4-31.

Figure 4-31. Your second TextBlock is now able to be read from right to left and is correct for the Arabic language.

As I mention earlier, this property applies to content controls as well as Text controls. For example, if we were to put a FlowDirection property of RightToLeft on the parent StackPanel, all of its children would inherit that property and thus all be aligned right. Try adding that property to the StackPanel, and you should see what I have in Figure 4-32.

Figure 4-32. Content Controls such as StackPanel can also have a FlowDirection property. And children of the control will inherit this property.

Improved Data Binding

Data Binding is an easy way for Silverlight controls to bind to data. That data can be either a set of predefined data or data of another object. For example, if you had a `String` property named `Foo` with a value of `Silverlight Rocks` you could, in XAML Data Bind a `TextBlock`'s `Text` value to the value of `Foo`, and the `TextBlock` would read `Silverlight Rocks`. Further, if the `TextBlock` had a Binding mode set to `TwoWay`, then if the `TextBlock`'s value were to change, `Foo` would change as well. Silverlight 4 has improved Data Binding in a few ways:

DependencyObject Binding

Now in Silverlight 4 you can bind to properties on a `DependencyObject` and not just on `FrameworkElements`. What, you ask is a `DependencyObject`? A `DependencyObject` is the base class of several important Silverlight classes such as `UIElements`, `Styles`, `Resource Dictionaries`, and `Transformations`. So now you can bind a Framework Element's X position in a `TranslateTransform` transformation to the value of a `Slider`. This will allow you to move the `Slider` and change the position of the `FrameworkElement`. Prior to Silverlight 4 this was not possible.

Data Validation and Data Binding

If a Silverlight entity implements the `IDataErrorInfo` interface and then is involved in a binding operation, it validates the bound properties and can then notify the UI of any binding errors and if the `NotifyOnValidationError` property is set to `True`, any error messages can be displayed. Basically this gives developers a way to know when binding errors have occurred via asynchronous server-side validation errors.

String Format, TargetNullValue, and FallbackValue

Silverlight 4 now allows you to tell the bound object how to display its data. For example, say you are binding to a `Date` object and want a particular format for that date, now you can simply set your binding expression to this:

```
<TextBox Text="{Binding Path=PublishedDate, Mode=OneWay, StringFormat='MM-dd-yyyy'}"/>
```

This will format your date to this format: `01-24-10` and override the default format of the `Date` object. Prior to Silverlight 4 the object would have to be manipulated in code-behind prior to populating the `TextBlock`.

You can now set a `FallbackValue` for a binding expression. If the binding fails for any reason, what will be displayed is the `FallbackValue`. Example:

```
<TextBox Text="{Binding Path=SomeBindingValue, Mode=TwoWay, FallbackValue=N/A}" />
```

`TargetNullValue` allows you to set a value if the binding expression encounters a null value. Example:

```
<TextBox Text="{Binding Path=QuantityOnHand, Mode=TwoWay, TargetNullValue=0}" />
```

Summary

Content or layout controls allow you to easily place content into your applications. You have gone through each of the major layout elements and actually created them with hands-on exercises. You also learned that each layout element has its own special ability:

- The Grid allows you to declare `Rows` and `Columns` so that you can then position objects precisely within that Grid.
- The Canvas allows you to specify where the content inside of it is placed by using the `Canvas.Top`, `Canvas.Left`, `Canvas.Right`, and `Canvas.Bottom` properties.
- The StackPanel positions its content automatically, but you can specify whether the content is stacked horizontally or vertically.
- The Border simply allows you to draw a `Stroke` around the content placed inside of it, as well as a `Background`.

You also learned about item controls such as a `ListBox`. You even learned how to create sample data and then bind a `ListBox`'s `ItemsSource` to it. This will prove very handy for testing when you start making your own data-driven Silverlight applications.

Finally, you learned about some new features of Silverlight 4. These are by no means *all* of the new features; features that are new to Silverlight 4 and not discussed in this chapter will be discussed in detail elsewhere in the book. In the next chapter I delve into the world of Silverlight animation and talk about how to accomplish it with timed Storyboards.

Chapter 5

Timed Storyboards:
Creating a Newton Cradle Application

What this chapter covers:

- Creating a simple Storyboard
- Types of Storyboard Animations
- How to use Storyboards to create a Silverlight Newton Cradle application
- What Behaviors are
- Using Behaviors to fire Storyboard Animations
- Modifying the Newton Cradle application to use Behaviors

You can use Storyboards to create all types of interactions with your user. For example, recently I made an information dropdown for a client. The dropdown had a paragraph or two of information, but the client didn't want all the information to be displayed unless the user was interested in reading it. So we decided to put in a More Information button that when clicked would turn the snippet of information into the full paragraphs. Further, the dropdown itself had to grow in size to be able to fit all of the new information. To do this I created two Storyboards, one named ShowMoreInfoSB (*SB* standing for Storyboard) and ShowLessInfoSB. In the ShowMoreInfoSB Storyboard I made the TextBlock containing the information grow to show all of its text and made the dropdown background longer so the information would not extend pass the dropdown. I did the opposite for the ShowLessInfoSB. When the More Information button was clicked, I toggled between firing off one of the two Storyboards. The control worked as designed, and I had a very happy client.

There are many more ways you can use Storyboards to create user interaction through Animation, but this is just a short, real-world example. After I briefly describe what Storyboards are, I walk you through an example of how to create a very simple Storyboard that moves a TextBlock across the screen.

What Are Storyboards?

Storyboards are simply a way to animate `Dependency` properties of objects in Silverlight. Animation through Storyboards can add so much to RIAs (Rich Internet Applications) by adding interactivity and movement. Storyboards are usually contained in XAML and executed in code in Silverlight, but more recently people have been using Behaviors to fire them, thus eliminating the need for code-behind. I talk more about Behaviors later in this chapter and in more depth in chapter 7.

Storyboards work by animating properties (`Dependency` Properties) over time. The properties that are animated are up to you; for instance, you can animate the `X` and `Y` properties of an object so that the object moves across the screen. But that's not all, because pretty much any property you can set on an object, such as `Fill` (color), `Width`, `Height`, `Text`, `Opacity`, and so on can be set in a Storyboard. As long as the value of the property is of type Double, Color, or Point, you can animate it.

You can also animate properties of other types using `ObjectAnimationUsingKeyFrames`; however, this type of Animation uses *discrete interpolation*, which means that the values cannot really animate but will rather jump from one value to the next. An example of this would be when you try and change the `Text` value of a `TextBlock` over a three-second Timespan; the `TextBlock` would have the original value until it hit three seconds and then would jump/switch to the new value. Many don't really consider this true animation, but it is very handy when you just need the value of something to change, as in my earlier More Information button example.

Creating a Simple Storyboard

Open Blend and create a new Silverlight application called `SimpleStoryboard`. You can see my settings in Figure 5-1.

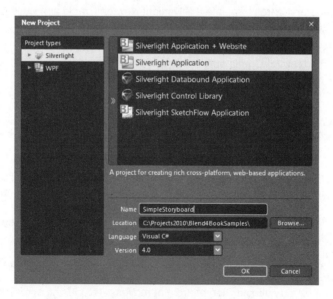

Figure 5-1. Create a new Silverlight application called `SimpleStoryboard`.

1. First, double-click the `TextBlock` control on the toolbar to add a `TextBlock` to the application.

2. Change the `TextBlock` to read "Silverlight rocks!" so that you have what I have in Figure 5-2.

Figure 5-2. A `TextBlock` that reads "Silverlight rocks!"

3. In the **Objects and Timeline** panel, rename the `TextBlock` to `MyTextBlock`.

4. Press F6 to enter Blend's Animation mode.

Notice how the **Objects and Timeline** panel moves to the bottom of the Blend IDE? This is to give the animator more physical space for an Animation Timeline. What's that you say? You don't see one of those? Well, you will once you create a Storyboard! So, let's do that now.

1. Click the **New Storyboard** icon with a plus symbol on it in the **Objects and Timeline** panel, as in Figure 5-3.

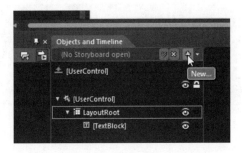

Figure 5-3. Create a new Storyboard.

2. When the **Create Storyboard Resource** dialog box appears, leave the default name and click **OK**.

Blend adds a Storyboard Timeline on the right of the **Objects and Timeline** panel, as shown in Figure 5-4.

CHAPTER 5

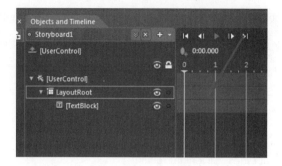

Figure 5-4. A Timeline has been added to the Objects and Timeline panel.

Blend also put a red line around the artboard and a red icon on the top left of it. This is to indicate to the animator that whatever is done from this point on is being recorded into the Storyboard you just created. To stop recording you can either click the red circle icon or close the Storyboard. Now let's start to add some animation!

1. Grab the yellow playhead in the Timeline and drag it out to the two-second mark of the Timeline, as I have done in Figure 5-5.

Figure 5-5. Move the playhead out to the two-second mark.

2. Now press the V key to activate the Selection tool, select the TextBlock, and move it to the bottom right of the artboard. You should have what I have in Figure 5-6.

Figure 5-6. Your TextBlock should now be in the right, lower corner of your artboard.

3. You can now click the Play Storyboard icon, as in Figure 5-7, to play your Storyboard and see how it looks when it fires in the running application.

98

Figure 5-7. The Play icon is just one of the controls you can use to test your Storyboards in Blend.

You can see there are other controls located in the same area that help you to test and manipulate your Storyboards before you use them in your running applications. The other controls are, in order, the Go to first frame, Go to previous frame, play, Go to next frame, and finally Go to last frame `Buttons`.

4. Now click the **Close Storyboard** icon to stop recording and close the Storyboard, as I am doing in Figure 5-8.

Figure 5-8. Close the Storyboard.

5. Press F6 to return out of the Animation mode.

6. Now we need to add a Behavior to start the Storyboard when the application begins. To do this, click the **Asset Library** button on the toolbar and under **Behaviors** click and hold the **ControlStoryboardAction** Behavior, as in Figure 5-9.

Figure 5-9. The ControlStoryboardAction in the Asset Library.

7. Drag this Behavior onto the `LayoutRoot` Grid in the **Objects and Timeline** panel, as I am doing in Figure 5-10, and release it.

Figure 5-10. Drag the ControlStoryboardAction Behavior to the LayoutRoot Grid.

    8. Now with the ControlStoryboardAction Behavior selected, go to the **Properties** panel and in the **Trigger** bucket change the **EventName** to Loaded, as shown in Figure 5-11.

Figure 5-11. Change the properties for the ControlStoryboardAction Behavior in the Properties panel.

    9. In the **Common Properties** bucket, change the Storyboard to the name of your Storyboard (mine was the default name of Storyboard1). See Figure 5-12.

Figure 5-12. Change the Storyboard property to the name of your Storyboard.

That's all you need to do! Press F5 to run the application and watch your `TextBlock` slide across the screen. Now that you know a little bit about how to create Storyboards, let's learn about them and then go on to make our Newton Cradle application.

Storyboard Animation Types

What, you might be asking, is an Animation anyway? Animations inherit from the `Timeline` object. So in their most basic form, Animations are Timelines. As such they have certain properties such as `Duration` for how long the Animation will last, `RepeatBehavior` that tells Animations whether they run once or repeat, `SpeedRatioProperty` that determines how fast the Animation progresses through the Timeline, and so on. As I mentioned earlier, in Silverlight you can animate any property as long as it is of types `Color`, `Double`, `Point`, or `Object` (`ObjectAnimationUsingKeyFrames`). All of these, save the `Object`, use either the `From/To` (as in the object is *instructed* to move *from* point X *to* point Y) type of Animation, or the `KeyFrame`-based Animation (where the object is *placed* in one `KeyFrame` at the beginning of the Animation and in another `KeyFrame` at the end of the Animation, and the computer fills in the gaps), while the `Object` can only make use of `KeyFrame`-based Animation. In the next section you will see each property's corresponding Animation type (`From/To` and `KeyFrame` based) as well an example of an Animation that can be produced using them.

Color

- `From/To` *Animation:* `ColorAnimation`
- `KeyFrame` *Animation:* `ColorAnimationUsingKeyFrames`
- *Example usage:* Animate the `Color` of a `Rectangle` (either `GradientBrush` or `SolidColorBrush`)

Point

- `From/To` *Animation:* `PointAnimation`
- `KeyFrame` *Animation:* `PointAnimationUsingKeyFrames`
- *Example usage:* Animate the Center Point of a `Rectangle`

Double

- `From/To` *Animation:* `DoubleAnimation`
- `KeyFrame` *Animation:* `DoubleAnimationUsingKeyFrames`
- *Example usage:* Animate the `Height` and/or `Width` of a `Rectangle`.

Animations also have a `TargetName` property and a `TargetProperty` property. As you have probably guessed, the `TargetName` is the name of the object that the Animation will take place upon, and the `TargetProperty` is the property that will be affected by the Animation. The following is a sample Storyboard that will make use of a `DoubleAnimationUsingKeyFrames`, a

ColorAnimationUsingKeyFrames, and a PointAnimationUsingKeyFrames that will make a Rectangle object named rectangle change its X and Y position, Height and Width and Color.

```xml
<Storyboard x:Name="SampleStoryboard">
                        <DoubleAnimationUsingKeyFrames
 Storyboard.TargetProperty="(UIElement.RenderTransform).
 (TransformGroup.Children)[3].(TranslateTransform.X)"
 Storyboard.TargetName="rectangle">
                                <EasingDoubleKeyFrame KeyTime="0:0:1"
 Value="152.517"/>
                        </DoubleAnimationUsingKeyFrames>
                        <DoubleAnimationUsingKeyFrames
 Storyboard.TargetProperty="(UIElement.RenderTransform).
 (TransformGroup.Children)[3].(TranslateTransform.Y)"
 Storyboard.TargetName="rectangle">
                                <EasingDoubleKeyFrame KeyTime="0:0:1"
 Value="27.66"/>
                        </DoubleAnimationUsingKeyFrames>
                        <ColorAnimationUsingKeyFrames
 Storyboard.TargetProperty="(Shape.Fill).(SolidColorBrush.Color)"
 Storyboard.TargetName="rectangle">
                                <EasingColorKeyFrame KeyTime="0:0:1"
 Value="#FFF11212"/>
                        </ColorAnimationUsingKeyFrames>
                        <DoubleAnimationUsingKeyFrames
 Storyboard.TargetProperty="(UIElement.RenderTransform).
 (TransformGroup.Children)[0].(ScaleTransform.ScaleY)"
 Storyboard.TargetName="rectangle">
                                <EasingDoubleKeyFrame KeyTime="0:0:1"
 Value="1.424"/>
                        </DoubleAnimationUsingKeyFrames>
                        <DoubleAnimationUsingKeyFrames
 Storyboard.TargetProperty="(UIElement.RenderTransform).
 (TransformGroup.Children)[0].(ScaleTransform.ScaleX)"
 Storyboard.TargetName="rectangle">
                                <EasingDoubleKeyFrame KeyTime="0:0:1"
 Value="1.88"/>
                        </DoubleAnimationUsingKeyFrames>
                        <PointAnimationUsingKeyFrames
 Storyboard.TargetProperty="(UIElement.RenderTransformOrigin)"
 Storyboard.TargetName="rectangle">
                                <EasingPointKeyFrame KeyTime="0:0:1"
 Value="0.809,0.202"/>
                        </PointAnimationUsingKeyFrames>
                </Storyboard>
```

As you can see from the preceding XAML code, a Storyboard is declared with the name SampleStoryboard. It then has a DoubleAnimationUsingKeyFrames which moves the Rectangle's (named rectangle) X position. And then the next DoubleAnimationUsingKeyFrames moves the Rectangle in Y space. There is then a ColorAnimationUsingKeyFrames node that changes the color of the Rectangle. The next DoubleAnimationUsingKeyFrames changes the scale of the Rectangle's Y scale. Then the next DoubleAnimationUsingKeyFrames changes the Rectangle's X scale. Finally, the last Animation, a PointAnimationUsingKeyFrames, moves the Rectangle.

Now that you know a little about Storyboards I would like to guide you through the development of your first Silverlight application that uses Storyboard Animations to duplication Newton's Cradle effect. If you don't know what Newton's Cradle is, go look it up on the Internet, I'll wait.

Creating the Newton's Cradle Application

Back already? Good, let's fire up Blend and create Newton's Cradle using Timed Storyboard Animations!

1. In Blend click File ➤ New Project, as I did back in Figure 5-1.

2. When the New Project dialog box appears (Figure 5-13), select Silverlight for the Project type.

3. Select the Silverlight 4 Application template.

4. Name the new Project NewtonCradle.

5. Click OK.

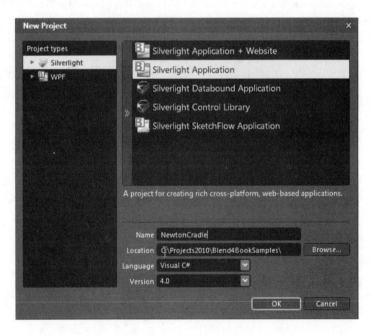

Figure 5-13. Create a new Silverlight project called NewtonCradle in Blend.

Now that you've created the new Silverlight project, you need to create a re-usable `UserControl` that will represent the balls that hang from the strings in a Newton's Cradle device. If you have never seen a Newton's Cradle device, or don't think you have, take a look at Figure 5-14 so you have a reference of what we are going to build.

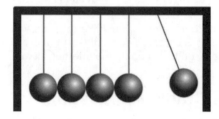

Figure 5-14. A Newton's Cradle device

Now we can start to create the `BallOnString` `UserControl`.

1. Select the Ellipse tool from the toolbar.

2. Hold down the Alt+Shift keys and draw an `Ellipse` on the artboard that is about 75×75.

3. In the **Properties** panel click the `Fill` property and then click "**Gradient brush,**" as I do in Figure 5-15.

Figure 5-15. Change the `Fill` to a gradient fill.

4. Now click the "**Radial gradient**" button as I do in Figure 5-16.

Figure 5-16. Change the gradient to a Radial gradient.

5. Select the "**Reverse gradient stops**" button, as shown in Figure 5-17.

Figure 5-17. Reverse the colors of the gradient stops.

6. Select the Gradient tool from the toolbar and adjust the gradient so it looks like what I have in Figure 5-18.

Figure 5-18. Use the Gradient tool and adjust your gradient to look like this.

7. Back in the **Properties** panel, select the Stroke property and click the "No brush" icon, as I am doing in Figure 5-19.

Figure 5-19. Remove the Stroke.

Now that we have the ball, we can draw the string.

1. From the toolbar click and hold the Ellipse tool until you see the Line tool and then click it, as I do in Figure 5-20.

Figure 5-20. Select the Line tool.

2. Hold down the Shift key to constrain the angle of your Line and draw a Line so that you have what I have in Figure 5-21. Note: because you just created an Ellipse with a radial Fill and no Stroke, you may need to make sure your newly created Line is selected and click the "**No brush**" button for the Fill and click the **Solid Color brush** for the Stroke in the **Properties** panel. With my Line selected, my **Properties** panel looks like what I have in Figure 5-22—make certain yours looks the same.

Figure 5-21. Draw a Line above the Ellipse.

Figure 5-22. You may have to adjust your `Line`'s Brushes settings to match what I have here.

Now that we have these two visuals set up, we can turn them into a `UserControl`.

1. In the **Objects and Timeline** panel, click the `Ellipse`, hold down the Control key, and click the `Line` to select them both.

2. Right-click and click **Make Into UserControl** to turn both into a `UserControl` so we can put multiple instances of it on the artboard.

3. When the **Make Into UserControl** dialog box appears, name the new `UserControl` `BallAndString` and click **OK,** as I am doing in Figure 5-23.

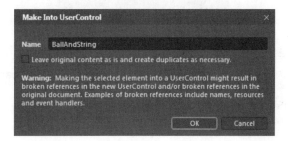

Figure 5-23. In the Make Into UserControl dialog box, name the `UserControl` `BallAndString`.

Blend then creates a new `UserControl` called `BallAndString` and places you into it. You should have what I have in Figure 5-24.

Figure 5-24. Your new `BallAndString` `UserControl`

Now you can switch back to `MainPage.xaml` and see that instead of an `Ellipse` and Path (for the `Line`) in your **Objects and Timeline** panel, you see an unnamed `UserControl` of type `BallAndString`. Figure 5-25 shows my **Objects and Timeline** panel.

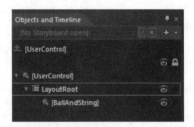

Figure 5-25. You can now see the `UserControl` in the Objects and Timeline panel.

Double-click the `BallAndString` `UserControl` in the **Objects and Timeline** panel and name it `Ball01` as it is always good to name objects that are interactive.

Now is a good time to talk about `RenderTransformOrigin`. The `RenderTransformOrigin` property sets the center point from which any `RenderTransform` Animation on the object will occur relative to the bounds of the object. By default the `RenderTransformOrigin` of any given `UserControl` will be in the center of the control. Thus, if we made an Animation that made this `UserControl` swing, the center of the Animation would be the center of the `UserControl`. In order to attain a convincing swing Animation, we need the center point to be at the very top center of the `UserControl`. To do this, follow these steps:

1. Locate the `BallAndString` `UserControl` in `MainPage.xaml` and press the V key to select your Selection tool.

2. Notice there is a small circular icon in the dead center no bigger than a lowercase o.

3. Place your mouse directly over this center point icon so that your cursor turns into an icon with four arrows facing outward, as shown in Figure 5-26.

Figure 5-26. Move the center point of the `UserControl`.

4. Now click and drag the center point to the very top, center of the `UserControl`, as I have done in Figure 5-27.

Figure 5-27. The center point is now at the top of the `UserControl`.

5. To test this move your cursor to the very bottom right of the `UserControl`, until your cursor turns into a two-sided curved arrow, and rotate the control. It should rotate from the very top center, as mine is doing in Figure 5-28.

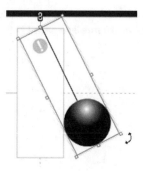

Figure 5-28. The `BallAndString` `UserControl` should now rotate from the center, top.

If your UserControl rotates like mine does in Figure 5-28, then you are ready to move on. If it does not, go back and re-read the last section and perform steps 1–5 again until you get it to rotate like mine does.

Now that you have one BallAndString UserControl set up, you can hold Control and press the Z key to undo the test rotation you just performed. We need to duplicate this control five more times so that we have six balls in total.

1. Select and move your current UserControl to the left of the artboard. Hold down the Alt key and click and drag a new instance of the UserControl out. Holding down Alt while clicking and dragging an object duplicates it in the Visual Tree. You can also accomplish this by selecting the UserControl and clicking Control+C to copy and Control+V to paste in a copy of the UserControl.

2. Do this four more times until you have six BallAndString UserControls lined up as I do in Figure 5-29.

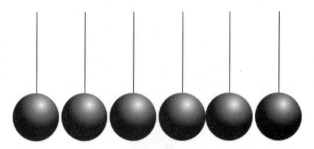

Figure 5-29. Put six instances of the BallAndString UserControl on the artboard.

3. Next select all your balls by either drawing an invisible box around them all or by holding down the Control key and clicking each one individually in the **Objects and Timeline** panel, or right on the artboard itself.

4. With them all selected, move them to the center of the artboard.

5. Double-click each one in the **Objects and Timeline** panel and name them Ball01 through Ball06 so that your **Objects and Timeline** panel look like what I have in Figure 5-30.

Figure 5-30. Name each instance of `BallAndString UserControls` so we can add them to the Storyboard.

The next thing you need to do is to create a stand that your balls will appear to swing from. You don't want people to think that these balls can swing from the sky, right? Do that now:

1. Draw a `Rectangle` on the artboard that covers all `BallAndString UserControls` and use the handles at the top left to give the corners a rounded edge, as I am doing in Figure 5-31.

Figure 5-31. Draw a `Rectangle` on the artboard.

2. Now right-click the newly created `Rectangle` and click **Path ➤ Convert to Path,** as I am doing in Figure 5-32.

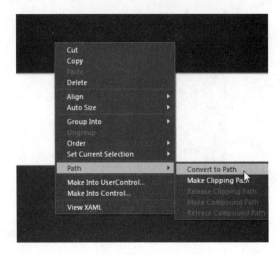

Figure 5-32. Convert the `Rectangle` to a Path.

3. With the `Rectangle` still selected, press Control+C to copy it and Control+V to paste a copy of it onto the artboard.

4. Hold down the Shift and Alt keys and make the Path on top smaller than the one under it.

5. Release the Shift and Alt keys and use the bottom scale handle to make the top Path longer than the one behind it, as I have done in Figure 5-33.

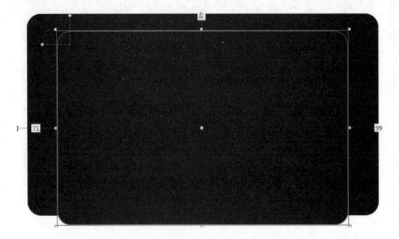

Figure 5-33. Add another `Rectangle` to the artboard.

6. Hold down Control and click the top, smaller Path *first* and then the second, larger Path so they are selected.

7. Right-click and click **Combine ➤ Subtract,** as I am doing in Figure 5-34.

Figure 5-34. Combine both Paths using the Subtract method.

You should then see something like what I have in Figure 5-35.

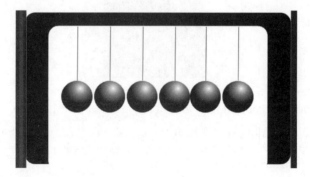

Figure 5-35. Your artboard should now look what I have here.

It's time to actually create our Animation Storyboards! Let's do that now:

1. Press F6 to go into Animation mode.

2. In the **Objects and Timeline** panel, which is now located on the bottom of the artboard, click the **New Storyboards** button as shown in Figure 5-36.

Figure 5-36. Create a new Storyboard.

3. In the **Create Storyboard Resource** dialog box, give the Storyboard the name SwingingSB, as I do in Figure 5-37.

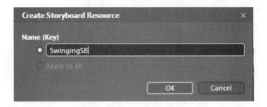

Figure 5-37. Name the new Storyboard SwingingSB.

4. Now you will see an empty Timeline. Move the playhead out to half a second, as I am doing in Figure 5-38.

Figure 5-38. Move the playhead out to half a second on the Storyboard Timeline.

5. Now select the very right most UserControl and put your cursor at the bottom right, until you see the cursor turn into a rotated two-sided arrow cursor, and rotate the UserControl –45 degrees, as I am doing in Figure 5-39.

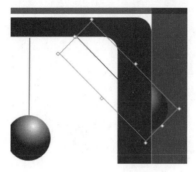

Figure 5-39. Rotate the right-most `UserControl` to –45 degrees.

6. Move your playhead out to 1 second and rotate the `UserControl` back to its original position, as I have done in Figure 5-40.

Figure 5-40. With the playhead at one second, rotate the right-most `UserControl` back to its default position.

7. With your playhead still at 1 second, you need to record the angle of the left-most `UserControl`. You do this by first moving it 15 degrees left (Figure 5-41) and then back to 0 degrees (Figure 5-42).

Figure 5-41. With the playhead at 1 second, move the left-most `UserControl` to 15 degrees.

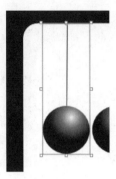

Figure 5-42. With the playhead still at 1 second, move the playhead back to the default position.

This may seem insignificant, but if you now look at your Timeline you will see a `KeyFrame` that has recorded the 0 angle of the left-most `UserControl`. This is because we don't want to start animating its angle until precisely now, and when it does start we want it to start an angle of 0. This `KeyFrame` is recording that 0 angle for us.

8. Now move your playhead out to 1.5 seconds and rotate the left-most `UserControl` to 45 degrees, as I am doing in Figure 5-43.

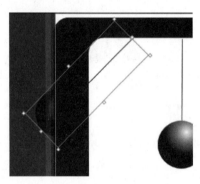

Figure 5-43. With the playhead at 1.5 seconds, rotate the `UserControl` to 45 degrees.

9. Finally, move your playhead out to 2 and rotate your `UserControl` back to its starting angle of 0. The Storyboard should now look like this:

    a. At .5 seconds move the right-most `UserControl` to an angle of –45 degrees.

    b. At 1 second the right-most `UserControl` should be back at its original position.

    c. At 1.5 seconds the left-most `UserControl` should be at an angle of 45 degrees.

    d. At 2 seconds the left-most `UserControl` should be back at its original position.

At this point you have finished with Blend and need to switch to Visual Studio to code up the project. In the **Projects** panel, right-click the Solution and left-click **Edit in Visual Studio, as shown** in Figure 5-44.

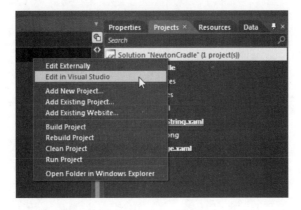

Figure 5-44. Edit the application in Visual Studio 2010.

1. Open `MainPage.xaml` and locate the `SwingingSB` Storyboard. It should look like this:

```
<Storyboard x:Name="SwingingSB">
```

2. Change it so that it has a `RepeatBehavior` of `Forever` like this:

```
<Storyboard x:Name="SwingingSB" RepeatBehavior="Forever">
```

3. Now open `MainPage.xaml.cs` and locate the `InitializeComponent()` call (see the following code in bold):

```
public partial class MainPage : UserControl
    {
    public MainPage()
    {
        // Required to initialize variables
        InitializeComponent();
    }
```

4. Under that line give the name of the Storyboard, type a period, and specify the `Begin()` command:

```
public MainPage()
    {
        // Required to initialize variables
        InitializeComponent();
        SwingingSB.Begin();
    }
```

Now press F5 to compile and run your application, and voilà! A working Newton Cradle with timed Storyboard Animations! (see Figure 5-45).

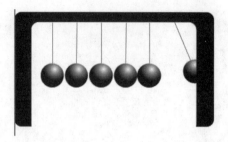

Figure 5-45. The running application will function just like a physical Newton Cradle.

Behaviors

Behaviors are simply classes of code that manipulate an object. An example would be a Behavior that changes the color of an object to, say, red. These Behaviors can then be attached to objects via drag and drop in Blend. The objects are then manipulated by the code that is contained in those classes. Behaviors allow designers to easily attach functionality to objects without having to write any code. Blend 4 comes with some pre-written Behaviors. You learn more about Behaviors in Chapter 7, but I want to show you how you could have made the Newton Cradle application you just completed run with no code-behind whatsoever. I'm going to make use of a Behavior that ships with Blend called `ControlStoryboardAction`.

1. The first thing you need to do is remove the line of code in `MainPage.xaml.cs` that reads:

```
SwingingSB.Begin();
```

To prove to yourself that the Newton Cradle application no longer functions, press F5, and you will see that there is no longer any Animation. That's because we are no longer telling the `SwingingSB` Storyboard to begin. Now switch back over to Blend and reload the application if asked.

Implementing the ControlStoryboardAction Behavior

Now that you're back in Blend, you can implement the `ControlStoryboardAction`.

1. Click the Asset Library tool on the toolbar and click the **Behaviors** tag, as I am doing in Figure 5-46.

Figure 5-46. Open the Asset Library.

2. Cick and hold The `ControlStoryboardAction` Behavior, drag it to the **Objects and Timeline** panel, and drop it on the Grid named `LayoutRoot`. Your **Objects and Timeline** panel should look like what I have in Figure 5-47.

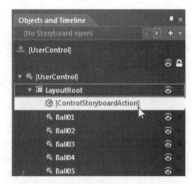

Figure 5-47. Add the `ControlStoryboardAction` Behavior to the `LayoutRoot` Grid of the application.

3. In the **Properties** panel, under the Trigger bucket, find the dropdown that says `EventName`. From that dropdown select **Loaded,** as I am doing in Figure 5-48. This means that this Behavior will begin when the `LayoutRoot` is loaded.

Figure 5-48. Change the `EventName` property to `Loaded` in the Trigger bucket of the Properties panel.

4. In the **Properties** panel find the **Common Properties** bucket, click the **Storyboard** dropdown, and change it to `SwingingSB`, like I am doing in Figure 5-49.

Figure 5-49. Change the Storyboard to `SwingingSB` in the Storyboard property in the Common Properties bucket of the Properties panel.

Now press F5 once again to run the application, and once again our Newton Cradle has animation. The only difference is that we are now firing the Storyboard without code-behind but with a Behavior instead! In short, instead of calling the Storyboards directly in code-behind, we are telling the Behavior to call it for us when the `LayoutRoot` is loaded.

A video tutorial of how to do timed Storyboards Animations can be found on my blog at: `http://www.windowspresentationfoundation.com/?p=60.` You can also find a tutorial on how to use Storyboards in conjunction with the Visual State Manager to make a slide in/out navigation bar here: `http://windowspresentationfoundation.com/?p=409.`

Summary

In this chapter you learned about Storyboards and how they make use of Animation objects to make things move in Silverlight. You then learned about the different types of Animations that exist in Silverlight. We even looked at sample code that makes use of all of the different types of Animations in one Storyboard. We then set off to create a sample application that uses Storyboard Animations to create a Newton Cradle. Originally we started off by firing off our Storyboard in code-behind, but then we learned of Behaviors that can help us easily attach pre-written code to objects. We were then able to remove the code-behind and use a Behavior that ships with Blend called `ControlStoryboardAction` to start the Storyboard for us when the `LayoutRoot` Grid is loaded. Next you are going to learn about the Visual State Manager (VSM) that allows us to easily wrap Storyboards into Visual States and easily fire them off.

To view this project in action go here:

`http://windowspresentationfoundation.com/SLSamples/NewtonCradle/`

The source code can be downloaded here:

`http://windowspresentationfoundation.com/SLSamples/NewtonCradle/NewtonCradle.zip`

Note: URLs are case sensitive.

> *When you try and run files/applications downloaded from the Internet, Visual Studio 2010 may give you a warning. Worry about any other files you download from the Internet, but not about mine; I promise they are safe and virus free! If, however, Visual Studio 2010 gives you compile errors when trying to run files that you have downloaded from me, please go here:* `http://blogs.msdn.com/b/brada/archive/2009/12/11/visual-studio-project-sample-loading-error-assembly-could-not-be-loaded-and-will-be-ignored-could-not-load-file-or-assembly-or-one-of-its-dependencies-operation-is-not-supported-exception-from-hresult-0x80131515.aspx` *and read how to fix this issue.*

Challenge: Animations in Silverlight have the ability to use Animation Easing. *Animation Easing* is a way to easily apply built-in Animation functions to your Storyboards. These Easing effects help make your Animation behave in a more realistic way. For example, here are a couple Animation easing functions:

- `CubicEase`: The Ease accelerates based on a cubic function.
- `CircleEase`: The Ease accelerates based on a circular function.

Further, these Animation functions have `EasingModes`, two of which are:

- `EaseOut`: The Ease occurs at the start of the Animation.
- `EaseIn`: The Ease begins at the end of the Animation.

I challenge you to use Easing Functions with Easing Modes to make the NewtonCradle application we made earlier act in a more natural way.

> *Hint: I have already given you the Function and Mode you need to complete the challenge.*
>
> *If you get stuck, my source code has the easing built in. Click on a KeyFrame and look in the Easing Bucket of the Properties panel to see the type of Easing Function and Mode any particular KeyFrame makes use of.*

Chapter 6

Using VSM and Blend 4's State Panel to Create a Silverlight Media Player

What this chapter covers:

- Understanding the Visual State Manager
- Understanding Blend 4's States panel
- Creating a Silverlight test project to show how to use VSM
- Creating a new Silverlight project
- Styling up a Media Player
- Adding Play, Pause, and Stop buttons
- Adding a `MediaElement` to the project
- Adding a `Source` and Clip region to the `MediaElement`
- Creating VSM States to hide and show the Play, Pause, and Stop buttons
- Wiring up the States and the Play, Pause, and Stop buttons using Behaviors

Silverlight 2 saw the addition of something called the Visual State Manager (VSM) that allows you to easily add States to any `UIElement` such as a `Button`, `Rectangle`, `Ellipse`, or even an entire `UserControl`. You can, of course, do this in code-behind, but it would be very tedious. For that reason Microsoft introduced the **States** panel. The **States** panel allows you to very easily and very quickly create States. Then all you need to do is wire up those States using Behaviors to trigger them in XAML with no code-behind whatsoever.

In this chapter I first show you how to use VSM to create States for a simple `Button` and wire up those States using Behaviors. I then show you how to take what you have learned and create a very highly styled Silverlight Media Player that makes use of VSM to show and hide the navigation buttons (Play, Pause, Stop). If you are like me and have absolutely no patience, you can navigate the following URL and see what the final Silverlight Media Player product will look like in action:

http://windowspresentationfoundation.com/BookProjects/SLVSMMediaPlayer/bin/Debug/Default.html

With that let's get to it!

The Visual State Manager (VSM)

Often when I explain VSM to developers they get confused and mistake the Visual State Manager for Blend's **States** panel. That being the case, I thought it best to clear up the difference between the two right off the bat. The *Visual State Manager* is the code that actually contains the States (in code) and executes the different States. By contrast Blend's **States** panel (explained and shown in depth in the next section) is the tool you will use to create the Visual States. Here is an example of Visual State Manager markup code in XAML.

```
<VisualStateManager.VisualStateGroups>
    <VisualStateGroup
        x:Name="MouseEnterLeaveStateGroup">
        <VisualStateGroup.Transitions>
            <VisualTransition
                GeneratedDuration="0:0:0.3" />
        </VisualStateGroup.Transitions>
        <VisualState
        x:Name="MouseEnter" />
    <VisualState
```

```
                x:Name="MouseLeave" />
        </VisualStateGroup>
</VisualStateManager.VisualStateGroups>
```

Let's quickly run through this code:

1. A `VisualStateManager.VisualStateGroups` is declared.

2. A `VisualStateGroup` is then declared and named `MouseEnterLeaveStateGroup`.

3. A default transition time is declared and tells all `VisualStates` in this group to take .5 seconds to execute

4. A `VisualState` named `MouseEnter` is declared with an empty Storyboard.

5. Another `VisualState` is declared called `MouseLeave` with an empty Storyboard.

The following is the accompanying C# code-behind that will execute the `MouseEnter` state when a `Button` named `MyBtn` is moused-over:

```csharp
void MyBtn_MouseEnter(object sender, MouseEventArgs e)
{
    VisualStateManager.GoToState(this, "MouseEnter", true);
}
```

Seems pretty straightforward, right? Next I explain and show you Blend's **States** panel.

Using Blend 4's States Panel

As I've said, Blend's **States** panel is how you create a VSM. You can see this panel in Figure 6-1.

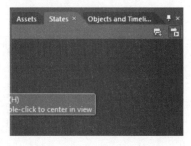

Figure 6-1. Blend 4's State panel above the Objects and Timeline panel.

This is a very hands-on book; so let's roll up our sleeves and create a new Silverlight application and use VSM and the State panel to create some States for a `Button`.

A Simple Silverlight Project

To show you how to quickly use VSM, we are going to make a simple sample application and create a StateGroup with States. Let's get to it!

1. Open Blend 4 and click **File ➤ New Project,** as I am doing in Figure 6-2.

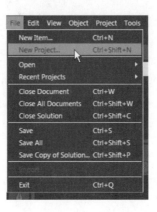

Figure 6-2. Create a New Project in Blend 4.

2. In the **New Project** dialog box, select **Silverlight Application**.

3. Name the project SimpleVSMProject.

4. Select the location where you want to save the project.

5. Click **OK** (see Figure 6-3).

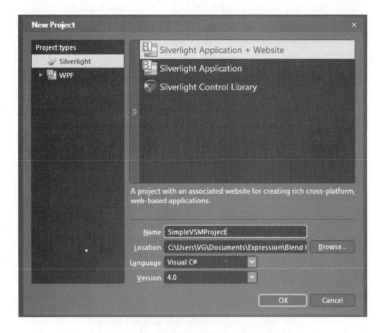

Figure 6-3. Make certain your New Project dialog box is the same as what is shown here.

6. Once Blend 4 has created the project, select the Rectangle tool from the toolbar, as I am doing in Figure 6-4.

Figure 6-4. Select the Rectangle tool.

7. Next draw a `Rectangle` that will act as a `Button` on the workspace, as I have done in Figure 6-5.

Figure 6-5. Draw a `Rectangle` control on the workspace.

8. Next select the `Rectangle` and in the **Properties** panel give it a name of `MyRectangle` and give it a solid color fill of black. See Figure 6-6.

Figure 6-6. Name and color the `Rectangle`.

Now you should have something like I have in Figure 6-7.

Figure 6-7. Your `Rectangle` should look like this.

9. Go over to Blend's **States** panel and click "**Add state group**," as I am about to do in Figure 6-8. Blend then highlights the new `StateGroup` so you can name it. Name the new `StateGroup` `MouseEnterLeaveStateGroup`, as I have done in Figure 6-9.

Figure 6-8. Add a new `StateGroup` in the States panel.

Figure 6-9. Name the `StateGroup`.

Notice that next to the `StateGroup` name you can see "0s." This represents the amount of time in seconds that it takes for the States (yet to be added) to complete.

10. Double-click this number and change it to **0.5**; this means your States will take 0.5 seconds to complete. Your **States** panel should look like what I have in Figure 6-10.

Figure 6-10. Your States panel should look like what I have here.

With the `VisualStateGroup` created you can now add a State (called a `VisualState` in code).

11. To add a State click the "**Add state**" button, as I am about to do in Figure 6-11.

Figure 6-11. Add a State to your `VisualStateGroup`.

12. Name your new State `MouseEnter`. Click the "**Add state**" button again and name the new State `MouseLeave`. Your **States** panel should look like what I have in Figure 6-12.

Figure 6-12. Your State panel should now have one `StateGroup` and two States.

129

I do not know if you noticed but once you created a new State, Blend placed a red line around your workspace to indicate that any action you perform on any `FrameworkElement` on the workspace is being recorded. I didn't have you perform any actions because you can simply click on a State anytime to start recording your actions.

13. So, go ahead and click on the `MouseEnter` State so the red line will appear around your workspace. Now change the fill color of your `Rectangle` to red, as I have done in Figure 6-13.

Figure 6-13. Change the `Rectangle` to be red.

14. Click the default **Base** State in the **States** panel so you are no longer recording your actions, as I have done in Figure 6-14.

Figure 6-14. Click the Base State.

Notice that the `Rectangle` is now black again. This is because in the default Base State the `Rectangle` is its original color. Now, you may be thinking that I am going to instruct you to click the `MouseLeave` State and do something to your `Rectangle`. I'm not. Why, you ask? Well, let's think of the behavior we want:

- When the application starts, we want the `Rectangle` to be its default color.
- When the `Rectangle` has a mouse over it, we want it to turn red.
- When the mouse moves off of the `Rectangle`, we want it to turn back to its default color of black.

This being the case, your `MouseLeave` State is already correct because if you click the `MouseLeave` State you will see that the `Rectangle` is already black. So you are probably asking yourself, why create a `MouseLeave` State if the default State of the `Rectangle` is black? That's a good question and one I had to ask myself when writing this chapter. If you don't add the `MouseLeave` State (that has the `Rectangle` with a fill of black), then when your mouse leaves the `Rectangle` in the running application it will stay Red. So, you need to have the `MouseLeave` State.

Now it is time to hook up the Visual States in the Visual State Group to the `MouseEnter` and `MouseLeave` events. Do that now:

1. On the toolbar click the **Assets** button.

2. Click the **Behaviors** bucket.

3. Click and hold the `GoToStateAction` Behavior and drop it onto `MyRectangle` in the **Objects and Timeline** panel (see Figure 6-15).

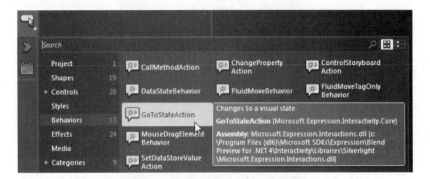

Figure 6-15. The `GoToStateAction` Behavior in the Asset Library.

4. Now go to the **Properties** panel and with the newly added Behavior selected in the **Objects and Timeline** panel, find the **Trigger** bucket.

5. Click the dropdown labeled `EventName` and select `MouseEnter`, as I am doing in Figure 6-16.

Figure 6-16. Change the `EventName` for the `GoToStateAction` Behavior to `MouseEnter`.

6. Now find the **Common Properties** in the **Properties** panel and Change the `StateName` to the `MouseEnter` State of the `MouseEnterLeaveStateGroup`, as I am doing in Figure 6-17.

Figure 6-17. Change the `StateName` property to `MouseEnter`.

7. Now drag another instance of the `GoToState` Behavior onto `MyRectangle` in the **Objects and Timeline** panel.

8. This time set the `EventName` to MouseLeave.

9. Change the `StateName` to `MouseLeave`.

10. Press F5 to compile and run the application; place your mouse over the `Rectangle` and notice how it turns red. Move it off the `Rectangle` and notice how it turns black again!

So, what's the big deal? True, this is not a very impressive implementation of VSM. With that, I want to show you how you can take full advantage of the powerful VSM to make a cool application. Next you are going to build a very styled media player and then use VSM to show and hide the video controls (Play, Pause, and Stop).

Creating a Media Player Using VSM

Before we get to it, I would like to give credit where credit is due. The design I am going to show you how to implement is loosely based on the Deadline Advertising website (http://www.dead-line.com), designed by my very talented friend, former colleague, and brand new daddy Mr. Chris McCall. It's shown in Figure 6-15.

Figure 6-18. The Web site `http://www.dead-line.com` designed by Chris McCall.

Creating the Silverlight Project in Blend 4

The first thing to do is close the current project in Blend and create a new Silverlight application. Name it `SLVSMMediaPlayer`. Your **New Project** dialog box should look like Figure 6-19.

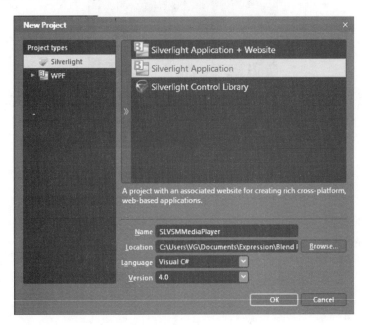

Figure 6-19. The Blend 4 New Project dialog box.

Designing the Navigation Orb

The next thing you need to do is to create the navigation orbs. These are going to be a series of Ellipses, one on top of the next, with different gradients. After we have the series of Ellipses the way we want them, you group them into a Canvas and tell Blend 4 to turn them into a Silverlight Button control. Let's start now:

1. On the Blend toolbar hold down the Rectangle tool until you see the option for the Ellipse tool.

2. Draw an Ellipse on the workspace, as in Figure 6-20.

Figure 6-20. Draw an Ellipse on the workspace.

3. With the Ellipse selected give it a **Gradient fill** in the **Properties** panel, as I am about to do in Figure 6-21.

Figure 6-21. Give the Ellipse a Gradient fill.

4. Adjust the color stops so that the Gradient goes from a gray to white color, as I have done in Figure 6-22.

Figure 6-22. Adjust the Gradient of the Ellipse.

    5. Now select the Stroke property and click "**No brush**," as in Figure 6-23.

Figure 6-23. Remove the Stroke from the Ellipse.

    6. In the **Objects and Timeline** panel, select the Grid named LayoutRoot.

    7. In the **Properties** panel change the background color from white to black.

    8. Now select the Ellipse again and press Control+C to copy it.

    9. Press Control+V to paste another Ellipse on top of it.

10. Hold down Alt (to make the `Ellipse` scale from the center).

11. Hold down Shift (to make the `Ellipse` stay symmetrical).

12. With the Selection tool selected, grab one of the corner Scale handles and move your mouse to make the top `Ellipse` smaller than the first, in Figure 6-24.

When doing detailed placement of vector graphics on Blend's artboard, it is sometimes easier to turn off snaplines. The icon for this is located just above the Results panel at the bottom of the Blend IDE.

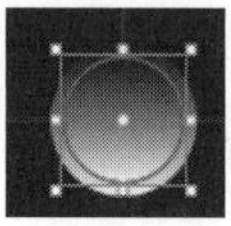

Figure 6-24. Scale the top `Ellipse` so that it is smaller than the bottom `Ellipse`.

13. Now change the top `Ellipse` to a solid color fill of black (it should turn black by default when you select **Solid Color**). See Figure 6-25.

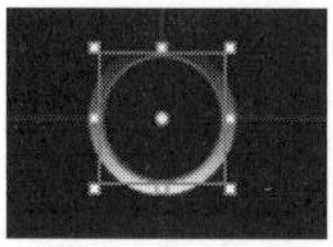

Figure 6-25. The top `Ellipse` should now be black.

14. Copy the topmost `Ellipse` and press Control+C to copy.

15. Press Control+V to paste in another `Ellipse`.

16. Set the new top `Ellipse` to have a linear Gradient and no `Stroke` so that you have what I have in Figure 6-26.

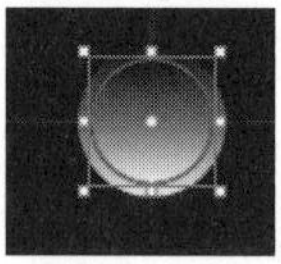

Figure 6-26. Add another `Ellipse`.

17. Now change the color stops so that the Gradient goes from white to white.

18. Select the right color stop.

19. Change the Alpha (see arrow in Figure 6-27) to be 0%.

Figure 6-27. Change the Gradient to go from white to white with the right white color with an Alpha of 0%.

You should now have something that looks like what I have in Figure 6-28.

Figure 6-28. This `Ellipse` has a linear Gradient that goes from white to white with the right color Alpha of 0.

20. Adjust the top `Ellipse` so that it is smaller and a little oblong until you have what I have in Figure 6-29.

Figure 6-29. Your top `Ellipse` should now look like this.

Looking at Chris's design, I see that the outer gray bezel (for lack of a better word) is smaller than what I have. So:

21. In the **Objects and Timeline** panel, select the `Ellipse` that is at the top of the Visual Tree (the one nearest the `LayoutRoot`, that is, the one at the bottom of the stack). See Figure 6-30.

Figure 6-30. Select the topmost `Ellipse` in the Visual Tree.

22. Now hold down Shift+Alt and use the scale handles to adjust the size of the `Ellipse` so you have what I have in Figure 6-31.

Figure 6-31. Your orb should look like this now.

I think that looks pretty good. At this point you are ready to group all your `Ellipses` into a Canvas and have Blend 4 turn them into a Silverlight Button control. Do that now:

23. With the Selection tool (the shortcut to select the Selection tool is the V key), draw a box around all of the `Ellipses` so they are all selected.

24. In the **Objects and Timeline** panel, right-click to bring up the context menu and then left-click **Group Into ➤ Canvas**, as I am about to do in Figure 6-32.

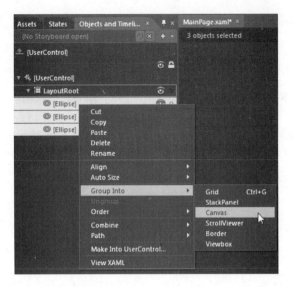

Figure 6-32. Group all `Ellipses` into a Canvas.

25. Now with the newly created Canvas selected, click **Tools ➤ Make Into Control**, as I am about to do in Figure 6-33.

26. When the Make Into Control dialog box appears, select Button as the control type, as I am doing in Figure 6-34.

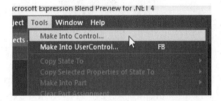

Figure 6-33. Make the new Canvas in a control.

Figure 6-34. Select Button as the control type.

27. In the **Name (Key)** section, give the new `Button` a Style name of `Style_OrbButton` and click OK.

Now you will see that in your **Objects and Timeline** panel you no longer have a Canvas with three `Ellipses` in it but rather a `Button` control. Notice, though, how the text of the `Button` is black and not centered on the `Button` (see Figure 6-35). We can fix that by using a `TextBlock` which gives more control for positioning and color. Let's do that now:

1. Select the `ContentPresenter` control from the **Objects and Timeline** panel. This control is what gives the `Button` its text. With the `ContentPresenter` selected, press Delete to delete the control.

Figure 6-35. The newly created `Button` control.

2. Click the `TextBlock` control from the toolbar and draw a `TextBlock` that is about double the length of the orb. Change its foreground color to white in the **Objects and Timeline** panel on top of the `Button`, as I have done in Figure 6-36.

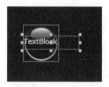

Figure 6-36. Draw a `TextBlock` with a white foreground color.

3. In the **Text** bucket of the **Properties** panel, click the **Paragraph** tab and then change the `TextAlignment` property from Left to Center, as I am doing in Figure 6-37.

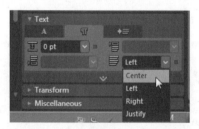

Figure 6-37. Change the `TextAlignment` property to Center.

4. Adjust your `TextBlock` so that it is centered on the background orbs, as I have done in Figure 6-38.

Figure 6-38. Center the `TextBlock` on the orbs.

Now no matter what the `Text` of the `Button` is it will be centered on the background orbs. The only problem that is if left like it currently is, every instance of the new `Button` control will have a `Text` value of `TextBlock`. We can use Template binding to make the `Text` always be the value of the `Content` property (set in XAML). Let's `TemplateBind` the `Text` property now:

5. In the **Common Properties** bucket of the **Properties** panel, locate the `Text` property and click the "**Advanced** property options" icon to the very right (which looks like a little white square), as I am doing in Figure 6-39:

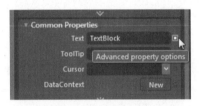

Figure 6-39. Click the "Advanced property options" icon.

6. Now click **Template Binding ➤ Content**, as I am doing in Figure 6-40. Notice now the text for the `Button` control changes to "Button."

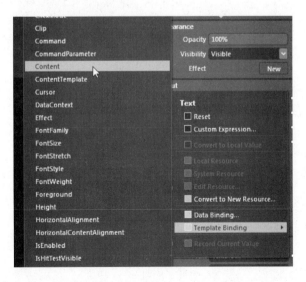

Figure 6-40. Template bind the `Text` to the `Content` property.

7. Now to stop editing the Style for the `Button`, click **[Button]** on the breadcrumb at the top right of the artboard, as I am doing in Figure 6-41.

Figure 6-41. The breadcrumb control.

8. Now with the Button selected in the **Objects and Timeline** panel, find the `Content` property in the **Common Properties** bucket of the **Properties** panel and change it from "Button" to "Play," as I am doing in Figure 6-42.

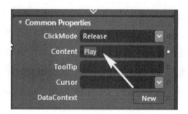

Figure 6-42. Change the default `Button` text to read "Play."

9. Press the Enter key and notice how the `Button` on the artboard changes to match what you just entered into the `Content` property field (see Figure 6-43).

Figure 6-43. Your new `Button` should now look like this.

10. Select the `Button` and copy and paste it two times, so that you have three orb `Buttons`, as shown in Figure 6-44.

Figure 6-44. You should now have three orb `Buttons` on the workspace.

Now you need to name each `Button` and give them the correct `Content` property (so they have the correct text).

1. Select the first orb and in the **Properties** panel name it `PlayBtn`.

2. In the **Common Properties** bucket of the **Properties** panel give it a `Content` property of `Play`.

3. Name the second orb `PauseBtn` with a `Content` of `Pause`.

4. Name the third orb `StopBtn` with a `Content` of `Stop` so that you have what I have in Figure 6-45.

Figure 6-45. Your `Buttons` should all be named and have the correct `Content` (text).

Creating the Backplate for the MediaElement

Now you need to create the background for your `MediaElement`. In looking at my project, I realized that I have left the default size of the application, which Blend set to a `Width` of 640 and a `Height` of 480. Let's go ahead and change that to a bigger size to give us a little breathing room.

1. Select the `UserControl` in the **Objects and Timeline** panel, as in Figure 6-46.

2. In the **Layout** bucket of the **Properties** panel, change the `Height` to 600 and the `Width` to 800.

Figure 6-46. Select the main `UserControl` in the Objects and Timeline panel.

Now that you have a little more space to work with, let's go ahead and create the `Backplate` for the `MediaElement`.

3. Select the Ellipse tool from the toolbar.

4. Hold down the Shift+Alt keys and draw an `Ellipse` on the workspace. Make it about the size I have in Figure 6-47.

> Resizing the main `UserControl` resized my `Buttons` and made them look strange. If this occurs to you, just use the resizing handles and make it the size it was before you did the resize.

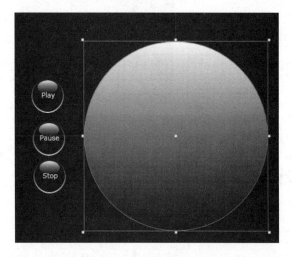

Figure 6-47. Draw an `Ellipse` on the workspace roughly 400×400.

5. Give the `Ellipse` a Gradient fill and no `Stroke`, as I have done in Figure 6-47.

6. Now copy and paste the `Backplate Ellipse` with a solid black fill.

7. Hold down the Shift+Alt keys and use the resize handles to make the top `Ellipse` a little smaller than the bottom one; give it a solid color fill of black, as in Figure 6-48.

Figure 6-48. Copy and paste a new `Ellipse` with a black fill.

It is starting to look good, but I think at this point it would look much better if we put a highlight effect on top of the `Backplate`, the same as we did for the `Buttons`. Let's do that now:

1. Copy and paste the `Ellipse` with the black fill.

2. Give it a Gradient fill.

3. Change the Gradient to go from white to white.

4. Select the right color stop and change the **Alpha** value to 0%.

5. Use the resize handles and make the `Ellipse` a little smaller and a little oblong so that you have something like Figure 6-49.

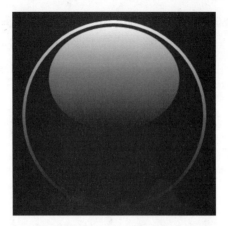

Figure 6-49. Give the topmost `Ellipse` a Gradient with the right color stop with an Alpha of 0.

You still need to tweak the Gradient a bit to get the effect we are looking for.

1.   Select the **Gradient** tool, as I am doing in Figure 6-50.

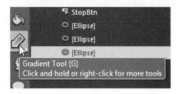

Figure 6-50. Select the Gradient tool.

2.   Select the highlight `Ellipse` and use the Brush Transform handles to adjust the Gradient so that it looks like what I have in Figure 6-51.

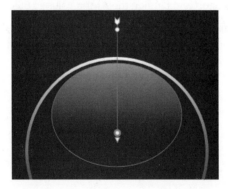

Figure 6-51. Adjust the Gradient with the Brush Transform tool.

The next thing I want you to do is to create another highlight Ellipse with a Radial Gradient fill. This one's a little trickier to conceptualize, so we'll do it a different way. This time, I give you the XAML so you can place it under the XAML of the last Ellipse in your markup. Once you've added the code, you can go ahead and use the **Brush Transform** tool to play around with the fill in Design mode to see how I accomplished this Gradient if you like. The code for this final highlight Ellipse is as follows:

```
<Ellipse Margin="298,250,292,188" RenderTransformOrigin="0.5,0.5">
                <Ellipse.RenderTransform>
                        <CompositeTransform Rotation="180"/>
                        </Ellipse.RenderTransform>
                        <Ellipse.Fill>
                                <RadialGradientBrush RadiusY="1.077" RadiusX="1.241"
  Center="0.46,0.567" GradientOrigin="0.46,0.567">
                                        <RadialGradientBrush.RelativeTransform>
                                                <CompositeTransform CenterY="0.567"
CenterX="0.46" Rotation="-17.915"/>
                                        </RadialGradientBrush.RelativeTransform>
                                        <GradientStop Color="White" Offset="1"/>
                                        <GradientStop Color="Transparent"
Offset="0.459"/>
                                        <GradientStop Color="White" Offset="0.577"/>
                                </RadialGradientBrush>
                        </Ellipse.Fill>
                </Ellipse>
```

You may have to move the new highlight Ellipse in Design view to get it in the correct position so that you have something like I have in Figure 6-52.

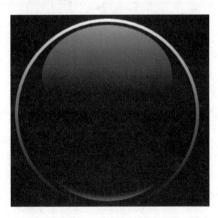

Figure 6-52. Your Backplate should look like this at the stage.

The next thing to do is add some decorative Ellipses and Rectangles. Do that now:

1. Select the Ellipse tool and hold down the Shift+Alt keys; draw an Ellipse on the workspace, as I have done in Figure 6-53.

Figure 6-53. Draw a decorative `Ellipse` on the workspace.

2. Give the new `Ellipse` a Gradient fill.

3. Add two new color stops to the center by clicking in the color bar twice, as I have done in Figure 6-54.

Figure 6-54. Add two color stops to the center of the Gradient.

4. Change the leftmost color stop to a color of #FF0D0F35.

5. Change the color of the color stop to the right of the one above to #FF878787.

6. Change the color stop to the right of the one above to #FF878787 as well.

Finally change the color stop of the far rightmost to #FF050620, so that you have what I have in Figure 6-55.

Figure 6-55. Your decorative `Ellipse` should look something like this.

7. Now copy and paste the decorative `Ellipse`.

8. Move the new `Ellipse` down below the one you copied from.

9. Hold down the Shift+Alt keys and make the new `Ellipse` a little smaller than the one you copied from.

10. Repeat the preceding steps until you have something like I have in Figure 6-56.

Figure 6-56. Decorative `Ellipses`.

Now you want to add some decorative `Rectangles` to the right of the Media Player.

1. Select the Rectangle tool from the toolbar.

2. Draw a `Rectangle`.

3. Give the `Rectangle` a Gradient fill.

4. Leave the default gradient.

5. Copy the `Rectangle` and make it smaller than the one you copied from.

6. Repeat these steps until you have something like what I have in Figure 6-57.

Figure 6-57. Decorative `Rectangles`.

At this stage your `Backplate` should look something like I have in Figure 6-58.

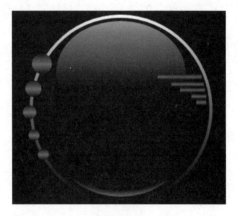

Figure 6-58. The Media Player Backplate.

1. In the **Objects and Timeline** panel, select all the `Ellipses` and `Rectangles` that comprise the `Backplate` and group them into a Canvas.

2. In the **Properties** panel name the newly created Canvas `Backplate`.

Adding the MediaElement

I think the `Backplate` looks pretty good at this stage, so I think you should add the `MediaElement`.

1. Click the **Asset Library**.

2. In the search field type **MediaElement**, as I have done in Figure 6-59.

3. When the `MediaElement` appears select it.

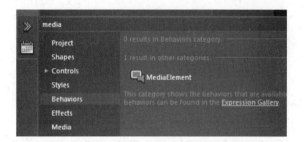

Figure 6-59. Find the `MediaElement` in the Asset Library.

4. Draw a `MediaElement` on the workspace, as I have done in Figure 6-60.

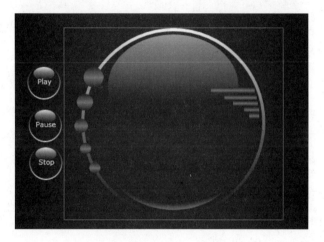

Figure 6-60. Draw a `MediaElement` on the workspace.

5. In the **Media** bucket of the **Properties** panel, click the "**Choose an image**" button, as I am about to do in Figure 6-61.

Figure 6-61. Click the "Choose an image" button.

6. Navigate to a video on your hard drive that is in WMV or MPEG format.

7. Double-click the video file.

8. Now select the `MediaElement` and name it `TheME` in the **Properties** panel.

You should see the `MediaElement` on the workspace populate with the first frame of your video file (see Figure 6-62). You may think it looks really bad, as the `MediaElement` is covering up most of the `Backplate`. You would be right to think such a thing. To fix this problem you can add a Clip Geometry. A *Clip Geometry* is simply a geometric shape that will clip or hide certain regions of the object being clipped.

Figure 6-62. The `MediaElement` with a `Source` video.

9. Select the Ellipse tool from the toolbar .

10. Hold the Shift+Alt keys and draw an `Ellipse` over the `MediaElement`, as I have done in Figure 6-63.

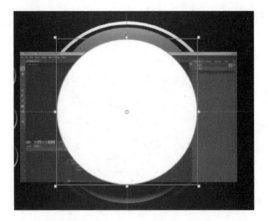

Figure 6-63. The `MediaElement` with an `Ellipse` over it.

11. Right-click the new `Ellipse` to bring up a context menu.

Left-click **Path** ➤ **Make Clipping Path**, as I am about to do in Figure 6-64.

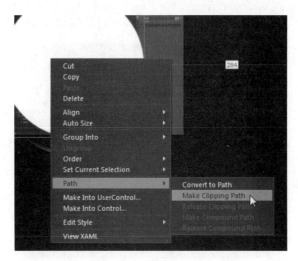

Figure 6-64. Turn the Ellipse into a Clipping Path.

12. When the **Make Clipping Path** dialog box pops up, select TheME, as I have done in Figure 6-65.

Click **OK**.

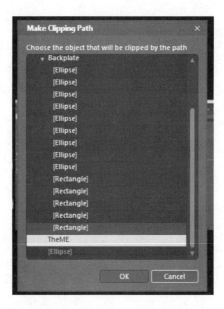

Figure 6-65. Select TheME from the dialog box.

Notice now the MediaElement named TheME is now clipped based on the shape of the Ellipse and the Ellipse has disappeared. At this point your MediaElement may need to be positioned to be in the center of the Backplate. See Figure 6-66.

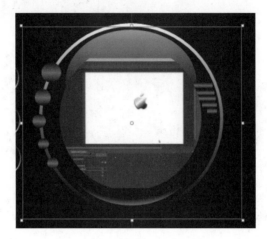

Figure 6-66. The MediaElement now has an Ellipse Clip Geometry.

You may notice that the MediaElement is sitting above the highlights and a little bit of the decorative Rectangles. To change that you need to move TheME into the Backplate Canvas and just under the highlight Ellipses.

1. Make sure the Backplate Canvas is expanded in the **Objects and Timeline** panel.

2. In the **Objects and Timeline** panel, select TheME.

3. Drag it to the correct place in the Backplate Canvas. See Figure 6-67.

Figure 6-67. Move `TheME` into the `Backplate` and under the highlight `Ellipse`s.

Your `MediaElement` and `Backplate` should look like what I have in Figure 6-68. We're now ready to position those navigation controls we created earlier so we can control the video.

Figure 6-68. The `MediaElement` in the `Backplate`.

Positioning the Navigation Buttons and the Backplate

The navigation Buttons and the Backplate are in the wrong places on my layout, so what I want you to do is to put the navigation Buttons on the right side of the Backplate and then center both items so that you have what I have in Figure 6-69.

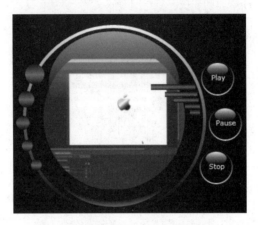

Figure 6-69. The correctly positioned Backplate and navigation Buttons.

Adding a Reflection

I promised you that this would be a highly styled Media Player, and what is any self-respecting styled application without reflections in this day and age? To accomplish that, we need to duplicate the Backplate, rotate it 360 degrees, and then add an OpacityMask to it so that it appears that our Media Player has a slight reflection. Let's do that now:

1. Select the Backplate in either the workspace or the Objects and Timeline panel.

2. Copy and paste another one into the workspace.

3. Name it BackplateReflection in the Properties panel and delete the MediaElement in the copy so you only have one MediaElement in your entire application.

4. Flip the Backplate to make it appear as a reflection, so it looks like what I have in Figure 6-70.

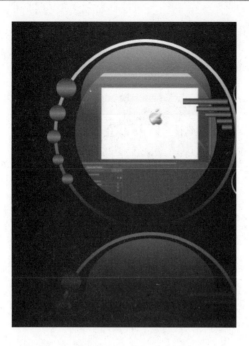

Figure 6-70. Copy, flip, and rename the reflection `Backplate`.

5. With `BackplateReflection` selected, go to the **Properties** panel and give it an `OpacityMask` with a Gradient, as I have done in Figure 6-71.

Figure 6-71. Give `BackplateReflection` an `OpacityMask`.

6. Set both color stops to be white.

7. Set the left color stop to an Alpha of 0%.

8.   Set the right color stop to an Alpha of 40%.

Use the Brush Transform tool and adjust the `OpacityMask` so it looks like what I have in Figure 6-72.

Figure 6-72. Adjust the `OpacityMask`.

Adding the States

Well, I think it is finally time for you to add the States, because you have now completed the final design. I know it is not quite as intricate as the design by Chris McCall, but remember I did say that this design was *loosely based* on his. What we want to happen via the use of the VSM is for the navigation `Buttons` and the design elements (`Ellipses` on the left and bars on the right) to disappear in a very cool way when the mouse moves off the entire Media Player and to do the opposite when the mouse moves over the player. With that, go ahead and add a State group.

1.   In the **States** panel click the **Add State Group** button.

2.   Name the new State `MouseEnterLeaveStateGroup`.

3.   Make the default transition time 0.5 seconds, as I have done in Figure 6-73.

Figure 6-73. Add a new `StateGroup` in Blend's State panel.

4.   Add two new States for `MouseEnter` and `MouseLeave`, as I have done in Figure 6-74.

Figure 6-74. Add the `MouseEnter` and `MouseLeave` States.

5. Now click the `MouseLeave` State and start recording what will occur when the mouse leaves the Media Player. I'm going to have the navigation `Buttons` animate and disappear when we leave the Media Player, and then animate back again when the mouse enters it. I'll also move the decorative elements off, and then back on again on `MouseEnter`.

6. I start by making my navigation `Buttons` spin around a few times and then shrink. See Figure 6-75.

7. Make the `Opacity` 0 in the **Properties** panel under the **Appearance** bucket. Do this for all three navigation `Buttons`.

Figure 6-75. Spin, Shrink, and make the navigation `Buttons` have an `Opacity` of 0 in the `MouseLeave` State.

8. Move your decorative `Ellipses` off the left of the Media Player, as in Figure 6-76.

9. Set their Opacity to 0 in the **Appearance** bucket of the **Properties** panel.

10. Scale the decorative `Rectangles` to be very small, as I have done in Figure 6-77.

11. Give them an Opacity of 0 in the Appearance bucket of the Properties panel.

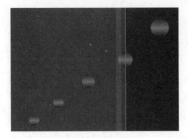

Figure 6-76. Move the decorative `Ellipses` off to the left of the Media Player and give them an `Opacity` of 0.

Figure 6-77. Scale down the decorative `Rectangles` and give them an `Opacity` of 0.

Your Media Player should now look like what I have in Figure 6-78 for the `MouseLeave` State.

Figure 6-78. Your Media Player should now look like this in the `MouseLeave` State.

Click the **Base** State, and your Media Player should be back to the default appearance, which is also how it appears in the `MouseEnter` State. Remember from our simple project earlier: because the `MouseEnter` State is supposed to look like the `Base` State we needn't do anything to it. Now we need to add the Behaviors to trigger the `MouseEnter` and `MouseLeave` States.

Using Behaviors to Trigger the MouseEnter and MouseLeave States

Now that we have our User Interface (UI) built and our different States, it is time to trigger those States. We could switch over to Visual Studio 2010 to do this in code-behind but we can do it all right in Blend using Triggers!

1. Click the Asset Library, click the **Behaviors** tab, and click and hold the `GoToStateAction` Behavior, as I am doing in Figure 6-79.

Figure 6-79. Find the `GoToStateAction` Behavior in the Asset Library.

2. Drag the `GoToStateAction` Behavior onto the `UserControl` in the **Objects and Timeline** panel, as I have done in Figure 6-80.

Figure 6-80. Drag the `GoToStateAction` Behavior onto [`UserControl`] in the Objects and Timeline panel.

3. Now go to the **Properties** panel and in the Trigger bucket change the `EventName` to `MouseLeave`.

4. In the **Properties** panel locate the **Common Properties** bucket and change the StateName to the MouseLeave State, so that your Properties panel looks like what I have in Figure 6-81.

Figure 6-81. Edit the properties for the GoToStateAction in the Properties panel.

5. Now drag another instance of the GoToState Behavior onto [UserControl] and this time in the **Properties** panel change the EventName to MouseEnter in the **Triggers** bucket and change the StateName in the **Common Properties** bucket to the MouseEnter State—so that your **Properties** panel for the second GoToStateAction Behavior looks like what I have in Figure 6-82.

Figure 6-82. Edit the properties for the second `GoToStateAction` Behavior.

6. Almost there… now add one more `GoToStateAction` Behaviors to [`UserControl`] and this time set the `EventName` in the **Triggers** bucket to `Loaded` and the `StateName` to the `MouseLeave` State. This will make the `Buttons` and decorations fly off screen as soon as the application is loaded. Your **Properties** panel should look like what I have in Figure 6-83.

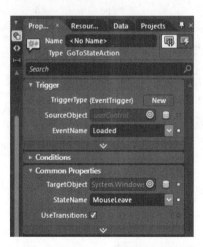

Figure 6-83. Edit the properties for the third and final `GoToStateAction` Behavior.

Now if you press F5 to run the application, you will see that the `Buttons` and decorations do in fact fly off when the application loads. Place your mouse over the application and watch as the `Buttons` and decorations fly back into view. Move your mouse off and watch them fly off again. Pretty cool, yes? The

VSM allowed us to quickly and easily create very cool transition effects for our Media Player, all without writing a *single* line of code.

Let's now talk about Easing functions that will make our animations a little more realistic and fun.

Adding Easing Functions to Animations to Make Them More Realistic and Fun

Now that we have our Visual States, we can use Easing functions to make them a little more life-like and cool. Easing functions are mathematical equations that simulate physics and allow your animations to move in a more realistic, lifelike way. Microsoft really stepped up its game with Easing functions in Blend 3, but I didn't really talk about them much in my last book. I decided to add a little bit about them in this publication. I want to change the default transition time for our Visual State Group from half a second to one full second and then add an Easing function called Bounce Out. This will have the effect of our animations starting off very smooth and then bouncing as they come to an end. You will understand more once you see the effect in action. Let's edit our Visual State Group and add the Easing function now:

1. In the **States** panel click the Easing button, which is on the left of the transition Time.

2. Click the dropdown arrow button on the right and then click the Bounce Out Easing function (see Figure 6-84).

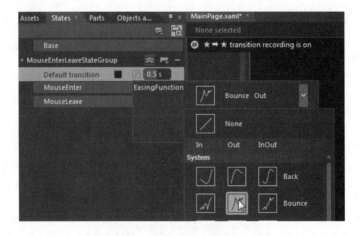

Figure 6-84. Adding an Easing Function to the Visual State Group.

3. Now change the Default Transition time to 1 second. This will allow a little more time for the animation to complete the bouncing. Half a second makes the objects bounce too fast and does not do the Easing function justice.

4. Press F5 to run the application and watch your Buttons and decorations bounce in and out of view. Cool, right?

Challenge: I have you add an Easing function to the default transition. But you can actually add different Easing functions to each of the Visual States (MouseEnter and MouseLeave). I want you to have the

Buttons and decorations Bounce Out on `MouseEnter` and then Bounce In on `MouseLeave`. If you need a hint, take a look at how my **States** panel has been modified (see Figure 6-85). (Only look at my **States** panel if you cannot figure it out yourself, because my hint *will* show you how meet the challenge.)

Figure 6-85. The hint to the challenge. Only read if you get stuck!

Adding Behaviors to Add the Play, Pause, and Stop Functionality

The behaviors required for this chapter are available for you to download here: `http://windowspresentationfoundation.com/Blend4Book/SL4Dlls.zip`. Save the file to your hard drive and extract the DLL files. Keep in mind where you extracted these DLL files, as you are going to use them in the next step.

1. In your project right-click the **Projects** panel, right-click the **References** folder, and left-click Add Reference.

2. Navigate to where you extracted the DLL files you just downloaded and select them, as I am doing in Figure 6-86.

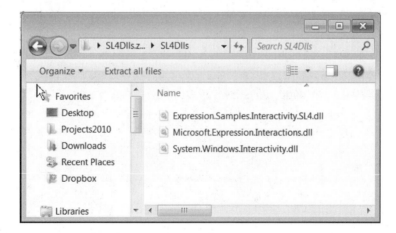

Figure 6-86. The SLADlls.zip you just downloaded.

3. Hold down the Control key, click `Expression.Samples.Interactivity.SL4.dll`, `Microsoft.Expression.Interactions`, and `System.Windows.Interactivity`, and click **OK.**

4. Click the Asset Library, click the **Behaviors** tab, and look for the `PlayMedia` behavior, as I have done in Figure 6-87.

Figure 6-87. The `PlayMedia` Behavior.

You may have to rebuild your solution before your Behaviors appear in the Asset Library.

5. Drag the `PlayMedia` Behavior and drop it onto the `PlayBtn` in the **Objects and Timeline** panel and let it go.

6. Now that the Behavior is attached to your `PlayBtn` you can select it, if it is not already in the **Objects and Timeline** panel, and go to the **Properties** panel to set the properties for this Behavior.

7. In the **Trigger** bucket of the **Properties** panel set the `EventName` to `Click`.

8. In the **Common Properties** bucket, find the `TargetObject` field. Click the Target Picker icon that looks like a mini dartboard (shown by the arrow in Figure 6-88).

Figure 6-88. The Target Picker icon looks like a little dartboard.

9. Now you will see that your cursor turns into an arrow and target icon. Click the `MediaElement` named `TheME` in the **Objects and Timeline** panel.

10. You have completed the Play button. Now from the Asset Library, drag an instance of the `PauseMedia` Behavior to the `PauseBtn`.

11. Again change the `EventName` to `Click` and set the `TargetObject` again using the Target Picker. You have completed the Pause button.

12. Finally, from the Asset Library drag an instance of the `StopMedia` Behavior to the Stop button, change the `EventName` to Stop, and use the Target Picker to set `TheME` to the `TargetObject` once again.

You have now wired up all three of your buttons: Play, Pause, and Stop. Press F5 to run the application and try out the different buttons. You have now a completed, functional Media Player that has very cool transition effects as well as functional media controls.

You can find my source code for both projects from this chapter here:

Simple VSM Project: `http://windowspresentationfoundation.com/Blend4Book/`

`SimpleVSMProject.zip`

Media Player: `http://windowspresentationfoundation.com/Blend4Book/SLVSMMediaPlayer.zip`

Summary

In this chapter you learned all about the Visual State Manager and Blend 4's **States** panel. You created a simple Silverlight application and created a `StateGroup` and two States to control how a simple `Rectangle` behaved when the mouse was over it and when the mouse was not. You then created another Silverlight project and styled up a cool looking Media Player. You also created a custom Silverlight `Button` Control. You used Behaviors to add the `MouseEnter` and `MouseLeave` functionality to switch between

Visual States. You finally installed the Expression Blend Samples and made use to the Media Behaviors to Play, Pause, and Stop the media. Nice job!

If you would like to email me a link to your video project, I would love to have a look—especially if you got all creative and deviated from the design instructions provided in this chapter. I'd also like to see what you have done with the Easing functions. You can email me at `wpfauthor@gmail.com`.

Chapter 7

Behaviors in Silverlight

What this chapter covers:

- What Behaviors are
- How to use Behaviors
- How to create your own custom Behavior

What Are Behaviors?

Behaviors were introduced with Blend 3 and have become an integral part of Silverlight development. Prior to Behaviors a developer or designer would have to switch over to Visual Studio to do things like control a `MediaElement`, hook up a Visual State of a Visual State Group, make an object draggable, change a property on the fly, or start a Storyboard. With the addition of Behaviors, that all changed. Now developers and designers can perform these actions by simply dragging a Behavior from the Asset Library right onto objects in either the artboard or the **Objects and Timeline** panel.

So then, what exactly is a Behavior? A *Behavior* is a reusable piece of interactivity, written in code (usually C#) and applied to objects in Expression Blend. For example, you can open the Asset Library and click the **Behaviors** tab. You can then click and drag a Behavior and drop it onto an object right on the artboard or even in the **Objects and Timeline** panel. That object will then have that Behavior attached to it. In this chapter I show you how to use some common Behaviors that ship with Blend 4, such as the `ControlStoryboardAction`, `MouseDragElementBehavior`, and the `ChangePropertyAction` Behaviors. I then show you how to create your very own simple Behavior in Visual Studio that you can then make use of in Blend. With that, let's explore some common Behaviors that ship with Blend 4.

A Behavior can be added programmatically in code-behind, but this is uncommon.

Using Behaviors

The first thing we are going to do is to open Blend and create a Silverlight 4 project and then use some of the Behaviors that ship with Blend 4. Let's do that now!

1. Click **File ➤ New Project.**

2. When the **New Project** dialog box appears, select **Silverlight** for the Project type, select **Silverlight Application** for the template, name the project UsingStoryboards, make certain **Visual C#** is selected for the language, and click **OK**. You should have what I have in Figure 7-1.

Figure 7-1. Create a new Silverlight 4 application named UsingStoryboards.

Now that we have our project created, we need some visuals to add behaviors to … or do we? We could have the background of the application itself change to a new color when the application is loaded. We can do that by applying a ChangePropertyAction Behavior to the LayoutRoot Grid (this is the Grid that is the default content container when a new Silverlight application is created). Let's do that now.

1. Click the Asset Library, click the **Behaviors** tab, and locate the ChangePropertyAction Behavior as I am doing in Figure 7-1.

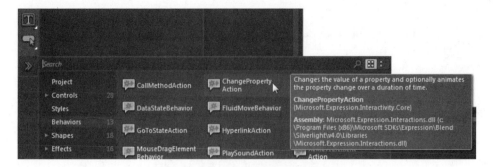

Figure 7-2. Locate the `ChangePropertyAction` Behavior in the Asset Library.

2. Click and drag this Behavior to the `LayoutRoot` Grid in the **Objects and Timeline** panel as I have done in Figure 7-3.

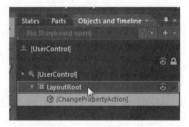

Figure 7-3. The `ChangePropertyAction` Behavior is now under the `LayoutRoot` Grid in the Objects and Timeline panel.

Now we can move over to the **Properties** panel and specify when the Behavior should fire, what property it should change, and what it should change that property to. Do that now.

1. With the `ChangePropertyAction` Behavior still selected in the **Objects and Timeline** panel, move over to the **Properties** panel.

2. In the **Trigger** bucket change the `EventName` dropdown to `Loaded`, as I do in Figure 7-4.

Figure 7-4. Change the `EventName` property to `Loaded`.

3. In the **Common Properties** bucket, change the `PropertyName` to `Background` as I do in Figure 7-5.

Figure 7-5. Change the `PropertyName` dropdown to `Background`.

4. Still in the **Common Properties** bucket, click "**Solid color brush,**" as I do in Figure 7-6.

Figure 7-6. Select the "Solid color brush" icon in the Common Properties bucket.

5. While still in the **Common Properties** bucket, click in the **Color Editor** to choose a color. This is the color that the `LayoutRoot Background` will change to when this Behavior fires (see Figure 7-7).

Figure 7-7. Select a new color in the Color Editor.

Now press F5 to compile and run the application and notice when it runs the Background changes to the color you just specified in the **Properties** panel for the Behavior. You have just used your very first Behavior! There are other Behaviors that are cool too. Close the application, and let's see the MouseDragElementBehavior Behavior in action.

1. The first thing to do is draw an Ellipse on the artboard with a blue fill so you have an object to apply the MouseDragElementBehavior Behavior to. Do that now so that you have what I have in Figure 7-8.

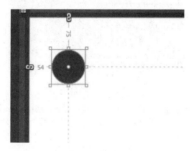

Figure 7-8. Draw a blue Ellipse on the artboard about 80×80.

2. Open the Asset Library and locate the MouseDragElementBehavior Behavior, as I have done in Figure 7-9.

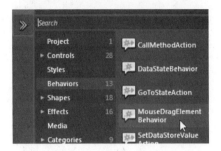

Figure 7-9. Locate the `MouseDragElementBehavior` Behavior in the Asset Library.

3. Drag the `MouseDragElementBehavior` Behavior to the `Ellipse` on the **Objects and Timeline** panel so that your **Objects and Timeline** panel looks like Figure 7-10.

> In the preceding example, I had you drag the Behavior right onto the object in the Objects and Timeline panel, but you should know that you can also drag Behaviors right onto objects in the artboard as well.

Figure 7-10. The `MouseDragElementBehavior` Behavior is now under the [Ellipse] in the Objects and Timeline panel.

Press F5 to run the application again and notice that you have an `Ellipse` on the page now. Use your mouse to click and drag the `Ellipse`. Notice how it drags—just that quickly we were able to make this object one that can be dragged about the page. If you ever made an object drag prior to the addition of Behaviors, you know it was a time-consuming, difficult task. The `MouseDragElementBehavior` Behavior allows us to accomplish this in less than a minute!

Now let's look at one more Behavior called the `ControlStoryboardAction` Behavior. To do this we need to create a simple Storyboard. Let's make a Storyboard now.

1. In Blend press F6 to enter the Animation workspace.

The Animation workspace has more vertical space to allow for easier viewing of your Objects and Timeline panel to create and view Storyboards.

2. Click the New Storyboard icon, as shown in Figure 7-11.

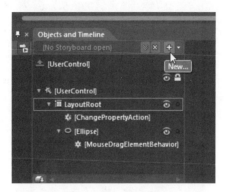

Figure 7-11. Click the New Storyboard icon.

3. When the New Storyboard dialog box appears, leave the default name of Storyboard1 and click **OK**.

4. When you see the Timeline appear, move the playhead out to 2 seconds, as I do in Figure 7-12.

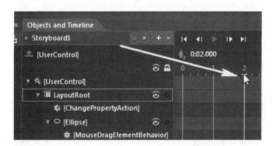

Figure 7-12. Move the playhead out to 2 seconds on the Timeline.

5. Now select your Ellipse and in the **Properties** panel locate the **Transform** bucket (you may have to click the arrow to reveal the content for the bucket).

6. Locate the **Projection** section and change the Y value to 160, as in Figure 7-13.

Having trouble finding properties in the Properties panel? You can always start typing whatever property you are looking for in the Search field at the top of the Properties panel. This will filter your properties for you. For example, say you want the `Projection Transform` *property. You can type* **Projection** *in the Search field, and every property with the letters* `Projection` *in it will be displayed. Other properties will be hidden. There is also a search field for the Asset Library.*

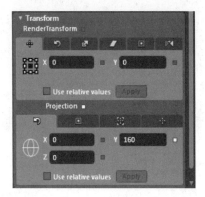

Figure 7-13. Change the Y property in the Projection section of the Transform bucket.

Notice how your Timeline now has a `KeyFrame` on it in the form a circular icon at the 2 second mark (see Figure 7-14).

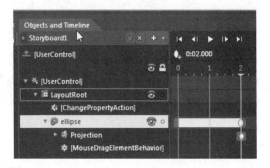

Figure 7-14. Blend added `KeyFrames` to the Timeline.

If you click the Play icon at the top of the Timeline panel, you will see how the Storyboard will affect the `Ellipse`. Now we need to set the `Repeat` Behavior for this Storyboard to `Forever` in XAML. Let's do that now.

You can also set the `RepeatBehavior` *in Blend by clicking the Storyboard in the Objects and Timeline panel and locating the property in the Properties panel.*

1. On the right of the Properties panel you will see the Split View icon, shown in Figure 7-15. Click that to view both the Design and XAML views.

Figure 7-15. Click the Split View icon.

2. In the XAML portion of the screen, locate the Storyboard with the `Key` of `Storyboard1` as I have done in Figure 7-16.

The name of a Storyboard is called the `Key` *property. The* `Key` *is how Storyboard and other resources are located in code.*

Figure 7-16. Locate `Storyboard1` in the XAML.

3. Change the XAML from:

```
<Storyboard x:Name="Storyboard1">
```

to:

```
<Storyboard x:Name="Storyboard1" RepeatBehavior="Forever">
```

4. Now close the Split view and go back to the Design view by clicking the Design View icon, as in Figure 7-17.

Figure 7-17. Click the Design View icon to return to the Design workspace.

5. Close the Storyboard by clicking the Close Storyboard button, as I am doing in Figure 7-18. Then click F6 to exit the Animation workspace and return to the Design workspace.

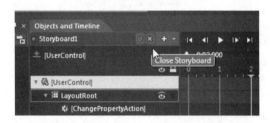

Figure 7-18. Close the Storyboard.

Now that we have created the Storyboard and given it a `Repeat` Behavior of `Forever`, we can go ahead and fire this Storyboard using the `ControlStoryboardAction` Behavior.

1. Click the Asset Library and locate the `ControlStoryboardAction` Behavior, as in Figure 7-19.

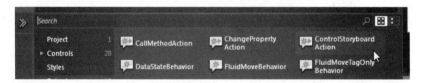

Figure 7-19. Locate the `ControlStoryboardAction` Behavior in the Asset Library.

2. Now click and drag that Behavior onto the `Ellipse`, as I have done in Figure 7-20.

Figure 7-20. The `ChangePropertyAction` Behavior is now under the `LayoutRoot` Grid.

3. Click the old `MouseDragElementBehavior` Behavior and press the Delete key to remove it. Then move to the **Properties** panel to adjust the settings for the `ControlStoryboardAction` Behavior.

4. In the **Trigger** bucket leave the default `EventName` of `MouseLeftButtonDown`.

5. In the **Common Properties** bucket, click the **Storyboard** dropdown and select our Storyboard named `Storyboard1`, as I am doing in Figure 7-21.

Figure 7-21. Change the Storyboard dropdown to `Storyboard1`.

Press F5 to run the application, click the `Ellipse`, and notice how it starts the Storyboard (named `Storyboard1`) and how it keeps repeating. Pretty cool, huh?

In this section we changed the `Background` property of the `LayoutRoot` Grid, made an `Ellipse` draggable, and then started a Storyboard when you clicked the `Ellipse`—*all* without writing a single line of code other than setting the `RepeatBehavior`, and we *could* have done that in Blend!

I think now you can see the power of Behaviors. Let's move on and see how easy it is to create your own simple Behavior in Visual Studio and then use it in Blend.

Creating Your Own Simple Behavior

1. Open Blend 4 and click **New ➤ Project**.

2. Create a new Silverlight application called `SimpleBehavior`, as I do in Figure 7-22.

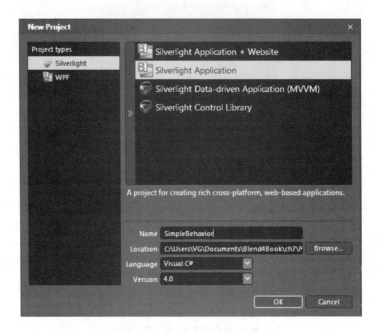

Figure 7-22. Create a new project in Blend called `SimpleBehavior`.

3. In the **Projects** panel right-click the Solution and left-click **Edit in Visual Studio,** as I am doing in Figure 7-23.

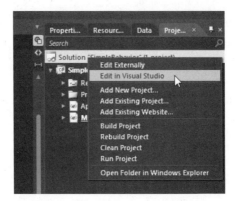

Figure 7-23. Edit the project in Visual Studio 2010.

Visual Studio 2010 will open. Here is where we are going to add our Behavior. We are going to create a Behavior that will make an object change color when the mouse is down and then return to its original color when the mouse is up. Let's do that now:

1. The first thing to do is add a new class to our project that will be our Behavior class. To do that right-click the project in Visual Studio's **Solution Explorer** and click **Add ➤ Class,** as I do in Figure 7-24.

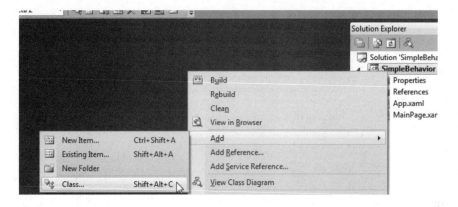

Figure 7-24. Add a new class to the project.

2. When the **Add New Item** dialog appears, name the class `FillBehavior` and click the **Add** button.

3. Now that you have the class created, you need to add a reference to the `DynamicLinkLibrary` (DLL) that allows you to create Behaviors. In the **Solution Explorer** right-click the References folder and left-click **Add Reference,** as in Figure 7-25.

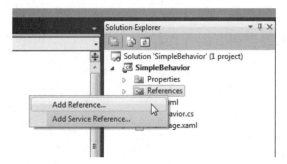

Figure 7-25. Add a Reference to the project.

4. Navigate to your `System.Windows.Interactivity dll`. Yours should also be located in `C:\Program Files (x86)\Microsoft SDKs\Expression\Blend\Silverlight\v4.0\Libraries\`, or wherever you installed Blend on your computer. When you find it select it and click **OK,** as I am doing in Figure 7-26.

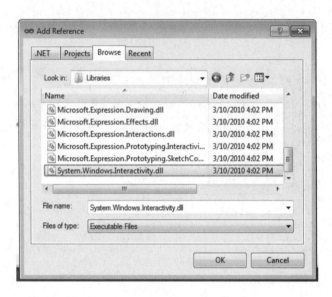

Figure 7-26. Locate `System.Windows.Interactivity` dll.

5.   Now that you have the DLL to be able to create Behaviors, you can start to turn your `FillBehavior` class into a Behavior. To do that put your cursor after `FillBehavior` and type ": `TargetedTriggerAction<FrameworkElement>`". Then press Control+. (period key), click `Using System.Windows.Interactivity,` and press the Enter key, as I do in Figure 7-27.

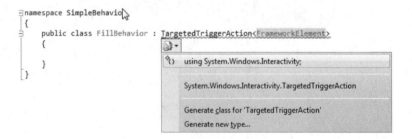

Figure 7-27. Tell Visual Studio to use `System.Windows.Interactivity` dll.

6.   You will see that there is still a blue indicator under the *T* in *TargetedTriggerAction*, indicating that there is more that Visual Studio can do for you (see Figure 7-28).

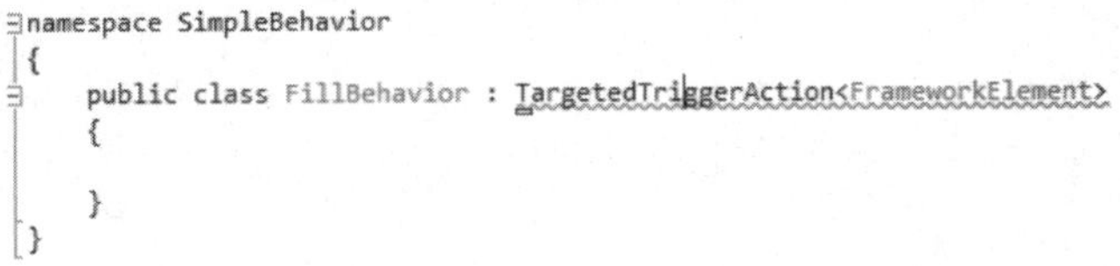

```
namespace SimpleBehavior
{
    public class FillBehavior : TargetedTriggerAction<FrameworkElement>
    {

    }
}
```

Figure 7-28. The blue indicator is informing you that Visual Studio would like to help you write some code.

7. Press Control+. (period key) again, and you will see that Visual Studio wants to implement the abstract class for you (Figure 7-29). Press the Enter key.

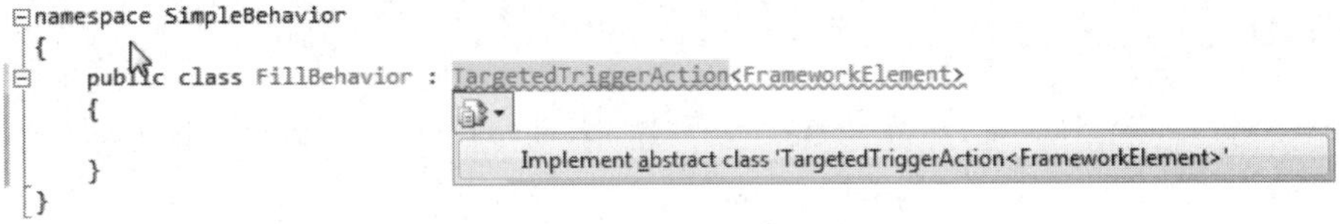

```
namespace SimpleBehavior
{
    public class FillBehavior : TargetedTriggerAction<FrameworkElement>
    {
        ⬦▾
              Implement abstract class 'TargetedTriggerAction<FrameworkElement>'
    }
}
```

Figure 7-29. Press Control+. (period) to have Visual Studio implement the abstract class for you.

Now you can see that Visual Studio went ahead and created a method for you, called Invoke (see Figure 7-30).

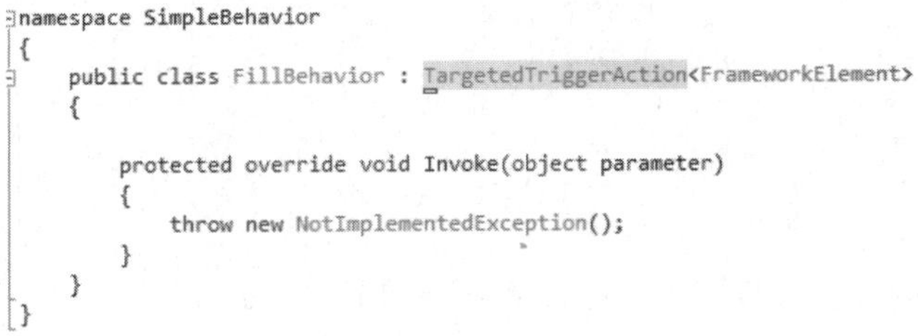

```
namespace SimpleBehavior
{
    public class FillBehavior : TargetedTriggerAction<FrameworkElement>
    {
        protected override void Invoke(object parameter)
        {
            throw new NotImplementedException();
        }
    }
}
```

Figure 7-30. Visual Studio implemented the abstract class for you.

This is the method that needs to be overridden for a Behavior. We could use this to add our MouseLeftButtonDown and MouseLeftButtonUp. But instead we are just going to delete the default code, as I do here:

```
protected override void Invoke(object parameter)
{

}
```

1. Above the Invoke method create two properties for the Shape and the OriginalColor, as I have done in the following bold code:

```
public class FillBehavior : TargetedTriggerAction<FrameworkElement>
{

    private Shape shape;
    private Brush originalColor;

    protected override void Invoke(object parameter)
    {

}
```

2. Go ahead and create an `OnAttached` override method, erase the default code, and set the shape to the `AssociatedObject`, as I do here:

```
public class FillBehavior : TargetedTriggerAction<FrameworkElement>
{

    private Shape shape;
    private Brush originalColor;

    protected override void Invoke(object parameter)
    {

    }

    protected override void OnAttached()
    {
            base.OnAttached();

    }
```

3. Now you can raise `MouseLeftButtonDown` and `MouseLeftButtoLeftButtonUp` events right in this method. Type **Shape.MouseLeftButtonDown +=** and press the Tab key twice to raise the event and create the event handler. Then do the same for `MouseLeftButtonUp` as I do here:

```
protected override void OnAttached()
{
    base.OnAttached();
    shape = this.AssociatedObject as Shape;
    shape.MouseLeftButtonDown += new
  MouseButtonEventHandler(shape_MouseLeftButtonDown);
    shape.MouseLeftButtonUp += new MouseButtonEventHandler(shape_MouseLeftButtonUp);

}

void shape_MouseLeftButtonUp(object sender, MouseButtonEventArgs e)
{
```

```
        throw new NotImplementedException();
}

void shape_MouseLeftButtonDown(object sender, MouseButtonEventArgs e)
{
        throw new NotImplementedException();
}
```

Now we are going to create a method that will get the original color of the shape object. Do that now:

1. Under where you raise the `MouseButtonUp` and `MouseButtonDown` events in the `Invoke` method, type `GetOriginalColor(shape);` and then press Control+. (period) again. Visual Studio will ask whether you want to generate the method for `GetOriginalColor`. You do, so press the Enter key. You should now have a method for `GetOriginalColor`, as I have below:

```
protected override void OnAttached()
{
        base.OnAttached();
        shape = this.AssociatedObject as Shape;
        shape.MouseLeftButtonDown += new
  MouseButtonEventHandler(shape_MouseLeftButtonDown);
        shape.MouseLeftButtonUp += new MouseButtonEventHandler(shape_MouseLeftButtonUp);
        GetOriginalColor(shape);
}

private void GetOriginalColor(Shape shape)
{
        throw new NotImplementedException();
}
```

2. Inside of this method you can get the original color of shape by deleting the default code and typing the following code:

```
void shape_MouseLeftButtonUp(object sender, MouseButtonEventArgs e)
{
        shape.Fill = originalColor;
}
```

3. Now on `MouseLeftButtonDown` you can set shape to a new color—say, red. Then on `MouseLeftButtonUp` you can change shape back to `originalColor`. Here is the code for this:

```
void shape_MouseLeftButtonUp(object sender, MouseButtonEventArgs e)
{
        shape.Fill = originalColor;
}

void shape_MouseLeftButtonDown(object sender, MouseButtonEventArgs e)
{
```

```
    shape.Fill = new SolidColorBrush(Colors.Red);
}
```

    4. Your completed code should now look like this:

```
namespace SimpleBehavior
{
    public class FillBehavior : TargetedTriggerAction<FrameworkElement>
    {

        private Shape shape;
        private Brush originalColor;

        protected override void Invoke(object parameter)
        {

        }

        protected override void OnAttached()
        {
            base.OnAttached();
        shape = this.AssociatedObject as Shape;
        shape.MouseLeftButtonDown += new
MouseButtonEventHandler(shape_MouseLeftButtonDown);
        shape.MouseLeftButtonUp += new
MouseButtonEventHandler(shape_MouseLeftButtonUp);
        GetOriginalColor(shape);
    }

    private void GetOriginalColor(Shape shape)
    {
        originalColor = shape.Fill as Brush;
    }

    void shape_MouseLeftButtonUp(object sender, MouseButtonEventArgs e)
    {
        shape.Fill = originalColor;
    }

    void shape_MouseLeftButtonDown(object sender, MouseButtonEventArgs e)
    {
        shape.Fill = new SolidColorBrush(Colors.Red);
    }
    }
}
```

Press F6 to recompile the application. Switch back to Blend and reload the application if prompted. Now it is time to actually add the FillBehavior to a Shape. To do that you need to first add a Shape such as a

Rectangle. Add a `Rectangle` to the artboard that is about 150 display units wide and 100 display units tall. Then set it to a solid color. I chose green for this example. You should have something like I have in Figure 7-31.

Figure 7-31. Draw a green `Rectangle` on the artboad.

Now we can add our new `FillBehavior` to this object.

1. Click the Asset Library and start to type **Fill** in the Search box. You should then see the `FillBehavior` show up, as in Figure 7-32.

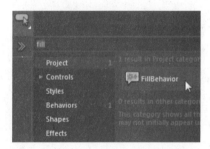

Figure 7-32. The `FillBehavior` is now located in the Asset Library.

2. Click and drag the `FillBehavior` onto the `Rectangle` in the **Objects and Timeline** panel, so you have what I have in Figure 7-33.

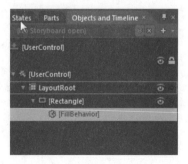

Figure 7-33. Your Objects and Timeline panel should now have the `FillBehavior` under the [Rectangle].

Now all you have to do is press F5 to compile and run the application, put your mouse cursor over the Rectangle, and notice nothing occurs (Figure 7-34). Click the Rectangle and notice how it changes colors to red just as we specified in the Behavior (Figure 7-35).

Figure 7-34. The Rectangle is originally green and will turn green again when the mouse button is up.

Figure 7-35. When clicked the Rectangle will turn red.

Summary

In this chapter you learned about Behaviors, which are basically encapsulated, reusable code that allow you to easily apply actions in Blend. Further, you created a new Silverlight 4 application where you learned how to apply some popular Behaviors in Blend such as the MouseDragElementBehavior, ControlStoryboardAction, and the ChangePropertyAction Behaviors. You then created a new Silverlight 4 application and learned how to add the System.Windows.Interactivity dll that allowed you to create your own Behavior called FillBehavior. You went into Blend and applied your new FillBehavior to a Rectangle. In the next chapter, you learn all about using XML in Silverlight applications.

You can find source code for both applications created in this chapter here:

http://windowspresentationfoundation.com/Blend4Book/UsingStoryboards.zip

http://windowspresentationfoundation.com/Blend4Book/SimpleBehavior.zip

You can watch a video tutorial of the above Behavior tutorial on my blog located here: http://www.windowspresentationfoundation.com/?p=36/

Chapter 8

The Silverlight MediaElement: Create a Video Player with a Custom UserControl, XML De-serialization, and Behaviors

What this chapter covers:

- Defining the Silverlight `MediaElement`
- Comparing Silverlight versus Flash for video
- Building a Silverlight media player
  - Parsing and de-serializing XML
  - Turning XML into native Silverlight data objects
  - Using the drag-and-drop Behavior
  - Creating a singleton `DataFactory`
  - Creating a custom `UserControl`

Because Silverlight 4 was designed to develop rich Internet applications (RIAs) with lots of embedded media such as video and audio, the `MediaElement` is a very important and useful tool, so I have decided to dedicate an entire chapter to it. The Silverlight `MediaElement` is a rectangular `UserControl` that can be used to play audio or video. In the current version of Silverlight, the `MediaElement` supports the following types of media:

- Raw video:
  - YV12: YCrCb(4:2:0)
  - RGBA: 32-bit Alpha RGB
  - WMV1: Windows Media Video (WMV) 7
  - WMV2: Windows Media Video (WMV) 8

- WMV3: Windows Media Video (WMV) 9
- WMVA: Windows Media Video Advanced Profile, non-VC-1
- WVC1: Windows Media Video Advanced Profile, VC-1
- H264 (ITU-T H.264 / ISO MPEG-4 AVC): H.264 and MP43 codecs.
- PlayReady DRM with MP4 (H264 and AAC-LC)
- Audio:
- WAV
- Microsoft Windows Media Audio v7, v8 and v9.x Standard (WMA Standard)
- Microsoft Windows Media Audio v9.x and v10 Professional (WMA Professional)
- ISO MPEG-1 Layer III (MP3)
- ISO Advanced Audio Coding (AAC)

In this chapter, I compare the pros and cons of using Silverlight instead of Flash for video and then I show you how to build a very cool, interactive Silverlight video player.

Choosing Between Silverlight and Flash for Video

If you have been paying any attention whatsoever to the world of RIA development over the past few years, you have undoubtedly heard the Flash vs. Silverlight debate. Staunch supporters of both technologies will recommend their preferred technology, even in the face of clear evidence that one is better than the other given the specific RIA requirements. Being a former Flash developer and a current Silverlight developer, I find it easy to objectively look at both Flash and Silverlight to determine which platform is better suited to handle the needs and requirements of the application that is to be developed. So, which one is better for video? The answer is that it depends on the requirements of the application. For example, if you have an RIA that streams video, you may want to use Silverlight: you can save on costs by streaming less overall bandwidth because of higher compression ratios in Silverlight video.

Choosing Silverlight

Here are some advantages to using Silverlight for video:

- Silverlight requires less bandwidth than the Flash to serve comparable-quality video.
- Silverlight does not require additional video codecs to play industry-standard video formats.
- Silverlight provides built-in content access protection known as Digital Rights Management (DRM).
- Silverlight automatically downgrades the quality of video, rather than stutters, when the incoming signal becomes weak (known as Adaptive Smooth Streaming).
- Silverlight has live and on-demand true HD (720p+). Internet Information Services (IIS, formerly IIS Media Pack), an integrated HTTP media delivery platform, features smooth streaming, which dynamically detects and seamlessly switches in real time the video quality of a media file delivered to Silverlight, based on local bandwidth and CPU conditions.

- Silverlight has more format choices. In addition to native support for VC-1/WMA, Silverlight 3 now offers users native support for MPEG-4–based H.264/AAC audio, enabling content distributors to deliver high-quality content to a wide variety of computers and devices.
- Silverlight has extensible media format support: With the new Raw AV pipeline, Silverlight can easily support a wide variety of third-party codecs. Audio and video can be decoded outside the runtime and rendered in Silverlight, extending format support beyond the native codecs.
- Silverlight has industry-leading content protection. Silverlight's DRM, powered by PlayReady Content Protection, enables protected in-browser experiences using Advances Encryption Standard (AES) encryption or Windows Media DRM.

Choosing Flash

And these are some advantages to using Flash for video:

- Nearly all web users have the Flash Player plug-in.
- Flash video requires much less CPU power, so it runs better on older machines and mobile phones.
- The Flash video encoder supports a wide range of video and animation formats that can be encoded into the FLV format. Here is a list of supported video and animation formats:
- Mobile Video (3G2)
    - GIF (animated GIF)
    - DLX (Sony VDU File Format Importer, Windows only)
    - DV (in a MOV or AVI container or as a containerless DV stream)
    - Flash Video (FLV, F4V)
    - M2T (Sony HDV)
    - MOV (QuickTime; in Windows, requires the QuickTime player)
    - MP4 (XDCAM EX)
    - MPEG-1, MPEG-2, and MPEG-4 formats (MPEG, MPE, MPG, M2V, MPA, MP2, M2A, MPV, M2P, M2T, AC3, MP4, M4V, M4A)
    - MTS (AVCHD)
    - Media eXchange Format (MXF)
    - Netshow (ASF, Windows only)
    - QuickTime (MOV; 16 bpc, requires QuickTime)
    - Video for Windows (AVI, WAV; requires QuickTime on Mac OS)
    - WMV (WMV, WMA, ASF; Windows only)

So what does this all mean? Basically, it means that you, as the developer, must decide what tool you need given the requirement of the RIA you are developing. In some cases, the tool will be Silverlight, and in others, it will be Flash.

Creating the Silverlight Video Player Application

In staying with my philosophy that the best way to learn is by hands-on experience, I am now going to show you how to build a fun, interactive Silverlight video player. I have decided that this particular application would be a good place to show you how to do some very cool things in Silverlight, such as the following:

- Using XML for data
- Making UI objects draggable using the `MouseDragElementBehavior` Behavior
- Creating a singleton `DataFactory`
- Making UI objects react when other UI objects are dropped on them

To develop this application, you will need at least three videos in the WMV format as well as corresponding JPG thumbnail images for each (I made my thumbnail images about 100 pixels wide and tall). For simplicity, I named my videos `video1.wmv`, `video2.wmv`, and so on, and my corresponding thumbnails `video1.jpg`, `video2.jpg`, and so on.

> *Windows Vista ships with sample WMV videos. These can usually be found in* `C:\Users\Public\Videos\Sample Videos`. *If you cannot find them there, search for* ***.wmv** *to find them. Windows 7 ships with one video called* `Wildlife.wmv` *located at* `C:\Users\Public\Videos\Sample Videos`.

With that, let's fire up Visual Studio 2010 and create our Silverlight video player:

1. Open Visual Studio.
2. Click **File ➤ New ➤ Project**.
3. In the **New Project** dialog box, select Silverlight for the **Project Type**.
4. Select Silverlight Application for the **Template**.
5. Type **SLVideoPlayer01** for the project **Name**.
6. Be sure to make a mental note where the project is being saved, so you can open it in Blend down the road (see Figure 8-1).

> *If you have forgotten where you have saved a project, you can right-click on any XAML file in Visual Studio 2010's Solution Explorer and left-click Open in Expression Blend.*

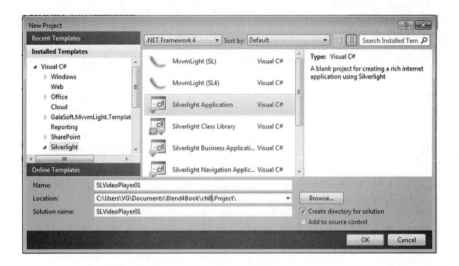

Figure 8-1. Create a new Silverlight project in Visual Studio 2010.

7. When the New Silverlight Application dialog box appears, check the box that reads "Host the Silverlight application in a new Web site," as shown in Figure 8-2. We need to do this so Visual Studio will set up an intranet site for us. If we don't, running the application merely opens the application on the hard drive, and a video will never play.

8. Click OK.

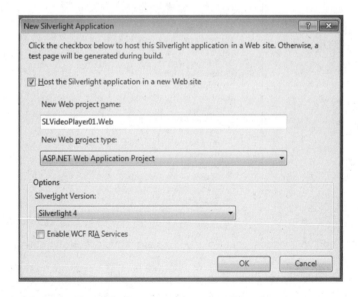

Figure 8-2. Opt to host the Silverlight application in a new web site.

The first thing to do is to import some videos into the application. We need to add the videos directly to the `SLVideoPlayer01.Web`'s `ClientBin` directory, or the videos won't play when we run the application.

1. In Solution Explorer, right-click `SLVideoPlayer01.Web`'s `ClientBin` and choose Add Existing Item, as shown in Figure 8-3.

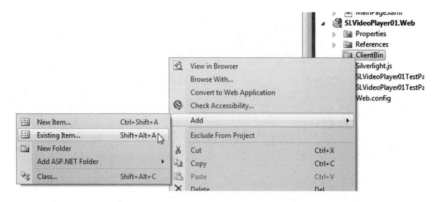

Figure 8-3. Add an existing item to `SLVideoPlayer01.Web`'s `ClientBin`.

2. Navigate to the location of your videos on your hard drive and double-click them so that you now have videos in your `ClientBin`, as shown in Figure 8-4.

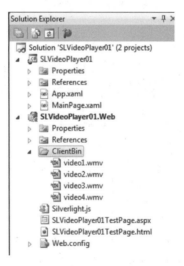

Figure 8-4. When you add your videos, your Solution Explorer should look something like this.

Now that videos are added, add the thumbnails.

3. Right-click `SLVideoPlayer01` (not `SLVideoPlayer01.Web`) in Solution Explorer and select **Add ➤ Existing Item.**

4. Navigate to your thumbnail images on your hard drive and select them.

Your Solution Explorer should look the one shown in Figure 8-5.

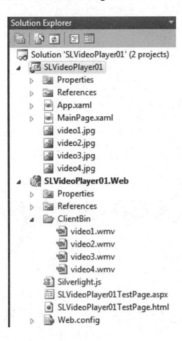

Figure 8-5. After you've added your thumbnails, Solution Explorer should look something like this.

With the videos and thumbnails included in the application, you need to create the XML that tells the application where to find these assets. Let's do that now:

5. In the `SLVideoPlayer01.Web` project, right-click ClientBin and click **Add New Item**.

6. In the **Add New Item** dialog box, select **Data for the Installed Templates**.

7. Select **XML File** for the file type.

8. Name the new XML file `videodata.xml`.

9. Select **Add,** as shown in Figure 8-6.

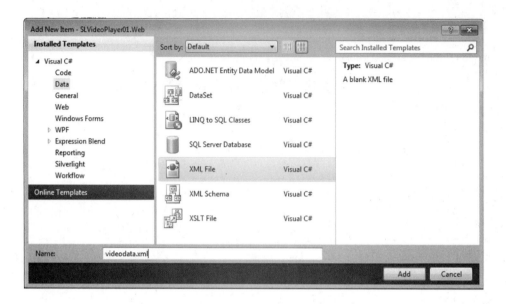

Figure 8-6. Add a new XML file to the application.

Your videodata.xml *file must be located in the* ClientBin *directory of your* SLVideoPlayer01.Web *project or it will not be located correctly.*

10. When the new file opens, change your code so it looks like the following (if you named your videos or thumbnails differently than I have, make sure your XML file reflects that):

```xml
<VideoData
  xmlns:xsd="http://www.w3.org/2001/XMLSchema"
  xmlns:xsi="http://www.w3.org/2001/XMLSchema-instance">
  <Video>
    <Url>video1.wmv</Url>
    <Title>Me Working</Title>
    <ThumbnailImage>video1.jpg</ThumbnailImage>
  </Video>
  <Video>
    <Url>video2.wmv</Url>
    <Title>Butterfly</Title>
    <ThumbnailImage>video2.jpg</ThumbnailImage>
  </Video>
  <Video>
    <Url>video3.wmv</Url>
    <Title>Bear</Title>
    <ThumbnailImage>video3.jpg</ThumbnailImage>
```

```
    </Video>
    <Video>
      <Url>video4.wmv</Url>
      <Title>IdentityMine</Title>
      <ThumbnailImage>video4.jpg</ThumbnailImage>
    </Video>
</VideoData>
```

For your convenience, you can download a text version of this XML file at http://windowspresentationfoundation.com/Blend4Book/videodata.txt.

Some browsers will show you the output of the XML rather than the code itself. If you end up seeing only **"video1.wmv video1.jpg video2.wmv video2.jpg video3.wmv video3.jpg video4.wmv video4.jpg"** *in your browser, right-click and click View Source to see the XML code that you can then copy and paste into your own XML file.*

Now that we have our assets imported and our XML file created, it is time to parse and serialize the XML file:

11. In Solution Explorer, click the + symbol next to MainPage.xaml in the `SLVideoPlayer01` project.

12. Double-click `MainPage.xaml.cs` to open it (see Figure 8-7).

Figure 8-7. Double-click in the Solution Explorer to open `MainPage.xaml.cs`.

13. Put your cursor right after the line that reads `InitializeComponent();` and press the Enter key to create an empty line.

14. Start typing **Loaded** and press the Enter key when Visual Studio's Intellisense tries to finish the line for you.

15. Type **+=** and press the Tab key twice so that Intellisense attaches the `RoutedEventHandler` and also generates the event handler method stub. Your code should look like the following:

```
namespace SLVideoPlayer01
{
    public partial class MainPage : UserControl
    {
        public MainPage()
        {
            InitializeComponent();
            Loaded += new RoutedEventHandler(MainPage_Loaded);
        }

        void MainPage_Loaded(object sender, RoutedEventArgs e)
        {
            throw new NotImplementedException();
        }
    }
}
```

16. Erase the line that reads "throw new…"

Here is where we would normally start to deal with the XML, but before we do, we need to add a reference to the .NET XML libraries so that our application knows how to deal with XML:

17. In Solution Explorer, right-click the References folder of the SLVideoPlayer01 project.

18. Left-click **Add Reference…**, as shown in Figure 8-8.

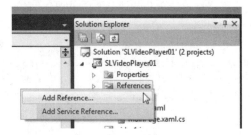

Figure 8-8. Add a reference to the SLVideoPlayer01 project.

19. When the **Add Reference** dialog box appears, make sure the **.NET** tab is selected.

20. Scroll down to System.Xml.Linq and System.Xml.Serialization.

21. Hold down the Ctrl key to select both of these and click **OK,** as shown in Figure 8-9.

Figure 8-9. Add a reference to `System.Xml.Linq` and `System.Xml.Serialization`.

Now that you have done this, you can start dealing with the XML in the `MainPage_Loaded` event handler:

22. Add the following code into the `MainPage_Loaded` event handler:

```
WebClient xmlClient = new WebClient();

xmlClient.DownloadStringCompleted += new
DownloadStringCompletedEventHandler(xmlClient_DownloadStringCompleted);
xmlClient.DownloadStringAsync(new Uri("videodata.xml", UriKind.RelativeOrAbsolute));
```

After you type **DownloadStringCompleted** type **+=** and press the Tab key twice to auto-complete raising the event and also automatically create the `xmlClient_DownloadStringCompleted` event handler.

Your code should now look like this:

```
public partial class MainPage : UserControl
    {
        public MainPage()
        {
         InitializeComponent();
         Loaded += new RoutedEventHandler(MainPage_Loaded);
        }

    void MainPage_Loaded(object sender, RoutedEventArgs e)
    {
        WebClient xmlClient = new WebClient();
```

```
    xmlClient.DownloadStringCompleted += new
    DownloadStringCompletedEventHandler(xmlClient_DownloadStringCompleted);
     xmlClient.DownloadStringAsync(new Uri("videodata.xml",
UriKind.RelativeOrAbsolute));
    }

        void xmlClient_DownloadStringCompleted(object sender,
        DownloadStringCompletedEventArgs e)
        {
                throw new NotImplementedException();
        }
    }
}
```

23. Erase the "throw new. . ." code.

24. Now we need to make sure that there was no error in the downloading process. To do that, we remove the default "throw new…" code and add the code that will only proceed if there is no error:

```
void xmlClient_DownloadStringCompleted(object sender,
DownloadStringCompletedEventArgs e
    {
        // if e.error is null we can proceed.
        if (e.Error == null)
        {

        }

    }
```

25. Next, we can create a string variable called xmlData and set it to the result of our DownloadStringCompleteEventArgs, which is a string of our XML video data.

26. We can then create MessageBox to make certain our data had been downloaded correctly.

```
void xmlClient_DownloadStringCompleted(object sender,
DownloadStringCompletedEventArgs e)
    {
        // if e.error is null we can proceed.
        if (e.Error == null)
        {
            string xmlData = e.Result;
            MessageBox.Show(xmlData);
        }

    }
```

Now, if you press F5 to compile and run the application, you should see something like what's shown in Figure 8-10.

```
<VideoData
 xmlns:xsd="http://www.w3.org/2001/XMLSchema"
 xmlns:xsi="http://www.w3.org/2001/XMLSchema-instance">
 <Video>
  <Url>video1.wmv</Url>
  <Title>Me Working</Title>
   <ThumbnailImage>video1.jpg</ThumbnailImage>
 </Video>
 <Video>
  <Url>video2.wmv</Url>
  <Title>Butterfly</Title>
   <ThumbnailImage>video2.jpg</ThumbnailImage>
 </Video>
 <Video>
  <Url>video3.wmv</Url>
  <Title>Bear</Title>
   <ThumbnailImage>video3.jpg</ThumbnailImage>
 </Video>
 <Video>
  <Url>video4.wmv</Url>
  <Title>IdentityMine</Title>
   <ThumbnailImage>video4.jpg</ThumbnailImage>
 </Video>
</VideoData>
```

Figure 8-10. The `MessageBox` shows that our data has been downloaded correctly.

Now that the XML has been properly downloaded, we need to deserialize the data into our own data. Before we do that, though, we need to add some classes that the data can serialize into. We are going to start by creating a `DataFactory`.

When we deserialize XML, it turns the data into data that the application understands.

The `DataFactory` is a convention that allows developers to place all their application data into one neat place for easy setting and retrieval. Close the web browser, and let's create the `DataFactory` now:

27. Right-click the `SLVideoPlayer01` project, and click **Add ➤ Class,** as shown in Figure 8-11.

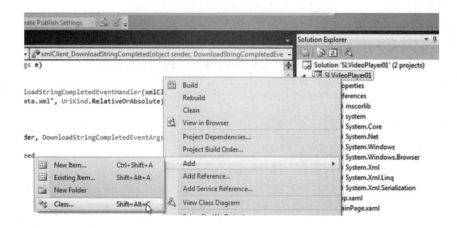

Figure 8-11. Add a new class to the SLVideoPlayer01 project.

28. In the **Add New Item** dialog box, name the new class DataFactory and click **Add**, as shown in Figure 8-12.

Figure 8-12. Name the new class DataFactory.

29. In the new class, we are going to create a new singleton (a class that can only be created or instantiated once) instance of DataFactory. This will allow us to create a CLR instance memory flow that we can then put our serialized data into for easy retrieval:

The Common Runtime Language (CLR) is the core .NET engine. The .NET libraries allow you to create applications that run on the CLR. The applications you create are thus merely an instance of the CLR.

```
namespace SLVideoPlayer01
{
    public class DataFactory
    {
        #region Singleton

        protected static DataFactory _Singleton = new DataFactory();
        public static DataFactory CLRInstance
        {
            get
            {
            return _Singleton;
            }
        }
        public DataFactory Instance
        {
            get
            {
                return CLRInstance;
            }
        }


        #endregion Singleton
    }
}
```

To keep the code clean, I have wrapped it in a region called `Singleton`. Such regions can be collapsed to make reading other parts of the code easier.

Now, we need to add a couple more classes, `VideoData` and `Video`:

1. Right-click `SLVideoPlayer01` and create a new class called `VideoData`.

2. Right-click `SLVideoPlayer01` and create a new class called `Video`.

3. Open `VideoData`.

4. The first thing to do in `VideoData` is specify the root (highest level node) of our XML file (note that you will need to right-click `XmlRoot` and resolve it to use `System.Xml.Serialization`). This tells the class where to start looking for data in the XML file. If we don't specify this, Silverlight won't know whitch XML node to start looking for data.

```
namespace SLVideoPlayer01
{
    [XmlRoot("VideoData")]
```

```
    public class VideoData
    {

    }
}
```

5. The next thing to do is extend `VideoData` to know that it is going to be a list of `Video` objects (note, you will also need to resolve `List` to use `System.Collections.Generic`):

```
namespace SLVideoPlayer01
{
    [XmlRoot("VideoData")]
    public class VideoData : List<Video>
    {

    }
}
```

6. Now, all we need to do is to create a private `_Video` variable of type `Video` and then create a public `Video` variable of type `Video`. These will be the individual data objects that are to be contained in our `Video` object. Each one will contain specific information such as the name of the video, the URL, and the name of the thumbnail image it is to display:

```
namespace SLVideoPlayer01
{
    [XmlRoot("VideoData")]
    public class VideoData : List<Video>
    {

    private Video _Video = null;
    public Video Video
        {
            get { return _Video; }
            set { _Video = value; }
        }
    }
}
```

We are finished with `VideoData`. Next open `Video` and modify it as follows:

1. We need to create string variables that correspond to our XML nodes (`URL`, `ThumbnailImage`, and `Title`):

```
namespace SLVideoPlayer01
{
    public class Video
    {
        private string _URL = "";
        public string URL
```

```
    {
        get { return _URL; }
        set { _URL = value; }
    }

    private string _Title = "";
    public string Title
    {
        get { return _Title; }
        set { _Title = value; }
    }

    private string _ThumbnailImage = "";
    public string ThumbnailImage
    {
        get { return _ThumbnailImage; }
        set { _ThumbnailImage = value; }
    }
  }
}
```

Now, go back to the `DataFactory` and create the `VideoData` object, which will give us access to `VideoData` via our CLR instance of `DataFactory`:

2. Create the `VideoData` object:

```
public class DataFactory
{
 #region Singleton

 protected static DataFactory _Singleton = new DataFactory();
 public static DataFactory CLRInstance
 {
     get
     {
         return _Singleton;
 }
 }
    public DataFactory Instance
    {
      get
      {
          return CLRInstance;
      }
 }

 #endregion Singleton
```

```
    private VideoData _VideoData = null;
    public VideoData VideoData
        {
        get { return _VideoData; }
        set { _VideoData = value; }
        }
    }
```

Now that you have done this, go back to `MainPage.xaml.cs` and continue to deserialize the data:

1. Deserialize the data and set it to the `DataFactory VideoData` object. This will turn the XML data into data that the application can understand:

```
void xmlClient_DownloadStringCompleted(object sender,
DownloadStringCompletedEventArgs e)
    {
        // if e.error is null we can proceed.
        if (e.Error == null)
        {
            string xmlData = e.Result;
            // comment out the MessageBox as we
            // now our XML is being parsed correctly
            //MessageBox.Show(xmlData);

            // Create the XmlSerializer
            XmlSerializer x = new XmlSerializer(typeof(VideoData));

            using (XmlReader reader = XmlReader.Create(new
StringReader(xmlData)))
            {
                // deserialize the XmlDate and set it to
                // our DataFactory VideoData object

                DataFactory.CLRInstance.VideoData =
(VideoData)x.Deserialize(reader);

            }
        }

    }
```

2. Remember, you will need to resolve `XmlReader` and `StringReader`.

Now that we have populated the `VideoData` object with `Video` objects by way of serialization, we need to make use of it. For each `Video` object in `VideoData`, we are going to add an instance of a custom `UserControl` called `UC_VideoDragger` (UC is short for *UserControl*).

1. Right-click `SLVideoPlayer01` in Solution Explorer.

2. Click **Add** ➤ **New Item**.

3. Click **Silverlight User Control**.

4. Name it `UC_VideoDragger`.

5. Click **Add** (see Figure 8-13).

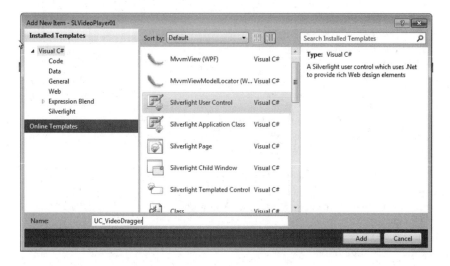

Figure 8-13. Create a new Silverlight `UserControl`.

6. In `UC_VideoDragger`'s XAML file, change the Height and Width to 100.

7. Change the `LayoutRoot` Grid to have a `Transparent` background.

8. Add a `StackPanel` with an `Orientation` of `Vertical` (so the pieces of content stack on top of each other).

9. Add an `Image` named `PreviewImage` with a `Height` of 80.

10. Add a `TextBlock` named `PreviewTextBlock` with a `TextAlignment` of `Center` and a `Foreground` of `Black`:

```
<UserControl
    x:Class="SLVideoPlayer01.UC_VideoDragger"
    xmlns="http://schemas.microsoft.com/winfx/2006/xaml/presentation"
    xmlns:x="http://schemas.microsoft.com/winfx/2006/xaml"
    xmlns:d="http://schemas.microsoft.com/expression/blend/2008"
    xmlns:mc="http://schemas.openxmlformats.org/markup-compatibility/2006"
    mc:Ignorable="d"
    Height="100"
    Width="100">
    <Grid
        x:Name="LayoutRoot"
```

```
            Background="Transparent">
        <StackPanel
            Orientation="Vertical">
            <Image
                x:Name="PreviewImage"
                Height="80" />
            <TextBlock
                x:Name="PreviewTextBlock"
                TextAlignment="Center"
                Foreground="Black" />
        </StackPanel>
    </Grid>
</UserControl>
```

Now that we have created the UserControl, we can go back to MainPage.xaml.cs and loop through our list of Video objects. For each one, we are going to create an instance of UC_VideoDragger and set its PreviewImage and PreviewTextBlock:

1. The first thing we need to do is to create a method called CreateVideoDraggerUserControls directly under the xmlClient_DownloadStringCompleted method:

```
void xmlClient_DownloadStringCompleted(object sender,
DownloadStringCompletedEventArgs e)
    {
        // if e.error is null we can proceed.
        if (e.Error == null)
        {
            string xmlData = e.Result;
            // comment out the MessageBox as we
            // now our XML is being parsed correctly
            //MessageBox.Show(xmlData);

            // Create the XmlSerializer
            XmlSerializer x = new XmlSerializer(typeof(VideoData));

            using (XmlReader reader = XmlReader.Create(new
StringReader(xmlData)))
            {
                // deserialize the XmlDate and set it to
                // our DataFactory VideoData object

                DataFactory.CLRInstance.VideoData =
(VideoData)x.Deserialize(reader);
            }
        }

    }
```

```
private void CreateVideoDraggerUserControls()
{

}
```

2.   In this new method, we are going to cycle through the `VideoData` list:

```
private void CreateVideoDraggerUserControls()
{
    foreach (Video v in DataFactory.CLRInstance.VideoData)
    {
    }
}
```

Here is where we are going to create a new instance of `UC_VideoDragger`. We can then set the `PreviewImage` and `PreviewTextBlock`. But we also need to be able to tell the `UC_VideoDragger` what the URL is for its video. There is no built-in property for this in `UC_VideoDragger`, so we are going to need to create a custom `DependencyProperty` to store this information:

3.   Open `UC_VideoDragger.xaml.cs` (note that this is the CS file, not the XAML file we were editing earlier) and create the `DependencyProperty` called `VideoURL`:

```
namespace SLVideoPlayer01
{
    public partial class UC_VideoDragger : UserControl
    {
        #region VideoURL (DependencyProperty)


        public string VideoURL
        {
            get { return (string)GetValue(VideoURLProperty); }
            set { SetValue(VideoURLProperty, value); }
        }
        public static readonly DependencyProperty VideoURLProperty =
        DependencyProperty.Register("VideoURL", typeof(string),
         typeof(UC_VideoDragger),
        new PropertyMetadata(string.Empty));

        #endregion


        public UC_VideoDragger()
        {
            InitializeComponent();
        }
    }
}
```

We are going to amend the application so you can drag a `UC_VideoDragger` onto a `MediaElement` to play the corresponding video. We also want the `UC_VideoDragger` to snap back to its original position when dropped. To do that, we need to store its X and Y positions when it is created. To do this, we can create two more `DependencyProperties` called `Xprop` and `Yprop`. Do that now:

```
namespace SLVideoPlayer01
{
    public partial class UC_VideoDragger : UserControl
    {
        #region VideoURL (DependencyProperty)


        public string VideoURL
        {
            get { return (string)GetValue(VideoURLProperty); }
            set { SetValue(VideoURLProperty, value); }
        }
        public static readonly DependencyProperty VideoURLProperty =
        DependencyProperty.Register("VideoURL", typeof(string),
        typeof(UC_VideoDragger),
        new PropertyMetadata(string.Empty));

        #endregion VideoURL

        #region Xprop (DependencyProperty)

public double Xprop
{
    get { return (double)GetValue(XpropProperty); }
    set { SetValue(XpropProperty, value); }
}
public static readonly DependencyProperty XpropProperty =
DependencyProperty.Register("Xprop", typeof(double),
typeof(UC_VideoDragger),
    new PropertyMetadata(0.0));

#endregion Xprop (DependencyProperty)

#region YProp (DependencyProperty)

public double YProp
{
    get { return (double)GetValue(YPropProperty); }
    set { SetValue(YPropProperty, value); }
}
public static readonly DependencyProperty YPropProperty =
DependencyProperty.Register("YProp", typeof(double),
typeof(UC_VideoDragger),
```

```
        new PropertyMetadata(0.0));

    #endregion YProp (DependencyProperty)

    public UC_VideoDragger()
    {
        InitializeComponent();
    }
    }
}
```

Now that we have stored the X and Y positions, we can go back to `MainPage.xaml.cs` and finish adding our `UC_VideoDraggers`:

1. We can make two private variables in `MainPage.xaml.cs` called `Xprop` and `Yprop`. You will see why in a bit:

```
public partial class MainPage : UserControl
    {
        private double Xprop = 10;
        private double Yprop = 10;
```

In `MainPage.xaml`, we need to add a `Canvas` that will hold our soon-to-be instances of `UC_VideoDragger`.

2. In `MainPage.xaml`, add a `Canvas` to the main grid and call it `DragCanvas`:

```
<UserControl x:Class="SLVideoPlayer01.MainPage"
    xmlns="http://schemas.microsoft.com/winfx/2006/xaml/presentation"
    xmlns:x="http://schemas.microsoft.com/winfx/2006/xaml"
    Width="400" Height="300">
    <Grid x:Name="LayoutRoot" Background="White">

        <Canvas
            x:Name="DragCanvas" />


    </Grid>
</UserControl>
```

Now we can go back to our `foreach` loop in `MainPage.xaml.cs`. You can see what we are doing by reading the commented code:

```
        private void CreateVideoDraggerUserControls()
        {
            foreach (Video v in DataFactory.CLRInstance.VideoData)
            {
                // instantiate a new instance of UC_VideoDragger called
```

videoDragger

```
            UC_VideoDragger videoDragger = new UC_VideoDragger();
            // set the PreviewImage source
            videoDragger.PreviewImage.Source = new BitmapImage(new

Uri(v.ThumbnailImage, UriKind.RelativeOrAbsolute));
        // set the video URl
        videoDragger.VideoURL = v.Url;

            // set the PreviewTextBlock Text
            videoDragger.PreviewTextBlock.Text = v.Title;
            // set the VideoURL DependencyProperty
            videoDragger.VideoURL = v.Url;
            // set the Xprop and Yprop to our local variables
(Xprop and Yprop)
            videoDragger.Xprop = Xprop;
            videoDragger.YProp = Yprop;
            // set the values for where the videoDragger appears
            videoDragger.SetValue(Canvas.LeftProperty, Xprop);
            videoDragger.SetValue(Canvas.TopProperty, Yprop);
            // set videoDragger so it has a hand cursor
            videoDragger.Cursor = Cursors.Hand;
            // add videoDragger to the workspace
            DragCanvas.Children.Add(videoDragger);
            // add 150 units to local Xprop
            Xprop += 150;
        }
```

> You will need to resolve BitmapImage in the preceding code by right-clicking on it and left-clicking Resolve.

As you can see in the preceding listing, we are accomplishing the following:

- Instantiating a new UC_VideoDragger called videoDragger
- Setting the Source and Text of the Image and TextBlock
- Setting the DependencyProperties for VideoURL, Xprop, and Yprop
- Setting where videoDragger will appear in the DragCanvas
- Setting the cursor of videoDragger to be a Hand cursor
- Adding videoDragger to DragCanvas
- Increasing the local Xprop by 150

At this point, if we run the application, we will not see anything. Why? Because we never called the CreateVideoDraggerUserControls method. Right after we serialize the XML, we need to call this method:

```
void xmlClient_DownloadStringCompleted(object sender,
 DownloadStringCompletedEventArgs e)
{
    // if e.error is null we can proceed.
    if (e.Error == null)
    {
        string xmlData = e.Result;
        // comment out the MessageBox as we know our XML is being parsed correctly
        //MessageBox.Show(xmlData);

        // Create the XmlSerializer
        XmlSerializer x = new XmlSerializer(typeof(VideoData));

        using (XmlReader reader = XmlReader.Create(new StringReader(xmlData)))
        {
            // deserialize the XmlDate and set it to
            // our DataFactory VideoData object

            DataFactory.CLRInstance.VideoData =
(VideoData)x.Deserialize(reader);
            CreateVideoDraggerUserControls();
        }
    }
}
```

Now, if you press F5 to compile and run the application, you should see something like I have in Figure 8-14.

Figure 8-14. The running application

Our application is coming along nicely, but we now need to add the ability to drag each UC_VideoDragger. In my last book, Behaviors were something relatively new to Silverlight, so I didn't talk about them much, if at all. To create the drag for the UC_VideoDragger controls, I had readers write a bunch of code. This version is going to be simpler because of Behaviors. In this book Behaviors are so important that they not only have their own chapter, they have caused the re-write of this and many *other* chapters. With that, let's use Behaviors to make the UC_VideoDraggers draggable.

Behaviors are commonly added in Blend by dragging and dropping them onto the target FrameworkElement. Here, though, we don't have anything to drag the Behaviors onto because our UC_VideoDraggers are being added programmatically. But don't fret, we can also add the drag Behavior programmatically as well. Before we do, though, we need to add a couple of references to the DLLs that make Behaviors possible. These DLLs are: the `System.Windows.Interactivity.dll` and the `Microsoft.Expression.Interactions.dll`. Let's add those now in Visual Studio.

1. In Visual Studio's Solution Explorer, right-click the `References` folder.

2. Click **Add Reference.**

3. When the **Add Reference** dialog box appears, click the **Browse** tab.

4. Navigate to `C:\Program Files (x86)\Microsoft SDKs\Expression\Blend\Silverlight\v4.0`.

> *The location of the Silverlight SDK mentioned in step 4 is the default location when Silverlight is installed; it could possibly be different on your individual machine. If this is the case, you can do a search on your machine for "SDKs" to locate yours.*

5. Locate the `System.Windows.Interactivity.dll` and double-click to add it to the project.

6. Start again from step 2 and this time add the `Microsoft.Expression.Interactions.dll` (you can see both DLLs in Figure 8-15).

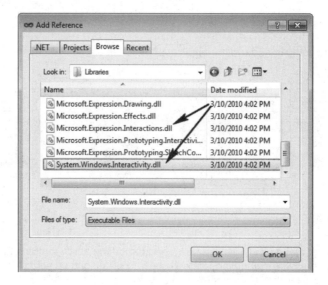

Figure 8-15. Add the `Microsoft.Expression.Interactions` and `System.Windows.Interactivity` DLLs to your application.

Now that you have added these DLLs you can go back the `foreach` statement in the `CreateVideoDraggerUserControls` method of `MainPage.xaml.cs`.

7. Just below where you increment XProp by 150, you can add the code to attach the MouseDragElementBehavior Behavior to the videoDragger variable:

```
private void CreateVideoDraggerUserControls()
{
    foreach (Video v in DataFactory.CLRInstance.VideoData)
    {
    // create a new instance of UC_VideoDragger
    //UC_VideoDragger videoDragger = new
    UC_VideoDragger videoDragger = new UC_VideoDragger();

    // set the PreviewImage source
    videoDragger.PreviewImage.Source = new BitmapImage(new Uri(v.ThumbnailImage,
riKind.RelativeOrAbsolute));

    // set the video URl
    videoDragger.VideoURL = v.Url;

    // set the PreviewTextBlock text
    videoDragger.PreviewTextBlock.Text = v.Title;

    // set the X and Y Prop to local values
    videoDragger.Xprop = Xprop;
    videoDragger.YProp = Yprop;

    // set the x and y location on the DragCanvas Canvas
    videoDragger.SetValue(Canvas.LeftProperty, Xprop);
    videoDragger.SetValue(Canvas.TopProperty, Yprop);

    // set the cursor to the Hand cursor
    videoDragger.Cursor = Cursors.Hand;

    // add videoDragger to the DragCanvas
    DragCanvas.Children.Add(videoDragger);

    // Add 150 units to XProp
    Xprop += 150;

    // Attach the MouseDragElementBehavior to videoDragger
    MouseDragElementBehavior dragBehavior = new MouseDragElementBehavior();
    dragBehavior.Attach(videoDragger);

    }
```

Now press F5 to compile and run the application; notice how your UC_VideoDragger controls can now be dragged about your application (see Figure 8-16).

Figure 8-16. You can now drag the `UC_VideoDraggers`.

Great! Next, when we drop the videos, we want the video associated with the dragger to start to play, and we want the dragger to snap back to its original position:

1. The first thing we need to do is to add a `MediaElement` to `MainPage.xaml`:

```
<UserControl
    xmlns="http://schemas.microsoft.com/winfx/2006/xaml/presentation"
    xmlns:x="http://schemas.microsoft.com/winfx/2006/xaml"
    xmlns:d="http://schemas.microsoft.com/expression/blend/2008"
    xmlns:mc="http://schemas.openxmlformats.org/markup-compatibility/2006"
    xmlns:i="http://schemas.microsoft.com/expression/2010/interactivity"
    xmlns:ei="http://schemas.microsoft.com/expression/2010/interactions"
    x:Class="SLVideoPlayer01.MainPage"
    mc:Ignorable="d"
    d:DesignHeight="300"
    d:DesignWidth="400">
    <Grid
    x:Name="LayoutRoot"
    Background="White">
<MediaElement
    x:Name="ME"
    Source="video1.wmv"
    Margin="140,160,360,260"
    AutoPlay="True"
    Position="00:00:03"
    Stretch="Uniform" />
    <Canvas
    x:Name="DragCanvas" />
    </Grid>
</UserControl>
```

The Margin *property for your* MediaElement *may be different from mine. If you run the application and don't see any video, set your* MediaElement *to have a margin of 0, run the application again, and adjust it accordingly.*

Notice that I set the Source of the MediaElement to be video1.wmv, and the MediaElement is set to auto play. So when you run your application, your video should start to play. But we want a UC_VideoDragger, if dragged and dropped onto the MediaElement, to start playing the video that is associated with the dragger. To do this we need to get a list of all visual elements in the visual tree. We then need to cycle through that list, and if that list contains a MediaElement, we need to set the Source of the MediaElement to the VideoURL property of the UC_VideoDragger:

To do this, go back in to your CreateVideoDraggerUserControls method in MainPage.xaml.cs and wire up a handler to an event right under where you increment XProp. In that new handler you will create the code that will cycle through all of the elements in the visual tree. When a MediaElement is located during that cycle, you will re-create the videoDragger and then use its URL property to set the Source of the MediaElement.

```
private void CreateVideoDraggerUserControls()
{
    foreach (Video v in DataFactory.CLRInstance.VideoData)
    {
        // create a new instance of UC_VideoDragger
        UC_VideoDragger videoDragger = new UC_VideoDragger();

        // set the PreviewImage source
        videoDragger.PreviewImage.Source = new BitmapImage(new
Uri(v.ThumbnailImage, UriKind.RelativeOrAbsolute));

        // set the video URl
        videoDragger.VideoURL = v.Url;

        // set the PreviewTextBlock text
        videoDragger.PreviewTextBlock.Text = v.Title;

        // set the X and Y Prop to local values
        videoDragger.Xprop = Xprop;
        videoDragger.YProp = Yprop;

        // set the x and y location on the DragCanvas Canvas
        videoDragger.SetValue(Canvas.LeftProperty, Xprop);
        videoDragger.SetValue(Canvas.TopProperty, Yprop);

        // set the cursor to the Hand cursor
        videoDragger.Cursor = Cursors.Hand;

        // add videoDragger to the DragCanvas
```

```
            DragCanvas.Children.Add(videoDragger);

            // Add 150 units to XProp
            Xprop += 150;

            // Attach the MouseDragElementBehavior to videoDragger
            MouseDragElementBehavior dragBehavior = new MouseDragElementBehavior();
            dragBehavior.Attach(videoDragger);

            videoDragger.MouseLeftButtonUp += new
MouseButtonEventHandler(videoDragger_MouseLeftButtonUp);
        }

}

void videoDragger_MouseLeftButtonUp(object sender, MouseButtonEventArgs e)
{
        // get a list of all visual elements in the VisualTree
        IEnumerable<UIElement> mylist =
VisualTreeHelper.FindElementsInHostCoordinates(e.GetPosition(this), this);

        //cycle through each element
        foreach (UIElement uie in mylist)
        {
            // if this element is a MediaElement
            if (uie is MediaElement)
            {
                // create a UC_VideoDragger element
                UC_VideoDragger videoDragger = sender as UC_VideoDragger;

                // make sure it is not null
                if (videoDragger != null)
                {
                    // pause the MediaElement (named ME)
                    ME.Pause();

                    // create the URI based upon the videoDragger
                    Uri srcUri = new Uri(videoDragger.VideoURL,
UriKind.RelativeOrAbsolute);

                    // set the Source of ME
                    ME.Source = srcUri;

                    // play the ME
                    ME.Play();
                }
            }
        }

}
```

The last thing you need to do is to have the videoDragger, if dropped onto the MediaElement, return to its original position. We can do this by creating a GeneralTransform to determine where the videoDragger originated from and then use a TranslateTransform to actually move it back to where it came from. See the code for this below in bold.

```
void videoDragger_MouseLeftButtonUp(object sender, MouseButtonEventArgs e)
{
    // get a list of all visual elements in the VisualTree
    IEnumerable<UIElement> mylist =
VisualTreeHelper.FindElementsInHostCoordinates(e.GetPosition(this), this);

    //cycle through each element
    foreach (UIElement uie in mylist)
    {
        // if this element is a MediaElement
        if (uie is MediaElement)
        {
            // create a UC_VideoDragger element
            UC_VideoDragger videoDragger = sender as UC_VideoDragger;

            // make sure it is not null
            if (videoDragger != null)
            {
                // pause the MediaElement (named ME)
                ME.Pause();

                // create the URI based upon the videoDragger
                Uri srcUri = new Uri(videoDragger.VideoURL,
UriKind.RelativeOrAbsolute);

                // set the Source of ME
                ME.Source = srcUri;

                // play the ME
                ME.Play();

                // Create a GenderalTransform to find out where the
videoDragger originated from
                GeneralTransform gtf =
videoDragger.TransformToVisual(videoDragger) as GeneralTransform;

                // Send it back to its orginal postion
                Point currentPoint = gtf.Transform(new Point(0, 0));
                videoDragger.RenderTransform = new TranslateTransform();
            }
        }
    }

}
```

If now you press F5 to compile and run the application, you will see that you can drag a UC_VideoDragger onto the MediaElement. The MediaElement will play the associated video, and the UC_VideoDragger will return to its original X and Y position. Cool, huh?

That's it! You have a cool Silverlight video player with drag capabilities. My challenge to you is to make the video for the UC_VideoDragger play when you click it.

You can download my source code for the project discussed in this chapter at http://windowspresentationfoundation.com/Blend4Book/SLVideoPlayer01.zip.

Summary

In this chapter, you learned about the Silverlight MediaElement and some situations where you would want to use Silverlight for video rather than Flash. You then created a Silverlight video player, complete with XML data, a DataFactory, and drag-and-drop capabilities.

If you would like to watch a video tutorial on how to do the above tutorial you can do so here: http://www.windowspresentationfoundation.com/?p=287.

You can also watch a video tutorial on how to use the MediaElement to create your own TutorialCam just like I use in my video tutorials: http://www.windowspresentationfoundation.com/?p=439.

In the next chapter, I examine events and event handlers, including the new Silverlight 4 right-click and MouseWheel event handling.

Chapter 9

Events and EventHandlers

What this chapter covers:

- What events and `EventHandlers` are
- Creating a project and exploring and creating some different events
- New events in Silverlight 4

Most Silverlight objects have a set of events that fire when users interact with them. You have already seen some events in earlier chapters. You also know that any method or function that is called when an event is fired is called an `EventHandler`. In this chapter I discuss the many different events that objects have, from the `Click` event to the new Silverlight 4 `MouseWheel` event. You are going to create `EventHandlers` for all these different events as well, so let's get started and create a new Silverlight project.

Creating the EventsAndEventHandlers project

As I have stated so many times before, this is a very hands-on book, so now would be a great time to create a new Silverlight 4 Application project and start exploring events and `EventHandlers` with practical examples (as you might have guessed, I am of the opinion that people learn best by doing rather than just reading). So let's get started:

1. Open Visual Studio 2010.

2. Select **File ➤ New ➤ Project**, and choose **Silverlight Application**.

3. Give the project the name `EventsAndEventHandlers`. Choose a location to save the project and click **OK** (see Figure 9-1). Click **OK** again when the **New Silverlight Application** dialog box appears.

Figure 9-1. Creating a new Silverlight Application project called `EventsAndEventHandlers` in Visual Studio 2010.

    4. Note where the project was created, as we are about to open it in Blend 4.

    5. Open Blend 4, navigate to where you saved the project, and open it.

    6. With your project open in Blend 4, double-click `MainPage.xaml` from the **Projects** panel, select the Button tool from the toolbar, and draw a `Button` control on the artboard like the one shown in Figure 9-2.

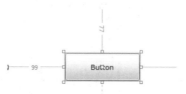

Figure 9-2. Drawing a `Button` control in the workspace in Blend.

    7. Build the project by pressing Ctrl+Shift+B, and switch back to Visual Studio 2010. When you're prompted to reload the project, select **Yes**.

    8. Now that you have a `Button` in the XAML, you need to give it a unique name so that you can control it programmatically in the C# of `MainPage.xaml.cs`. So in `MainPage.xaml`, locate the XAML for your `Button`, and give it the name of `MyButton` as shown in the following code:

```
<UserControl
    x:Class="EventsAndEventHandlers.MainPage"
```

```
xmlns="http://schemas.microsoft.com/winfx/2006/xaml/presentation"
xmlns:x="http://schemas.microsoft.com/winfx/2006/xaml"
xmlns:d="http://schemas.microsoft.com/expression/blend/2008"
xmlns:mc="http://schemas.openxmlformats.org/markup-compatibility/2006"
mc:Ignorable="d"
d:DesignHeight="300"
d:DesignWidth="400">
<Grid
    x:Name="LayoutRoot"
    Background="White">
    <Button
        x:Name="MyButton"
        Content="Button"
        Height="43"
        Margin="99,77,182,0"
        VerticalAlignment="Top" />
</Grid>
</UserControl>
```

> For easier-to-read XAML, you can restructure your code so that each property is on its own line as I have done with the preceding `Button` code.

9. Press F6 to recompile the project without running it.

10. Now that you have named your `Button` and recompiled the application, open `MainPage.xaml.cs` and in the constructor below the code that reads `InitializeComponent();`, type the Button name followed by a . (period). You will see an IntelliSense dropdown menu of the events that your `Button` has. Events have an icon that looks like a lightning bolt next to them.

Let's go over the events that you would commonly use for a `Button`.

Click

`Click`, obviously, is the event that occurs when the `Button` is clicked.

1. Directly under the `InitializeComponent();` line of code, type **click**. Then type **+=** and press the Tab key twice. Visual Studio 2010 attaches the `Click` event to the `EventHandler` method stub for you. My code follows:

```
namespace EventsAndEventHandlers
{
    public partial class MainPage : UserControl
    {
        public MainPage()
```

```
    {
        InitializeComponent();
        MyButton.Click += new RoutedEventHandler(MyButton_Click);
    }

    void MyButton_Click(object sender, RoutedEventArgs e)
    {
        throw new NotImplementedException();
    }

}
}
```

2. In the new method stub, remove the default text of `throw new NotImplementedException();`. Replace it with a `MessageBox`. This will allow us to show the user a message when a `Click` has occurred. See the following code:

```
namespace EventsAndEventHandlers
{
    public partial class MainPage : UserControl
    {
        public MainPage()
        {
            InitializeComponent();
            MyButton.Click += new RoutedEventHandler(MyButton_Click);
        }

        void MyButton_Click(object sender, RoutedEventArgs e)
        {
            MessageBox.Show("I was clicked");
        }

    }
}
```

3. Press F5 to compile and run the application.

4. Now you can click the `Button` and see a `MessageBox` with the message "I was clicked."

That was simple enough, so let's move on to mouse events.

Mouse Events

In C#, there are many ways to handle events that involve users interacting with objects using the mouse. I will now discuss some of these events. It is also important to note that you are going to create examples of these events using a `Button` control, but most of these events can just as easily be applied to other objects, such as a simple Rectangle, a `MediaElement`, or even the main application itself.

Before I start talking about these events, you'll need to do some maintenance to your application to give you some breathing room:

1. Make sure your application is saved and switch back to Blend 4.

2. Change the width and height of your application to 800×600, respectively. I find the easiest way to do this is to alter the XAML in the Split view and just change the `Height` and `Width` properties in the `UserControl` node to 800 and 600 (by default, Visual Studio made my Page 400×300).

I find developing visually in Blend 4 easier with the Design view rather than the Split view, as I do most of my XAML coding in Visual Studio 2010—primarily because it formats my code and Blend 4 does not. With its new size, the application in Blend should look similar to the one shown in Figure 9-3.

Figure 9-3. After changing the size of the application, your application should resemble this.

3. With the `Button` selected, go to the **Common Properties** bucket of the **Properties** panel and change the **Content** property to read "**Press Me!**".

4. In XAML view, your code should look similar to this:

```
<UserControl
    x:Class="EventsAndEventHandlers.MainPage"
    xmlns="http://schemas.microsoft.com/winfx/2006/xaml/presentation"
    xmlns:x="http://schemas.microsoft.com/winfx/2006/xaml"
    xmlns:d="http://schemas.microsoft.com/expression/blend/2008"
    xmlns:mc="http://schemas.openxmlformats.org/markup-compatibility/2006"
    mc:Ignorable="d"
    d:DesignHeight="600"
    d:DesignWidth="800">
    <Grid
        x:Name="LayoutRoot"
        Background="White">
        <Button
```

```
            x:Name="MyButton"
            Content="Press Me!"
            Height="43"
            Margin="99,77,182,0"
            VerticalAlignment="Top" />

    </Grid>
</UserControl>
```

5. Press Ctrl+Shift+B to compile the application.

MouseEnter and MouseLeave

MouseEnter and MouseLeave are two very important events. Most rich media applications have buttons that do something when your mouse is over them and then do something else when your mouse leaves them, and these events enable you to provide this type of functionality. For example, navigation buttons commonly glow when your mouse is over them, and the glow disappears when your mouse moves away. In Flash and JavaScript, these are commonly known as RollOver and RollOut states, but in Silverlight and Blend they are known as MouseEnter and MouseLeave, respectively. Try out these events yourself in the following sections.

MouseEnter

As you can probably guess, a MouseEnter event is fired when the user moves the mouse over an object. To see how this works, you'll add the MouseEnter event and EventHandler to the MyButton control. In the last edition I showed how to create these events in Visual Studio with C#. In this book I focus more on Blend and therefore will show how to create these events in Blend. Let's do that now.

1. In Blend make sure that the Button (named MyButton) is selected, and in the **Properties** panel click the **Events** icon, as I am doing in Figure 9-4.

Figure 9-4. Click the Events button in Blend.

2. You will then see a list of Events that are applicable to the Button object. Find the MouseEnter event and double-click it to create the event, as I am doing in Figure 9-5.

Figure 9-5. The `MouseEnter` event is created in Blend.

3. Blend will then open the `MainPage.xaml.cs` code-behind page and show you the newly created event:

```
private void MyButton_MouseEnter(object sender, System.Windows.Input.MouseEventArgs
e)
{
    // TODO: Add event handler implementation here.
}
```

4. You can see mine in Figure 9-6. Then under the commented default line of code that reads "`// TODO: Add event handler implementation here.`" add a `MessageBox`, as I am doing in Figure 9-7.

```
27
28          private void MyButton_MouseEnter(object sender, System.Windows.Input.MouseEventArgs e)
29          {
30              // TODO: Add event handler implementation here.
31          }
32
33      }
34  }
```

Figure 9-6. The C# that Blend created for you.

```
private void MyButton_MouseEnter(object sender, System.Windows.Input.MouseEventArgs
e)
{
    // TODO: Add event handler implementation here.
    MessageBox.Show("MyButton was MouseEntered");
}
```

```
private void MyButton_MouseEnter(object sender, System.Windows.Input.MouseEventArgs e)
{
    // TODO: Add event handler implementation here.
    MessageBox.Show("MyButton was MouseEntered");
}
```

Figure 9-7. The code with the `MessageBox` added.

   4.   Press F5 to compile and run the application. Place your mouse pointer over the `Button` and you will see a `MessageBox` appear (see Figure 9-8).

Figure 9-8. The `MouseEnter` event was fired.

Let's move on to looking at the `MouseLeave` event.

MouseLeave

Click the tab at the top of Blend for `MainPage.xaml` (shown in Figure 9-9) to return to the XAML and with `MyButton` selected go back to the **Events** in the **Properties** panel and double-click the `MouseLeave` event. This will create the `MouseLeave` event for you in code-behind. You can see my code in Figure 9-10.

Figure 9-9. Click the `MainPage.xaml` tab to return to `MainPage`.

```
private void MyButton_MouseLeave(object sender, System.Windows.Input.MouseEventArgs e)
{
    // TODO: Add event handler implementation here.
}
```

```
private void MyButton_MouseLeave(object sender, System.Windows.Input.MouseEventArgs e)
{
    // TODO: Add event handler implementation here.
}
```

Figure 9-10. Blend creates the `MouseLeave` code.

```
private void MyButton_MouseLeave(object sender, System.Windows.Input.MouseEventArgs
e)
{
    // TODO: Add event handler implementation here.
    MessageBox.Show("MyButton was MouseLeave");
}
```

1. Add a `MessageBox` for `MouseLeave`, as I am doing in Figure 9-11.

```
private void MyButton_MouseLeave(object sender, System.Windows.Input.MouseEventArgs e)
{
    // TODO: Add event handler implementation here.
    MessageBox.Show("MyButton was MouseLeave");
}
```

Figure 9-11. Add a `MessageBox` for `MouseLeave`.

2. When you press F5 to run the application, now you will see the `MessageBox` for `MouseLeave` as shown in Figure 9-12.

Figure 9-12. The `MouseLeave` event fires this `MessageBox`.

MouseLeftButtonDown

The `MouseLeftButtonDown` event is fired when you click your left mouse button on an object. This seems pretty straightforward, but there is a catch: if you were to listen for the `MouseLeftButtonDown` event on your `Button`, you would not get any results, because a `Button` control has a `Click` event. So, you may be asking, why would you want to use a `MouseLeftButtonDown` event on a `Button`? Good question; the simple answer is you wouldn't because the `MouseLeftButtonDown` event is primarily used for controls that do not have a `Click` event such a Grid. That being said, let's create an event for a `MouseLeftButtonDown` event on the application's main `Grid` named `LayoutRoot`. An event like this would be useful in an application such as one that draws when the mouse is down and stops when the mouse is up. In this case we would need to know when both events take place.

1. In Blend switch back to `MainPage.xaml` and choose your selection tool by pressing the V key and select the `LayoutRoot` Grid in the **Objects and Timeline** panel like I have done in Figure 9-13.

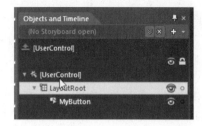

Figure 9-13. Select the LayoutRoot Grid in the Objects and Timeline panel.

2. Next move to the **Properties** panel and locate the event for MouseLeftButtonDown and double-click it, as I have done in Figure 9-14.

Figure 9-14. Double-click the MouseLeftButtonDown event in Blend.

3. Once Blend opens the code-behind for MainPage.xaml.cs and creates the MouseLeftButtonDown event, go ahead and insert a MessageBox that reads: " MouseLeftButtonDown event fired" as I have done in Figure 9-15.

```
private void LayoutRoot_MouseLeftButtonDown(object sender,
 System.Windows.Input.MouseButtonEventArgs e)
{
        // TODO: Add event handler implementation here.
        MessageBox.Show("MouseLeftButton down event fired");
}
```

```
private void LayoutRoot_MouseLeftButtonDown(object sender, System.Windows.Input.MouseButtonEventArgs e)
{
    // TODO: Add event handler implementation here.
    MessageBox.Show("MouseLeftButtonDown event fired");
}
```

Figure 9-15. Add a `MessageBox` to the `MouseLeftButtonDown` event handler.

4. Run the application and try it out. As you can see in Figure 9-16, you get the results you would expect.

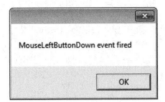

Figure 9-16. The `MessageBox` fires when you click on the `LayoutRoot` Grid.

MouseLeftButtonUp

The `MouseLeftButtonUp` event is much like the `MouseLeftButtonDown` event except it fires when, of course, the left mouse button is released over an object. Go ahead and follow the steps above to:

1. In Blend select the `LayoutRoot` Grid in the **Objects and Timeline** panel.

2. In the Properties panel Events section, double-click the `MouseLeftButtonUp` event to have Blend create the event handler in code.

3. Alter the default code to add a `MessageBox` that displays "MouseLeftButtonUp event fired".

Your code should look like this:

```
private void LayoutRoot_MouseLeftButtonUp(object sender,↵
System.Windows.Input.MouseButtonEventArgs e)
{
    // TODO: Add event handler implementation here.
    MessageBox.Show("MouseLeftButtonUp event fired");
}
```

These are just some of the common events that are able to be reacted to in Silverlight. As you continue with Silverlight, you will see there are many more that can help make your Silverlight applications more interactive. Even though many events shipped with Silverlight 3, you will find that there have been some very handy additional events added in Silverlight 4. Let's take a look at some of them now.

New Events in Silverlight 4

With the release of Silverlight 4, there is now support for some new events that make for better User Experiences (UX) and all around better Rich Internet Applications (RIAs) in general. Let's explore some of these new events.

Right-Click

Right-click is an event that was added with the release of Silverlight 4 and is one that is a very important part of allowing Silverlight to behave like typical desktop software applications such as Microsoft Word. In Word you know that if you right-click something you often get some kind of contextual menu that allows you to perform certain actions such as changing the size of the font. Figure 9-17 shows what happens when you right-click text in Microsoft Word.

Figure 9-17. Right-clicking text in Microsoft Word brings up this contextual menu.

To show how Silverlight 4's new Right-click event can be useful, let's try and make our application do something similar to what Word does. To start create an image like I have in Figure 9-17, save it to your hard drive and return to Blend.

> *I have uploaded my image just in case you don't know how or don't have time to make one:* http://www.windowspresentationfoundation.com/bookDownloads/RightClickImg.jpg

1. In Blend right-click on the EventsAndEventHandlers project in the **Projects** and click **Add Existing Item,** as I am doing in Figure 9-18.

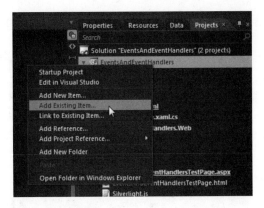

Figure 9-18. Add Existing Item to the project.

2. Navigate to where you saved your image that looks like Figure 9-17 and double-click it to add it to the project.

3. Drag the image from the **Projects** panel to the artboard so that you have your image sitting on your artboard, as shown in Figure 9-19.

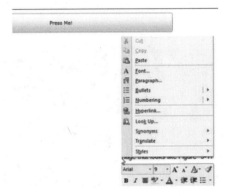

Figure 9-19. Drag the image to the artboard.

4. Switch back to the **Properties** panel. It is probably still showing the **Events,** so click the **Properties** icon to switch back to **Properties**. The **Properties** icon is shown in Figure 9-20:

Figure 9-20. Click the Properties icon to view the properties of the selected objects.

5. With the Image selected go to the **Appearance** bucket and change the Opacity property to 0 to make it invisible, as I am doing in Figure 9-21.

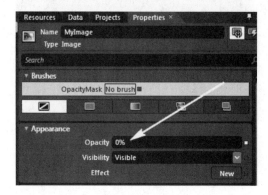

Figure 9-21. Change the Visibility to Collapsed for the Image.

6. Give the image a Name property of MyImage.

7. Click the **Events** icon in the **Properties** panel to view the Events again. Locate the MouseRightButtonDown event and double-click it. Blend will create the event and event handler as shown in Figure 9-22

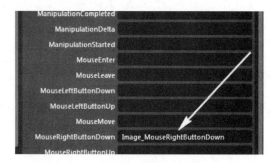

Figure 9-22. Create the MouseRightButtonDown event.

8. In MainPage.xaml.cs, locate the newly created event and change the Opacity to 1 (100%) as I do here:

```
private void Image_MouseRightButtonDown(object sender,↵
 System.Windows.Input.MouseButtonEventArgs e)
{
    MyImage.Opacity = 1;
}
```

> *If you didn't want the Silverlight context menu to appear you could simple write "e.Handled = true;" in the event handler.*

9. Run the application and right-click in the area where `MyImage` should be if you could see it. Notice how it appears (see Figure 9-23).

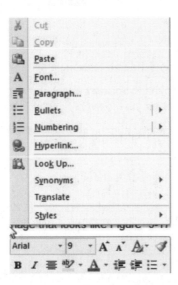

Figure 9-23. `MyImage` now shows up when you right-click it.

> *Challenge: Make `MyImage` have an `Opacity` of 0 again when you `MouseRightButtonUp`.*

MouseWheel

`MouseWheel` is another important event that allows Silverlight 4 to provide the good UX that we have become so used to. For example, say we have an image that is not fully shown but has scrollbars; we know that if we use our mouse and drag the scrollbars the image will scroll. But we also have become used to the idea that if we see scrollbars we can also use our `MouseWheel` to scroll. As it turns out Microsoft has made the implementation of this event quite easy. Any object that can have scrollbars, such as a `ScrollViewer`, `ListBox`, or `DataGrid` already has `MouseWheel` implemented, and we don't have to write any special code to make it work; it just does out of the box. But we can write code to use `MouseWheel` on items that don't have scrollbars. For instance, we could use the `MouseWheel` event to change the size of an object—say, a Rectangle. Let's do that now.

1. In Blend create a Rectangle with an explicit `Height` and `Width` of 100 and a solid red fill, as I have done in Figure 9-24.

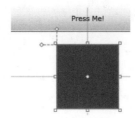

Figure 9-24. A Rectangle with a red fill.

2. In the **Properties** panel name the new Rectangle `MyRect`.

3. Switch to the **Events** tab in the **Properties** panel and, with `MyRect` still selected, double-click the `MouseWheel` property to create the event handler in the `Mainpage` code-behind.

4. In the `MouseWheel` event handler add the code to change the `Height` of the Rectangle, as I do here:

```
private void MyRect_MouseWheel(object sender,
System.Windows.Input.MouseWheelEventArgs e)
{
    // TODO: Add event handler implementation here.
    double RectHeight = MyRect.Height;
    double RectWidth = MyRect.Width;
    int delta = e.Delta;
}
```

If you run the application now you will see that when you click the red Rectangle and then scroll your `MouseWheel` up and down, you can change the `Height` of the Rectangle. Pretty cool, huh?

Drop Target Events

Silverlight 4 now has the ability to use the application as a *drop target*. That is, you can drop items from your hard drive right onto your Silverlight 4 applications and interact with them. To show how cool this feature is, let's make a simple little demo application that allows you to drop an image onto your Silverlight 4 application, and your application will then display that image.

1. In Visual Studio 2010 create a new application called `ImageDrop`. Select **Silverlight Application** for the template, as I am doing in Figure 9-25.

Figure 9-25. Create a new Silverlight application called `ImageDrop`.

2. When the New Silverlight Application dialog box appears, uncheck **"Host the Silverlight application in a new website"** and click **OK**.

3. In `MainPage.xaml` in the very first `UserControl` section, add a new property at the very end called `AllowDrop` and set it to `True` (seen in Figure 9-26). This tells the application that we are going to allow content to be dropped onto it.

```
<UserControl x:Class="ImageDrop.MainPage"
    xmlns="http://schemas.microsoft.com/winfx/2006/xaml/presentation"
    xmlns:x="http://schemas.microsoft.com/winfx/2006/xaml"
    xmlns:d="http://schemas.microsoft.com/expression/blend/2008"
    xmlns:mc="http://schemas.openxmlformats.org/markup-compatibility"
    mc:Ignorable="d"
    d:DesignHeight="300" d:DesignWidth="400" AllowDrop="True">
```

Figure 9-26. Set `AllowDrop` to true.

4. The first thing to do is to add the `Drop` event. Open `MainPage.xaml.cs` and under the `InitializeComponent();` call add the word `Drop` and type +=. Press the Tab key twice to raise the event and have Visual Studio generate the event handler. You can see my code here:

```
namespace ImageDrop
```

```
{
    public partial class MainPage : UserControl
    {
        public MainPage()
        {
            InitializeComponent();
            Drop += new DragEventHandler(MainPage_Drop);
        }

        void MainPage_Drop(object sender, DragEventArgs e)
        {
            throw new NotImplementedException();
        }
    }
}
```

5. Now to make sure we are catching the Drop event property, add a simple MessageBox to the MainPage_Drop event handler as I do in the following code:

```
void MainPage_Drop(object sender, DragEventArgs e)
{
    MessageBox.Show("DROP");
}
```

6. Press F5 to run the application and drop an image from your hard drive onto the running application. You should see something like I have in Figure 9-27.

I had you drop an image onto your Silverlight application, but it should be noted that this can be done with other objects, such as text, XAML, Word files, and many more.

Figure 9-27. This MessageBox ensures we are catching the Drop event.

I've just showed you that we can react to the Drop event, but what if we wanted to actually do something more interesting? What if when we drop an image onto our application, we actually then display that image? Let's do that now.

7. We need to add a few variables:

- First we need to get the `FrameworkElement` that was dropped on and call that the `fe`.
- We need to get the `objectName`.
- We need to get the `dataObject`.
- We need to get the files that we dropped onto the application (see the following code for this).

```
void MainPage_Drop(object sender, DragEventArgs e)
{
    FrameworkElement fe = sender as FrameworkElement;
    String objectName = fe.Name;
    IDataObject dataObject = e.Data as IDataObject;
    FileInfo[] files = dataObject.GetData(DataFormats.FileDrop) as FileInfo[];
}
```

8. You will have to resolve `FileInfo[]`. You can do this by right-clicking it and left-clicking `Resolve`, or clicking `FileInfo` and pressing Control+. (period key), as I am doing in Figure 9-28.

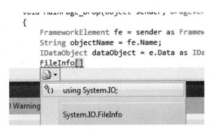

Figure 9-28. Resolve `FileInfo[]`.

9. Because `files` is a collection, you need to cycle through it to look for the `.jpg` (image) extension. For now, when we find the right file we are just going to display a simple `MessageBox` alert to let us know we are on the correct track. If this works we can then remove the `MessageBox` and actually re-create the image.

```
void MainPage_Drop(object sender, DragEventArgs e)
{
    FrameworkElement fe = sender as FrameworkElement;
    String objectName = fe.Name;
    IDataObject dataObject = e.Data as IDataObject;
    FileInfo[] files = dataObject.GetData(DataFormats.FileDrop) as FileInfo[];

    foreach (FileInfo file in files)
    {
        if (file.Extension.ToUpper() == ".JPG")
        {

            MessageBox.Show("I am an IMAGE");
```

```
    }
  }
}
```

10. Run the application and drag a non-image onto the app—nothing should occur. Then drag an image onto the app and let it go. You should get the alert that we set above.

11. To handle what occurs if we have an image, we need to create an IO stream and read the file. An *IO Stream* is simply a generic stream of the bytes that make up any file. We can create a new `BitmapImage` and then set its `Source` to the stream (see the following code).

```
FrameworkElement fe = sender as FrameworkElement;
String objectName = fe.Name;
IDataObject dataObject = e.Data as IDataObject;
FileInfo[] files = dataObject.GetData(DataFormats.FileDrop) as FileInfo[];

foreach (FileInfo file in files)
{
    if (file.Extension == ".JPG")
    {
        using (var stream = file.OpenRead())
        {
            var imageSource = new BitmapImage();
            imageSource.SetSource(stream);
        }
    }
}
```

You will also need to resolve `BitmapImage`.

12. Now that we already have our `BitmapImage` with a `Source` set to the raw bytes of the dropped image, all we need to do is simply create a new `Image` control, set its `Source` to the `BitmapImage Source` we created earlier, give it a `Height` of 300 (the `Width` will automatically set itself while keeping its aspect ratio), and then add it to the main Grid of the application named `LayoutRoot`:

```
FrameworkElement fe = sender as FrameworkElement;
String objectName = fe.Name;
IDataObject dataObject = e.Data as IDataObject;
FileInfo[] files = dataObject.GetData(DataFormats.FileDrop) as FileInfo[];

foreach (FileInfo file in files)
{
    if (file.Extension == ".JPG")
    {
```

```
            using (var stream = file.OpenRead())
            {
                var imageSource = new BitmapImage();
                imageSource.SetSource(stream);

            Image img = new Image();
            img.Source = imageSource;
            img.Height = 300;
            LayoutRoot.Children.Add(img);


        }
    }
  }
}
```

So now if you press F5 and run the application, you can drag images onto it and it will add a new image every time you drag and drop one (see Figure 9-29).

Figure 9-29. You can now add images to the running application by dragging and dropping them on to it.

You can find the source code for both of the applications I created in this chapter here: http://windowspresentationfoundation.com/Blend4Book/Ch9Projects.zip

For more information about MouseWheel events, you can watch Jesse Liberty's video here: http://www.silverlight.net/learn/videos/all/mousewheel-api/

For more on Right-click events, you can watch Tim Heuer's video here: http://www.silverlight.net/learn/videos/all/right-click-mouse-events/

For a very in depth look at using Silverlight as drop targets, you can watch Jesse Liberty's very impressive video here: http://www.silverlight.net/learn/videos/all/silverlight-controls-drop-targets/

Summary

In this chapter you learned about some very common events and even some very new events that were included in the Silverlight 4. You even learned how to use them in a practical manner by making an application that allows you to add images to it by simply dragging then and dropping them right onto the application. There are more events that are now part of Silverlight that we will talk about when we discuss Out Of the Browser (OOB) applications in Chapter 14, such as the `DragMove`, `DragResize`, `Maximize`, `Minimize`, and `Close` events. In the next chapter I discuss Classes and Interfaces in depth, as mastery of these will ensure you will become a well-rounded Silverlight developer.

Chapter 10

Classes and Interfaces

What this chapter covers:

- Learning about different types of classes
- Using interfaces to create polymorphic classes

As I briefly discuss in Chapter 3, *classes* are a very important construct of Object-Oriented Programming and can be considered a blueprint for creating objects. Further, these classes encapsulate State and Behavior. Behavior is encapsulated into *methods* (sometimes referred to as *functions*), and State is encapsulated in data placeholders called *member variables*, also known as *properties*. There are different types of classes, and we will go over many of them in this chapter. Similar to classes are an Object-Oriented Programming construct called *interfaces*. I show you how you can use interfaces in order to create polymorphic classes. Finally I show you a typical scenario in which one would want to re-factor behaviors into a separate class object.

Static Classes vs. Concrete Classes

You already know quite a bit about creating classes, as we created a few of them back in Chapter 3. We had to create an instance of those classes before we could use them. The opposite of this is known as a Static class, which is a class that has methods that can be run without actually instantiating an instance of the class. A concrete class, like we created back in Chapter 3, on the other hand, is a class that can have both static or concrete members, methods, or properties. If the member—say, a method—is concrete, the class would need to be instantiated before it is used. For example, say I create a concrete class named `Peter`. In the `Peter` class I have a concrete property named `Occupation`. I also have a concrete method that encapsulates a Behavior—let's call that method `GotoTheGym`. In order for me to be able to read or set the `Occupation` property or for me to make use of the `GotoTheGym` method, I would have to create an instance of the `Peter` class like so:

```
Peter myPeterInstance = new Peter();
```

Now I can set the `Occupation` property like so:

```
myPeterInstance.Occupation = "IT Engineer";
```

I can also use the methods of the `Peter` class like so:

```
myPeterInstance.GotoTheGym();
```

I find that static classes are very good for helper classes that encapsulate functionality that is used throughout an application. I have a free online video tutorial that explains how to make a Storyboard helper class: at `http://www.windowspresentationfoundation.com/?p=94`. It basically shows you how to make a static class called `SBFader` to fade in and out Silverlight `FrameworkElements`. As I stated earlier, you do not need to instantiate these classes to use them. You simply give the class name and then the method name like this:

```
SBFader.FadeIn(frameworkElement);
```

> In this specific class you need to pass in the `FrameworkElement` you want to fade in, but this is specific to this class.

Abstract Classes

An *abstract* class, sometimes referred to as a *base* class or *superclass*, is a class that cannot be instantiated. These classes are designed to be parent classes that child classes can inherit from (I discuss class inheritance in Chapter 3). Abstract classes contain undefined and unimplemented abstract method bodies that the children are required to implement and define. It is this construct that allows for polymorphic classes, as the parent abstract class only requires that the concrete child (instantiated) classes only define and implement its methods and do not care how those child classes actually implement them. It is this that allows two different child concrete classes to implement the parent's abstract methods differently, thus creating polymorphic classes. I show you an example of this later in the chapter.

Sealed Classes

The *sealed modifier* is used to make certain that the class cannot be used as a base class for another class. This also means that a sealed class cannot be an abstract class. Declaring a class as sealed also enables some runtime optimizations. The most notable optimization occurs because it is possible to transform virtual function member invocations on sealed class instances into nonvirtual invocations.

Partial Classes

Partial classes are classes that can be split over multiple definitions. This is usually done to deal with large amounts of code. In Silverlight, however, this is common in `UserControls` because the XAML portion and the C# (or VB) code-behind files are both partial classes that are merged by the complier at runtime. As a matter of fact, when you create a new Silverlight project, you will see that a default `MainPage.xaml` with a code-behind page of `MainPage.xaml.cs` is created for you. These two files are in fact partial classes, as you can see here:

```
namespace SLApplication
{
        public partial class MainPage : UserControl
        {
                public MainPage()
                {
                        // Required to initialize variables
                        InitializeComponent();
                }
        }
}
```

`InitializeComponent();` is the method that actually instructs the compiler to merge the two partial class classes definitions into one class.

Singleton Classes

As the name implies the *singleton* design pattern is designed to restrict instantiation of a class to one, and only one, object. This is quite useful when only one instance of a particular class is needed. A good example would be a *data* class; such a class usually contains all the data to be used across the entire application. There is no need for more than one instance of such a class, so it makes sense to make it a singleton. Singletons are also useful when you want to have access to a lot of data globally throughout your application. Instead of having a lot of different global variables, you can have just one singleton and have all of your variables in it. Those variables are then accessible globally by accessing the singleton. We actually made use of a singleton when we created the `DataFactory` back in Chapter 8 for this exact reason; that is, we wanted to keep track of the video data throughout the application, so instead of making each of those variables globally accessible, we just accessed them via a singleton.

Private vs. Public Access Modifiers (Public and Private Classes)

Both classes and class members (properties and methods) can be declared as *public* or *private* (among others). Following are examples of both private and public classes:

```
public class PublicClass
{

}

private class PrivateClass
{

}
```

If you were to declare a public class and then in that same file declare a private class, only the public class (in the same file) would have access to it. More commonly, though, classes are declared as public, and certain members are declared as private or public. If a property of a class is set to private, then it can only be set within the class itself. Further, even if the class is instantiated, the private members cannot be accessed from outside the class. For example, if we made the Occupation property private in the Peter class we created earlier, and then instantiated an instance of Peter, we would not be able to read or write the value of that property.

Internal Classes

Internal classes are classes that are only accessible from other classes located in the same project or assembly. So, if you were to create a new Silverlight project called MySLProject and create an internal class called MyInternalClass, you would be able to asses it from anywhere in MySLProject. If you were to add a new project to MySLProject called MyNewSLProject and then tried to access MyInternalClass from it, you be unable to. It is also worth noting that if you do not declare a class modifier, then by default the class will be internal.

Protected Classes

Protected classes are like private classes in that they can be nested classes that can be accessed from the public class they are nested in. But unlike private classes, protected classes can be accessed from subclasses of the class that defines the protected class or classes.

Interfaces

Interfaces describe a group of Behaviors that can belong to any class. They are made up mostly of methods and properties. Any class that implements an interface is required to implement all the methods and/or properties of that Interface. This allows for polymorphic classes, because each class can implement the methods and properties of the interface differently. Also, any class that implements a particular interface is guaranteed to contain all the methods and properties that interface defines. In order to better demonstrate this, let's go ahead and create a new Silverlight project called InterfaceProject (see my settings in Figure 10-1) in Visual Studio:

Figure 10-1. Create a new Silverlight project called `InterfaceProject`.

When the New Silverlight Application dialog box appears, uncheck "Host the Silverlight application in a new Web site" and click OK, as I am about to do in Figure 10-2.

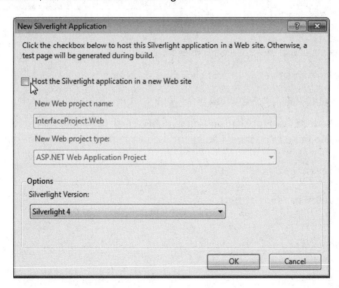

Figure 10-2. Uncheck "Host the Silverlight application in a new Web site" and click OK.

Now that we have done that, let's create a superclass called `Vehicle`. This class will be the base class for all of our other types of `Vehicles`, namely `Car`, `Motorcycle`, `Airplane`, `Scooter`, and `Skateboard`.

Vehicle is going to implement two interfaces, one called `IModeOfTransportation` (how the vehicle moves, wheels, wings, and so on) that has a method called `ShowModeOfTransportation` and a second interface, `INumberOfSeats` (how many seats the vehicle has), that has a method called `ShowNumberOfSeats`. In `Vehicle` we are going to implement `ShowModeOfTransportation` as an abstract method. This will require classes that derive from it to implement the method. And then we are going to implement `ShowNumberOfSeats` as a virtual method, which means that classes that derive from `Vehicle` can choose to implement it or not. If they do they can override the default method, if not they will inherit the parent's implementation. So, let's create `Vehicle` now:

1. Right-click the project in Visual Studio's Solution Explorer.

2. Left-click on Add ➤ Class, as I am doing in Figure 10-3.

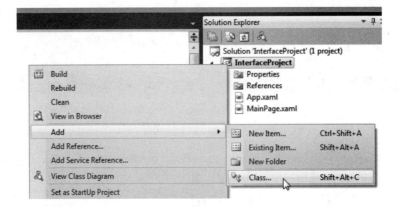

Figure 10-3. Add a new class in the Solution Explorer.

3. Name the new class `Vehicle` and click the Add button.

4. Repeat this process but name the new class `IModeOfTransporation`.

5. Change `IModeOfTransporation` from a public class to an interface (interfaces are public by default, so no need to declare it as such). You can see my code here:

```
namespace InterfaceProject
{
    interface IModeOfTransporation
    {

    }
}
```

6. Add a method in `IModeOfTransporation` called `ShowModeOfTransporation`, as I do in the following code. Notice there is no method body.

```
namespace InterfaceProject
{
    interface IModeOfTransporation
```

```
    {
        void ShowModeOfTransporation();
    }
}
```

7. Create a new class called `INumberOfSeats` and change it to an interface, as I do here:

```
namespace InterfaceProject
{
    interface INumberOfSeats
    {

    }
}
```

8. Add a method called `ShowNumberOfSeats`, as I do here:

```
namespace InterfaceProject
{
    interface INumberOfSeats
    {
        void ShowNumberOfSeats();
    }
}
```

9. Now we need to go into `Vehicle` and have it implement `IModeOfTransporation` and `INumberOfSeats` by adding ": IModeOfTransporation" after the class declaration, as follows:

```
namespace InterfaceProject
{
    public class Vehicle : IModeOfTransporation
    {

    }
}
```

10. When you see the helper icon appear, click it (or press Control+. (period)) and click "Implement interface 'IModeOfTransporation'," as I am about to do in Figure 10-4.

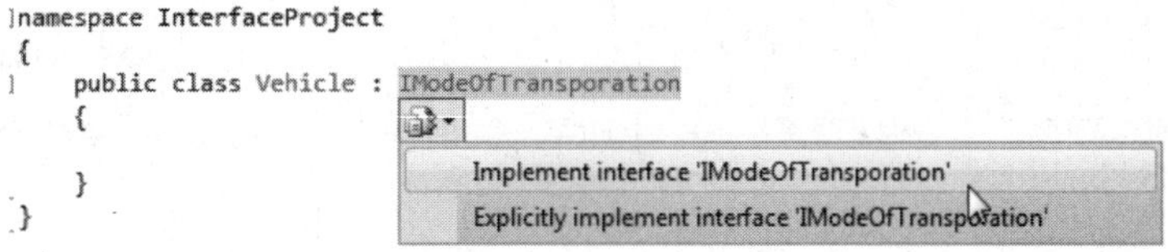

```
]namespace InterfaceProject
 {
]    public class Vehicle : IModeOfTransporation
     {
                              [icon]
     }
 }
```

| Implement interface 'IModeOfTransporation' |
| Explicitly implement interface 'IModeOfTransporation' |

Figure 10-4. Implement `IModeOfTransporation`.

You can see the resulting code here:

```
namespace InterfaceProject
{

    public class Vehicle : IModeOfTransporation
    {

        #region IModeOfTransporation Members

        public void ShowModeOfTransporation()
        {
            throw new NotImplementedException();
        }

        #endregion
    }
}
```

11. Now change the `Vehicle` class to be abstract so that it cannot be instantiated, as follows:

```
public abstract class Vehicle : IModeOfTransporation
 {
```

12. While still inside the `Vehicle` class, change `ShowModeOfTransporation` to make it abstract and remove the auto-generated method body (this also means that there is no method body). You can see my code here:

```
namespace InterfaceProject
{

    public abstract class Vehicle : IModeOfTransporation
    {

        #region IModeOfTransporation Members

        public abstract void ShowModeOfTransporation();

        #endregion
    }
}
```

13. Now make `Vehicle` also implement `INumberOfSeats` and press Control+. (period) to implement the interface (see the following code):

```
namespace InterfaceProject
{

    public abstract class Vehicle : IModeOfTransporation, INumberOfSeats
```

```
    {

        #region IModeOfTransporation Members

        public abstract void ShowModeOfTransporation();

        #endregion

        #region INumberOfSeats Members

        public  void ShowNumberOfSeats()
        {
            throw new NotImplementedException();
        }

        #endregion
    }
}
```

Because we don't want to force the child classes to implement this method, we are going to make it virtual and also provide a default implementation that the children can inherit. We are going to just write a message in Visual Studio's Debug window whenever this default implementation is fired. Let's do that now:

14. Change the method to be virtual, and erase the default "Throw new…" as I do here:

```
public virtual void ShowNumberOfSeats()
{

}
```

15. Inside the method type **Debug** and press Control+. (period). Highlight "using System.Diagnostics;" and press Enter, as I am about to do in Figure 10-5.

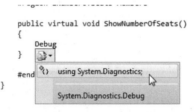

Figure 10-5. Resolve the debug command namespace.

16. Now write a default debug message as follows:

```
public virtual void ShowNumberOfSeats()
{
    Debug.WriteLine("Vehicle has no seats by default");
```

```
        }
```

Now that we are done with our superclass and our two Interfaces, it is time to go ahead and create some child classes that derive from `Vehicle`.

17. In the Solution Explorer right-click the project and click Add ➤ Class;

18. Name the new class `Car` and click Add.

19. Have the new `Car` class extent the `Vehicle` class, as I do here:

```
namespace InterfaceProject
{
    public class Car : Vehicle
    {

    }
}
```

20. Press Control+. (period) and when Intellisense gives you the option click "Implement abstract class 'Vehicle'," as I am doing in Figure 10-6:

Figure 10-6. Implement the `Vehicle` class.

Your code should now look like this for the `Car` class:

```
namespace InterfaceProject
{
    public class Car : Vehicle
    {

        public override void ShowModeOfTransporation()
        {
            throw new NotImplementedException();
        }
    }
}
```

Notice that only the `ModeOfTransportation` was implemented. This is because we implemented it in `Vehicle` as abstract, meaning that children of `Vehicle` are required to implement it. Conversely we implemented `NumberOfSeats` as virtual, so that the children could choose to implement it or not. So, let's go ahead and override the default implementation of NumberOfSeats in the Car class now. You can see my code here:

```
namespace InterfaceProject
{
    public class Car : Vehicle
    {

        public override void ShowModeOfTransporation()
        {
            throw new NotImplementedException();
        }

        public override void ShowNumberOfSeats()
        {
            base.ShowNumberOfSeats();
            Debug.WriteLine("A Car has four seats");
        }
    }
}
```

You will have to resolve the debug *command to use System.Diagnostic.dll.*

21. Now erase the default "Throw new…." code from ModeOfTransporation and put in another debug statemen, as I do here:

```
namespace InterfaceProject
{
    public class Car : Vehicle
    {

        public override void ShowModeOfTransporation()
        {
            Debug.WriteLine("A Car's mode of transportation is Wheels");
        }

        public override void ShowNumberOfSeats()
        {
            base.ShowNumberOfSeats();
            Debug.WriteLine("A Car has four seats");
        }
    }
}
```

22. Before we get ahead of ourselves, let's open MainPage.xaml.cs and instantiate a Car. Notice that in the code that follows I declare c as a Vehicle. I could have declared it as a Car by typing **Car c = new Car();**. But because `Vehicle` is the superclass for `Car`, I can do it either way (see the following code):

```
namespace InterfaceProject
{
    public partial class MainPage : UserControl
    {
        public MainPage()
        {
            InitializeComponent();
            Vehicle c = new Car();
            c.ShowModeOfTransporation();
            c.ShowNumberOfSeats();
        }
    }
}
```

23. If you press F5 to compile and run the application, you can see in Visual Studio's Output window the `debug` statements, as I have in Figure 10-7.

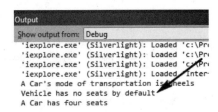

Figure 10-7. You can see the `debug` statements in Visual Studio's Output window.

Thus far all we have done is to create an abstract superclass that implements two interfaces: `IModeOfTransportation` and `INumberOfSeats`. The superclass implements the first interface as an abstract method with no method body. This requires that children implement the method themselves. The superclass implements the second interface as a virtual method and defines a default method body that the children can inherit. The children may also choose to override this method. We then create a `Car` class that extends the `Vehicle` class. We then chose to override both methods and put in some `debug` statements. So, you may be asking how this makes polymorphic classes. Well, let's stop the running project and add another class called `Airplane`, and I will show you how.

24. Right-click the project in Visual Studio's Solution Explorer and click Add ➤ Class.

25. Name the new class `Airplane` and click Add.

26. Have the new class extend the `Vehicle` class and implement both interfaces so that your code looks like what I have here:

```
namespace InterfaceProject
{
    public class Airplane : Vehicle
```

```
    {

        public override void ShowModeOfTransporation()
        {
            throw new NotImplementedException();
        }

        public override void ShowNumberOfSeats()
        {
            base.ShowNumberOfSeats();
        }
    }
}
```

27. Now put in some debug statements. You will have to resolve the debug namespace:

```
namespace InterfaceProject
{
    public class Airplane : Vehicle
    {

        public override void ShowModeOfTransporation()
        {
            Debug.WriteLine("An airplane's mode of transportation is Wings");
        }

        public override void ShowNumberOfSeats()
        {
            base.ShowNumberOfSeats();

            Debug.WriteLine("A Plane has hundreds  of seats");
        }
    }
}
```

28. Go into MainPage.xaml.cs and create a new Plane object, as I do here:

```
namespace InterfaceProject
{
    public partial class MainPage : UserControl
    {
        public MainPage()
        {
            InitializeComponent();
            Vehicle c = new Car();
            c.ShowModeOfTransporation();
            c.ShowNumberOfSeats();

            Vehicle a = new Airplane();
```

```
                a.ShowModeOfTransporation();
                a.ShowNumberOfSeats();
            }
        }
}
```

Now if you press F5 to compile and run the application, in your Output window you should see what I have in Figure 10-8.

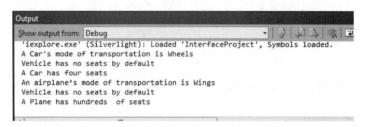

Figure 10-8. Your Output window should now look like this.

Notice that you not only have the overridden debug statements of "A Plane has hundreds of seats" and "a Car has four seats", but also have the default debug statement of "vehicle has no seats by default". That is because in our overridden methods for ShowNumberOfSeats we run the base method like this:

base.ShowNumberOfSeats();

This means that the base method is first run, and then our overridden code comes next. If we removed this line, then only the overridden code would run and we would not see the default message of "vehicle has no seats by default".

Now you have two polymorphic classes in Car and Airplane, because they both implement their parent's method differently.

My project is here: http://www.windowspresentationfoundation.com/ Blend4Book/ InterfaceProject.zip

Summary

In this chapter you learned about the different types of classes and when to use them. You also learned about interfaces and you then created a project that shows you how you can use interfaces and superclasses to create polymorphic child classes. These polymorphic classes have the ability to override the methods of their parent classes and have implementations different from other child classes. In Chapter 11 we are going to learn about a very powerful feature in Silverlight: the ability to re-use objects by making use of templatizing. This is done using ControlTemplates, Styles, and custom UserControls.

Chapter 11

Styles, Control Templates, and Custom UserControls

- Understanding how Styles work with ControlTemplates
- Understanding ControlTemplates
- Creating a Button ControlTemplate
- Creating Styles and using them to override default Silverlight styles
- Using Styles to mandate how controls display their content
- Using ResourceDictionaries
- Applying Resources to Silverlight controls
- Using Styles and ControlTemplates to create your own custom Silverlight UserControls
- Creating and using custom UserControls
- Using DependencyProperties and custom DependencyProperties

A very important concept in Object-Oriented Programming (OOP) is that you should be able to create something once and use it over and over again. This generally means that you can reuse a Resource in one application, but Silverlight takes this concept even further and allows you to reuse a Resource across multiple applications. Styles, ControlTemplates, and UserControls allow you to do just that. I have been working with Silverlight since before it was officially released some years ago, and in that time I have been able to create my own libraries of Resources that I can now reuse in new applications that I create. This allows me to develop new applications faster because I do not have to create new Resources every time I need them. For example, say I have an application that requires a good video player. All I need to do it is to add the reference to my already existing video player in my new application, and voilà! I have a video player in my new application. In this chapter you are going to create a Style for a Silverlight Button that will contain a ControlTemplate that has the Button display an Image control. You are then going to create a Resource Dictionary and move the Button Style to it. Finally, you are going to take everything you have learned and create a custom UserControl.

Understanding the ControlTemplate

A `ControlTemplate` is nothing more than a Resource, usually defined in a `Style`, which allows you to specify the way a control is displayed in the Visual Tree. It literally allows you to build a template for a Silverlight control, hence the name `ControlTemplate`. You can create `ControlTemplates` for a host of Silverlight controls, such as `Buttons`, `ListBoxes`, and so on. Further, once you create a `ControlTemplate`, say for a `Button`, you are then able to make use of that Resource throughout your application. Let's move forward and create a new Silverlight project, create a `ControlTemplate`, and then apply that `ControlTemplate` to other controls.

> A `ControlTemplate` *can be defined right in the control's XAML (called inline), but it is best practice to define them in a Resource.*

Creating a Button ControlTemplate with a Style

Let's start off by creating a new Silverlight application project in Blend:

1. Open Blend 4.

2. Select **Silverlight Application** from the installed templates.

3. Enter a project name of `ControlTemplateProject` and click **OK** (see Figure 11-1).

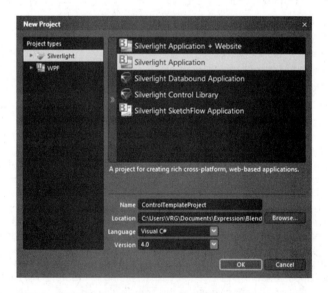

Figure 11-1. Create a new Silverlight 4 application in Blend.

In this project, you are going to create a `ControlTemplate` for a Silverlight `Button` control. You are then going to create a few Silverlight `Buttons` and apply your new `ControlTemplate` to them to see how simple it is to reuse a `ControlTemplate` Resource. So, let's get started:

1. Select the Rectangle tool from the toolbar.

2. Draw a `Rectangle` on the artboard roughly 100 display units wide and 25 display units tall.

3. Click the Selection tool from the toolbar (or press the V key to get the Selection tool).

4. Use the radius handles on the top left of the `Rectangle` to give it rounded edges, so you have what I have in Figure 11-2.

Figure 11-2. You now should have a `Rectangle` on your artboard that looks like what I have here.

5. With the `Rectangle` still selected, go to the **Brushes** bucket of the **Properties** panel and click the **Fill** property.

6. Click the **Gradient brush** icon to give the `Rectangle` a gradient fill, as I am doing in Figure 11-3.

Figure 11-3. Give your new `Rectangle` a gradient fill.

7. Play around with the two colors of the gradient until you are satisfied with the way it looks. I have left the default gradient fill for my `Rectangle`.

8. Now you are going to tell Blend that you would like to use this as a `Style` for a `Button` control. The easiest way to do this is to right-click the `Rectangle` and left-click **Make into Control**.

9. When the **Make Into Control** dialog box appears, select **Button** for the **Control Type** and name the new `Style` `GradientButtonStyle`, as I have done in Figure 11-4. Click **OK**.

Figure 11-4. Create a `Style` from your `Rectangle` called `GradientButtonStyle`.

Blend then wraps your `Rectangle` into a Grid, along with a `ContentPresenter` (which displays the `Button's Text`). You are still in `MainPage.xaml`, but you are actually editing the `GradientButtonStyle`. You can see this by looking at the top of the Visual Tree in the **Objects and Timeline** panel, where it says GradientButtonStyle (shown in Figure 11-5), or by the breadcrumb control that says **[Button] ➤ Template** (shown in Figure 11-6).

Figure 11-5. The top of the Objects and Timeline panel shows you are editing the `GradientButtonStyle`.

Figure 11-6. The breadcrumb control shows you that you are editing the template for a `Button` control.

If you wanted to stop editing this `Style`, you could either click the arrow icon next to the text GradientButtonStyle in the Objects and Timeline panel or you could click the word [Button] in the breadcrumb control. To start editing the Style once again, all you would have to do is click Template on the breadcrumb control.

Now, the newly created Button control, formerly a Rectangle, has all the capabilities of a normal Silverlight Button control, but the difference is that instead of using Silverlight's basic Button Style, it uses yours. Pretty cool, huh? You'll give your new Button a little functionality to prove it is just like any other Silverlight standard Button control—but before you do, I think it would be good to delve into the XAML and see exactly what Blend did for you under the hood, so to speak.

1. Click the XAML icon shown in Figure 11-7.

Figure 11-7. This button will show you the XAML for whatever page you are on.

When you click that button, you should see the following XAML code:

```xml
<UserControl
xmlns="http://schemas.microsoft.com/winfx/2006/xaml/presentation"
xmlns:x="http://schemas.microsoft.com/winfx/2006/xaml"
x:Class="ControlTemplateProject.MainPage"
Width="640" Height="480">
<UserControl.Resources>
    <Style x:Key="GradientButtonStyle" TargetType="Button">
        <Setter Property="Template">
            <Setter.Value>
                <ControlTemplate TargetType="Button">
                    <Grid>
                        <Rectangle RadiusY="9" RadiusX="9"
Stroke="Black">
                            <Rectangle.Fill>
                                <LinearGradientBrush
EndPoint="0.5,1" StartPoint="0.5,0">
                                    <GradientStop Color="Black"
Offset="0"/>
                                    <GradientStop Color="White"
Offset="1"/>
                                </LinearGradientBrush>
                            </Rectangle.Fill>
                        </Rectangle>
                        <ContentPresenter HorizontalAlignment=
```

```
                "{TemplateBinding HorizontalContentAlignment}" VerticalAlignment=
                "{TemplateBinding VerticalContentAlignment}"/>
                                </Grid>
                            </ControlTemplate>
                    </Setter.Value>
                </Setter>
            </Style>
        </UserControl.Resources>

        <Grid x:Name="LayoutRoot" Background="White">
            <Button Content="Button" Height="35" Margin="176,75,319,0"
        Style="{StaticResource
          GradientButtonStyle}" VerticalAlignment="Top" Width="145"/>
            </Grid>
        </UserControl>
```

Notice that inside of the main Grid, named LayoutRoot, there is only one UIElement which is a Button control. In the XAML for that control you can see that it is using GradientButtonStyle for its Style. Then if you look in the UserControl.Resources you will see our GradientButtonStyle Style. It has a property called ControlTemplate that contains a Grid with the Rectangle we created along with a ContentPresenter.

Creating ResourceDictionaries

Styles allow you to set properties for controls. In a project, say you have a lot of ListBoxes that want to look very different from an ordinary ListBox (with the default style). You could create a Style that defines how a ListBox should look and then apply that Style to any other ListBox you want. However, what if you want to reuse your Style in another XAML file other than MainPage.xaml? To reuse a Style in another XAML file, you can define it in a file called a Resource Dictionary that is accessible to your entire application, not just MainPage.xaml. In fact, it is best practice to put all of your Styles in a Resource Dictionary. I walk you through the steps for creating a Resource Dictionary for your ControlTemplateProject project now:

1. Click the **Design** button located just above the **XAML** button to switch back to the Design view. Then exit style editing mode by clicking the Return scope button in the **Objects and Timeline** panel.

2. On the toolbar, click the **Asset Library** button and do a search for listbox.

3. When you see the ListBox control appear, click it.

4. Draw a ListBox in the workspace with a **Width** of about **200** and a **Height** of about **400** display units.

5. Right-click the ListBox and select **Edit Template ➤ Edit a Copy**. This will create a Style for the ListBox that we can edit.

6. In the **Create Style Resource** dialog box, give the new Style Resource a name of MyListBoxStyle.

7. In the **Define in** section of the dialog box, find where it says **Resource Dictionary**. Notice that **Resource Dictionary** is grayed out, because there is no **Resource Dictionary** yet. To create one, click the **New** button.

8. Blend then opens a **Resource Dictionary** dialog box and asks what name you want to give to your new **Resource Dictionary**. Name it `ApplicationResourceDict` and click **OK**.

9. Notice now that the **Resource Dictionary** option is no longer gray. Blend has also selected it for you and entered the name of the newly created **Resource Dictionary**, `ApplicationResourceDict`. Click **OK**.

Blend opens the newly created `ApplicationResourceDict.xaml` file. Here, you can edit the `Style` of `MyListBoxStyle` to change the way the `ListBox` is displayed:

1. Select `[Border]` (a `Border` control) from the **Objects and Timeline** panel.

2. In the **Properties** panel under the **Layout** section, change the **HorizontalAlignment** property from the default **Stretch** to **Center** (see Figure 11-8).

Figure 11-8. Change the HorizontalAlignment property to Center.

Notice now that the `ListBox` contents change to center alignment. If you go back to `MainPage.xaml`, by clicking the **Return Scope to [UserControl]** button located at the very top of the Visual Tree (see Figure 11-9) you see . . . wait, nothing! That is because the `ListBox` does not have any content yet. To add items, continue with these steps:

3. Right-click the `ListBox` and click **Add ListBoxItem**.

4. Repeat one time to add a total of two generic `ListBoxItems`.

Figure 11-9. Stop editing the `ListBox` `Style`.

Now you can see that the `ListBoxItems` are positioned in the center of the `ListBox`, as shown in Figure 11-10.

Figure 11-10. The `ListBox` items are now centered.

What if you wanted to create a new `ListBox` and apply your new `Style` to it? Here is how that is done:

5. From the Asset Library select the ListBox tool and draw a `ListBox` on the workspace.

6. Right-click the new `ListBox` and click **Add ListBoxItem**.

7. Repeat the previous step twice to add two more generic `ListBoxItems` (for a total of three `ListBoxItems`).

8. Right-click the new `ListBox` (not the `ListBoxItems`) and click **Edit Template ➤ Apply Resource ➤ MyListBoxStyle**.

Notice how right away the `ListBoxItems` jump to center alignment. Pretty cool, huh? This is useful because it easily allows us to modify the way a `ListBox` displays its content. In a large application, this can save vast amounts of time.

Overriding Default Styles for Controls

You may be thinking to yourself, "Big deal!" I wouldn't blame you, because this is a pretty boring example of applying `Styles`. To show you the *real* power of `Styles`, let me present you with a scenario that I recently faced. In an application I was working on, I had to populate a `ListBox` with PNG images. That was easy enough to do with `Styles`, but when one of the `ListBox` items (a PNG image) was selected, the background of that `ListBoxItem` turned blue. Turning blue when selected is the default `Behavior` of a `ListBox`. If you want to see this `Behavior` for yourself, press F5 to run the application and click one of the `ListBox` items; you will see its background turn blue.

This default `Behavior` presented a problem for me in my application, because the designer thought it looked horrible and said that the blue background was not what he had in mind when conceptualizing the application. So, I was tasked with getting rid of the background. After some thought, I eventually came up with the idea to use `Styles` to override the default `Behavior`. This, to me, did seem like a big deal, and I feel it would be a good exercise for you to duplicate the steps I followed to override the default `Behavior` of the `ListBox`:

1. In `MainPage.xaml`, select just one `ListBoxItem` from one of the two existing `ListBoxes` currently on the artboard in the **Objects and Timeline** panel.

2. Right-click the `ListBoxItem` and select **Edit Template ➤ Edit a Copy**.

3. Leave the default name of `ListBoxItemStyle1` and select the **Resource Dictionary** that you created earlier, named `ApplicationResourceDict`.

4. In order to see the current States, click each State in the **States** panel. These are the defined States, which are shown in Figure 11-11:

    -   `Normal`
    -   `MouseOver`
    -   `Disabled`
    -   `Unfocused`
    -   `Focused`
    -   `AfterLoaded`
    -   `BeforeLoaded`
    -   `BeforUnloaded`
    -   `SelectedUnfocused`
    -   `Unselected`
    -   `Selected`

Figure 11-11. The States panel shows all the States for a `ListBoxItem`.

5. To change the `Selected` state, click the `Selected` state in the **State** panel.

6. Notice that the `ListBoxItem`'s background becomes blue (see Figure 11-12).

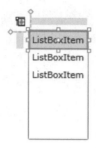

Figure 11-12. The Selected State for a ListBoxItem is blue.

7. To change this Behavior, select fillColor2 in the **Objects and Timeline** panel as shown in Figure 11-13.

Figure 11-13. Select fillColor2 in the Objects and Timeline panel.

8. Click the "**Advanced property options**" button next to the **Fill** field in the **Brushes** bucket of the **Properties** panel (see Figure 11-14).

Figure 11-14. Click the Advanced Options button.

9. Click **Reset** as shown in Figure 11-15.

Figure 11-15. Click the Reset button to reset the Fill for `fillColor2`.

Now if you look at the `ListBoxItem` on the workspace, you can see that it no longer has a blue background. If you were to run the application and select this particular `ListBoxItem`, you would see that nothing happens to the background at all, no matter what you do to it. Thus, we have overridden the default Behavior for this particular `ListBoxItem`.

But now, you have to tell all the other `ListBoxItems` to make use of the same `Style`, or they will use their default Behavior. In the States panel click the Base State to stop editing the Selected State. And then click the "**Return to scope**" button (with the arrow icon) at the top of the **Objects and Timeline** panel to stop editing the `ListBoxItem Style`. You are now ready to make the other `ListBoxItems` use the new `Style`, which doesn't turn the item blue when it is selected.

10. Select each additional `ListBoxItem`, right-click it, select **Edit Template ➤ Apply Resource**, and select **ListBoxItemStyle1**.

11. Recompile the application by pressing F5, and test it by selecting different `ListBoxItems`.

Instead of applying the `Style` *to each individual* `ListBoxItem` *you could set the* `ItemContainerStyle` *property directly on the parent* `ListBox`. *I chose to have you do it on each individual* `ListBoxItem` *to get familiar with the process.*

Notice that when you click any `ListBoxItem`, the background stays the same color? The only thing you do see is a blue line appear around the `ListBoxItem`. This is a good thing, because without it we would never know when a `ListBoxItem` was actually selected. We could though, if we wanted, remove this functionality by editing the `Focused` State.

Now you know what a `Style` is and how to create one. You also now know how to apply a `Style` to a control of the same type, and how to create a Resource Dictionary that contains your `Styles` that will be available to all XAML pages of your project. Finally, you have seen how `Styles` can be very useful in a real-world situation by giving you the ability to override a control's default Behavior by using a Visual State manager to set the control's properties, such as the `Selected` state of a `ListBoxItem` control. Now that you understand `Styles`, you can get back to your `Button` control and do some really fun stuff.

Adding Your Button Style to Your Resource Dictionary

So you now understand the way that the Button control you have made is displayed inside of a Style. If you look at MainPage.xaml, you can see the Button control Style called GradientButtonStyle defined in a section called UserControl.Resources. Earlier in this section, you learned that it is best practice to put all of your Styles in a Resource Dictionary, and you even learned how to do that. So, why did I have you create your Button control Style inside of your MainPage.xaml if it is not best practice to do so? Did I make a mistake? Actually, yes I did, but this mistake will allow me to show you how to fix a common error that I find many developers tend to make, and that is defining Resources such as Styles in the XAML page they are working on rather than in a Resource Dictionary. So, next you'll move your GradientButtonStyle Resource from MainPage.xaml to ApplicationResourceDictionary.xaml:

1. Open MainPage.xaml in XAML view.

2. Select the following code for the GradientButtonStyle Style and cut it out of the XAML (by right-clicking and selecting **Cut**, pressing Ctrl+X, or by selecting **Edit ➤ Cut**).

3. Open ApplicationResourceDict.xaml and paste this Style right above the MyListBoxStyle Style.

4. Run the application again by pressing F5.

> *Another way to move a* Style *to the Resource Dictionary would be to open Blend's Resource tab and drag and drop the* Style *from* MainPage *to the* ApplicationResourceDict.xaml *in the Resources tab.*

Notice that the Button looks exactly the way it did before, but rather than getting its Style from the MainPage.xaml's UserControl.Resources, it is getting it from ApplicationResourceDict.xaml. That was very simple indeed—but now that you have done this, you can use this Style throughout your application, which would be handy if you created an application with many different XAML pages.

Creating Custom UserControls

A UserControl in Silverlight allows you to create specifically designed controls for your applications. This is not to be confused with custom controls. Creating a custom control is a little more difficult to do but is handy when you want to create a control that other developers can then use Styles to change the look of, and use it in their own applications. UserControls are what you will be creating for your applications as a developer. You can specify how your custom controls look as well as applying EventHandlers for their Behavior. In the preceding exercises, you used a Style with a ControlTemplate to make your Buttons look a certain way. What if you wanted to simplify that process—that is, avoid having to create a Button in the workspace and then tell that Button to use the Style Resource with your ControlTemplate in it? In this exercise, I am going to show you how to create a Silverlight custom UserControl that will act much like a built-in Silverlight Button. Let's get started.

1. Go back to your ControlTemplateProject in Blend 4.

2. In the **Projects** panel, right-click `ControlTemplateProject` and select **Add New Item,** as shown in Figure 11-16.

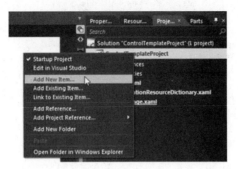

Figure 11-16. Add a new item to your project.

3. In the **New Item** dialog box, select `UserControl` and name it `UC_GreenButton` (see Figure 11-17).

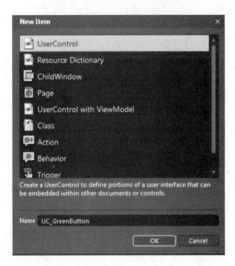

Figure 11-17. Select `UserControl` and name the new `UserControl` `UC_GreenButton`.

4. When Blend creates and opens the new `UserControl`, draw a green `Rectangle` in the top-left corner with rounded edges, as shown in Figure 11-18. Mine is roughly 100 display units wide and 50 display units tall.

Figure 11-18. Draw a green `Rectangle` in the top-left corner with rounded edges.

5. Next, copy (Ctrl+C) the green `Rectangle` and paste (Ctrl+V) a new one.

6. Remove the stroke from the new `Rectangle`.

7. Change the **fill** to be a gradient that goes from white to white.

8. Change the bottom gradient to have an **Alpha** of **0%,** so that the **Brushes** bucket of the **Properties** panel for your new `Rectangle` looks like the one shown in Figure 11-19.

Figure 11-19. Your new `Rectangle` should have these color settings in the Brushes bucket of the Properties panel.

9. Now make your top `Rectangle` smaller than the one behind it, so it looks like what I have in Figure 11-20.

Figure 11-20. Your two `Rectangles` should now look like this.

STYLES, CONTROL TEMPLATES, AND CUSTOM USERCONTROLS

10. Go ahead and add a `TextBlock` with a font size of 14 on top of both `Rectangles` and set its `Text` property to read "**Click Me**," as shown in Figure 11-21.

Figure 11-21. Add a `TextBlock` on top of both `Rectangles`.

11. What we are going to need to do now is Select [UserControl] from the Objects and Timeline panel and resize the `UserControl` so it is slightly bigger than the largest `Rectangle`.

Now that we have our `UserControl` looking like a cool button, let's go in and add some mouse States to it, namely, `MouseEnter` and `MouseLeave`.

12. In the **States** panel, click the "**Add state group**" button, as shown in Figure 11-22.

Figure 11-22. Add a State group.

13. Name the new State group `MouseStates` and set the **Default transition** time to **.3** seconds, as shown in Figure 11-23.

Figure 11-23. Add a State group named `MouseStates` with a default transition time of .3 seconds.

14. Click the **Add State** button, as I am doing in Figure 11-24, and name the State `Enter`.

Figure 11-24. Add a new State to your State group.

15. Make a new State and name this one Leave. Your State panel should look like what I have in Figure 11-25.

Figure 11-25. Your State panel should now look like this.

16. Next, click the Enter State and notice the red line that appears around the workspace indicating that changes are being recorded into that State.

17. Click the bottom, green Rectangle and change it to **red** in the **Brushes** bucket of the **Properties** panel.

18. Stop editing the State by clicking the Base State in the States panel.

19. Press Control+Shift+B to rebuild your application.

Now when the Enter state is fired, it will turn the black Rectangle to red. If you want to see these States in action prior to building and running your application, you can click the "**Turn on transition preview**" toggle button (shown in Figure 11-26) and then click **Enter and Leave States** to see the way they will actually look when fired. Now all we need to do it make use of our new control. To do this click the MainPage.xaml tabk to go back to MainPage. You will see that there is no instance of your UC_GreenButton control. Let's change that now:

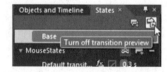

Figure 11-26. This button allows you to preview your States in Design mode.

1. Click the Asset Library and in the search field start typing **uc**, and you should see the UC_GreenButton, as I do in Figure 11-27.

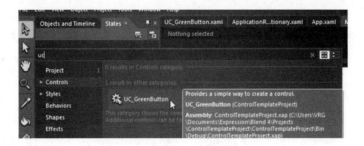

Figure 11-27. The UC_GreenButton shows up in the Asset Library.

2. Select the UserControl and draw one out on the artboard. You will see what I have in Figure 11-28.

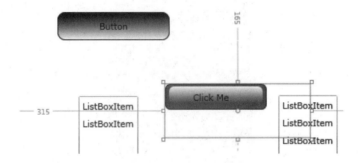

Figure 11-28. An instance of UC_GreenButton on the artboard in MainPage.xaml.

Now all we need to do its wire up the States using Behaviors.

1. Switch back over to UC_GreenButton, click the Asset Library, and start to type **goto** in the search field (see Figure 11-29).

2. When you see GotoStateAction click and drag an instance of it onto [UserControl] in the Objects and Timeline panel and drop it.

Figure 11-29. The GotoStateAction in the Asset Library.

3. With the newly added Behavior selected in the **Objects and Timeline** panel, change the `EventName` to `MouseEnter` in the **Trigger** bucket of the **Properties** panel (see Figure 11-30).

4. Change the `StateName` property to the `Enter` State in the **Common Properties** bucket of the **Properties** panel (see Figure 11-30) .

5. Add another `GotoStateAction` to the [UserControl].

6. With this new Behavior selected in the **Objects and Timeline** panel, change its `EventName` property to `MouseLeave` in the **Trigger** bucket of the **Properties** panel (see Figure 11-31).

7. Change the `StateName` property to the `Leave` State in the **Common Properties** bucket of the **Properties** panel (see Figure 11-31).

Figure 11-30. This is how the Common Properties and Triggers buckets should be set for the first `GotoStateAction`.

Figure 11-31. This is how the Common Properties and Triggers buckets should be set for the second `GotoStateAction`.

Now if you press F5 to compile and run the application, you can put your mouse cursor over the `UC_GreenButton UserControl`, and it will turn red and back to green when your mouse leaves it.

Demystifying the DependencyProperty

Throughout this book, you have worked with many Silverlight controls such as `Buttons`, `Rectangles`, and `MediaElements`. Because you have worked with these controls and did things such as set the `Source` property of a `MediaElement` or the `Fill` property of a `Rectangle`, you already have experience in working with `DependencyProperties` because `Fill` and `Source` are `DependencyProperties`. So, in their simplest form, and trust me they can get much more complicated, `DependencyProperties` are properties that allow you to manage in C# or XAML how controls look and behave. `DependencyProperties` are unique in quite a few ways:

DataBinding: When you bind to a `DependencyProperty` those bindings will automatically update if the property value changes. This will not be the case with a normal `.NET` property.

Styles: `Styles` and `Templates` are two motivating factors in the decision to use a `DependencyProperty` over a regular `.NET` property. `Styles` interact with the property systems because they often contain "setters" for some of their properties. Typically, the most important property they set is the `Template` to define its visual appearance.

Animations: In order for an object to be animated in Silverlight, the object's `Target` property must be a `DependencyProperty`.

Property-changed Behavior: Silverlight `DependencyProperties` have the ability to specify a property-changed callback event. This allows the developer to respond and make changes whenever the value of a `DependencyProperty` changes.

Default value and `ClearValue`: `DependencyProperties` allow you to specify a default value. This ensures that an acceptable value for your property will exist at all times. `ClearValue` can be used to set your `DependencyProperty` back to its default value.

`DependencyProperties` *must be registered:* In order to make use of a `DependencyProperty` you must first register it, usually in C#. This allows you to have a highly customized `DependencyProperty`. For example, when you register a `DependencyProperty` you have options such as specifying a `Callback` method that will fire whenever the value of your `DependencyProperty` changes. To use this feature, you must specify the type of object the `DependencyProperty` is, such as `String`, `ControlTemplate`, and so on.

Let's take a look at a simple `Button` with a `Background DependencyProperty` set to `Blue` and a `Content` `DependencyProperty` set to `"Dependency Properties Rock!"`:

```
<Button Background="Blue" Content="Dependency Properties Rock!"/>
```

When you set the `Background` property to `Blue`, the XAML loader type converter converts it into a Silverlight `Color` using the `SolidColorBrush`. Silverlight provides a variety of ways syntactically for setting these properties in both XAML and C#. If you give the `Button` a `Name`, like this:

```
<Button x:Name="MyButton" Background="Blue"
Content="Dependency Properties Rock!"/>
```

…you can go into the code-behind file and set the `Background` property with code like this:

```
// create a variable of the type SolidColorBrush
// and set it to a new Red SolidColorBrush
SolidColorBrush myBrush = new SolidColorBrush(Colors.Red);
// apply the new variable to the Background of MyButton
MyButton.Background = myBrush;
```

This is all fine, and I am sure you understand `DependencyProperties`, but what if you have a situation where there is no `DependencyProperty` that meets your needs? Say, for example, you want to be able to set the text on a custom `UserControl`. Sounds a lot like the issue we are having right now, doesn't it? Well, for times like this, Silverlight allows us to register our very own custom `DependencyProperties`. We are going to have to open our `ControlTemplateProject` solution in Visual Studio 2010 to accomplish this feat. So fire up Visual Studio 2010, and let's open `UC_GreenButton.xaml.cs` and register our own custom `DependencyProperty` called `GreenButtonsText`: (you can see my newly added code in bold as follows):

```
using System.Windows;
using System.Windows.Controls;
using System.Windows.Documents;
using System.Windows.Ink;
using System.Windows.Input;
using System.Windows.Media;
using System.Windows.Media.Animation;
using System.Windows.Shapes;

namespace ControlTemplateProject
{
        public partial class UC_GreenButton : UserControl
        {


    #region GreenButtonsTextProperty DP

    public static readonly DependencyProperty GreenButtonsTextProperty =
    DependencyProperty.Register(
        "GreenButtonsText", typeof(String),
            typeof(UC_GreenButton), null);
    public String GreenButtonsText
    {
        get { return (String)GetValue(GreenButtonsTextProperty); }
        set { SetValue(GreenButtonsTextProperty, value); }
    }

    #endregion GreenButtonsTextProperty DP
```

```
        public UC_GreenButton()
        {
                // Required to initialize variables
                InitializeComponent();
        }
    }
}
```

Now that we have registered our `DependencyProperty` we need to have the `TextBlock` of our `UserControl` show that text. Before we can write the C# code to do that, we need to save our changes and switch back to Blend and give the `TextBlock` a `Name` property. This is required when you are going to code against an object.

1. Switch back to Blend, go into `UC_GreenButton`, and select the `TextBlock` by clicking it.

2. The first thing we need to do is to make the `TextBlock` the same length as the `UserControl`. You can see that I have done this in Figure 11-32.

Figure 11-32. Make the `TextBlock` the same length as the `UserControl`.

3. With the `TextBlock` still selected, go into the **Text** bucket of the **Properties** panel, click the **Paragraph** tab, and change the alignment to **Center**, as I have done in Figure 11-33.

Figure 11-33. Change the alignment for the `TextBlock` to Center.

4. In the **Name** field at the very top of the **Properties** panel, change the `Name` of the `TextBlock` to `MainText`, as I have done in Figure 11-34.

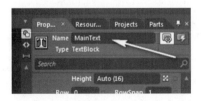

Figure 11-34. Give the `TextBlock` a `Name` property of `MainText`.

Now that you have named the `TextBlock`, we need to make sure it doesn't keep its default `Text` of "TextBlock." We actually want it to be the value of our `DependencyProperty`. But first we should give that a value, as up until now we have only registered it. Let's do that now:

1. Switch to `MainPage.xaml` and select your `UC_GreenButton` control.

2. In the **Miscellaneous** bucket of the **Properties** panel, you should now see the GreenButtonsText field (see Figure 11-35). Pretty neat how Blend picked that up, isn't it?

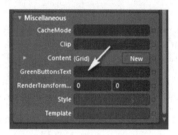

Figure 11-35. Blend now has a field for our new `DependencyProperty`.

3. Click in that field, type **Click Here**, and press Enter.

Now that our `DependencyProperty` has a value of "Click Here," we can Data Bind the `Text` property of the `MainText` `TextBlock`. Let's do that now!

4. Switch to `UC_GreenButton.xaml` in Blend and select the `MainText` `TextBlock`.

5. In the **Common Properties** bucket of the **Properties** panel, click the **Advanced Options** button, as I am doing in Figure 11-36.

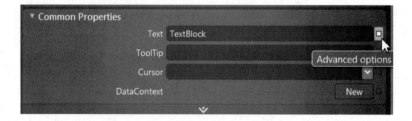

Figure 11-36. Click the Advanced Options button for the `TextBlock`.

6. Click **Data Binding**, as I am doing in Figure 11-37.

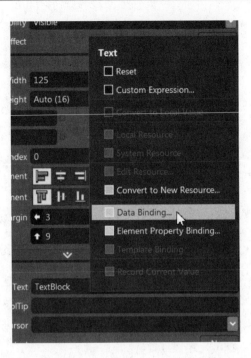

Figure 11-37. Click Data Binding in the Advanced Options menu.

7. When the **Create Data Binding** dialog box appears

    a. Select the **Element Property** tab.

    b. In the **Scene elements** box select **userControl.**

    c. In the **Properties** box select **GreenButtonsText.**

    d. Click the **OK** button (see Figure 11-38).

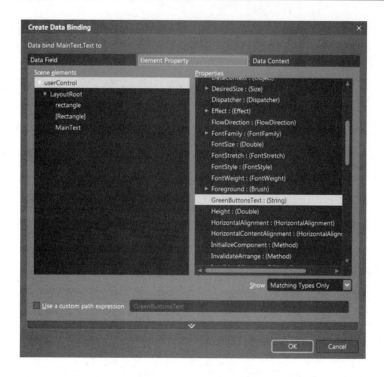

Figure 11-38. Data Binding to the `UserControls GreenButtonsText DependencyProperty`.

8. Press Control+Shift+B to rebuild again, switch back to `MainPage.xaml`, and notice how your `UC_GreenButton` changes to read "Click Here"! See Figure 11-39.

Figure 11-39. Our `UC_GreenButton` now shows the correct text in Blend.

You have successfully created your first custom `UserControl`, complete with a new `DependencyProperty` that allows you to specify right in Blend's Properties panel the text that the `UserControl` will display.

My project: `http://www.windowspresentationfoundation.com/Blend4Book/ControlTemplateProject.zip`

For some additional information on Data Binding, watch my free Silverlight video tutorial called "Working with Data in Blend": `http://www.windowspresentationfoundation.com/?p=56`

For information on how to use Template Binding, watch my video tutorial on that here:
`http://windowspresentationfoundation.com/Tutorials/TempBinding/Default.html`

Summary

In this chapter, you learned about `Styles` and how they work with `ControlTemplates`. You also learned that you can overwrite the default `Styles` provided by Silverlight controls, such as `ListBoxes` using `Styles`. You then learned how easy it is to apply Resources to controls in Silverlight, as well as the value of keeping your Resources, such as `Styles`, in a Resource Dictionary. You learned how to create your very own Silverlight custom `UserControl` complete with mouse States. You then learned about `DependencyProperties` and even how to register and make use of your own custom `DependencyProperty`, which then becomes an additional property of the object, just like built-in properties such as `Background`, `Width`, and `Height`.

Thus far, we have been using only built-in Silverlight panels such as StackPanel, Grid, and Canvas. Each of these panels lays out its children in a different way. What if none of these panels meets our requirements? In that case, we would need a custom panel. In the next chapter, I show you how to build just such a custom Silverlight panel.

Chapter 12

Writing a Custom Content Panel

What this chapter covers:

- How to write a custom Silverlight panel

Recently I was tasked with creating an image viewer that held thumbnails of lots of images. The problem was that I had to at least partially show all the thumbnail images that were all held in an `ObservableCollection`. Further, because the images were held in an `ObservableCollection` of data, I could never know how many images would be in the collection at any one time. For this reason, it was an obvious choice to put the thumbnails into a `StackPanel` and let the `StackPanel` arrange its children.

The catch with this is that a `StackPanel` can only arrange its children vertically or horizontally, and with a lot of thumbnail images that would just take up too much space. So, I decided to arrange the thumbnails in Z space (one on top of the other) rather than in X or Y space (arranged left/right or top/bottom). The problem is that no panel currently exists in Silverlight that can arrange its children in Z space. So, my final answer was to create a brand new Silverlight panel that *does*, in fact, arrange its children in Z space, as the following illustration shows. Notice how each image is slightly off-center and rotated, as if dropped onto a surface. That is what I am going to show you how to do in this chapter.

Creating the Project

The first thing to do is open Visual Studio and create a new Silverlight project called `CustomZStackPanelProject`. Use the settings shown in Figure 12-1.

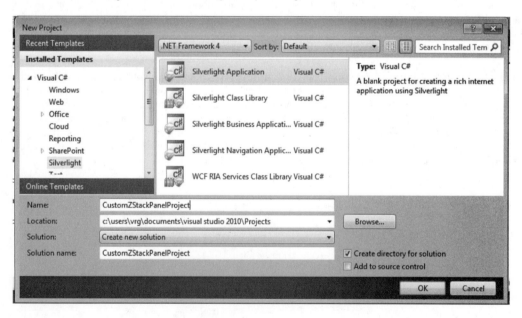

Figure 12-1. Create a new project called `CustomZStackPanelProject` in Visual Studio.

The next thing to do is define the settings for the new Silverlight application. Basically Visual Studio is asking whether we want to create an ASP.NET intranet site. This means that Silverlight will simulate a web site when the application is run. Otherwise, when the application is run, Silverlight will just open the file location on the hard drive. For the purposes of this exercise, hosting a ASP.NET Web site would be overkill.

1. When the **New Silverlight Application** dialog box appears, uncheck "**Host the Silverlight application in a new Web site**" and click **OK** (see Figure 12-2).

> If you check the "**Host the Silverlight application in a new Web site**" box, Visual Studio will create a server web site that acts as an intranet site. If this box is unchecked, Visual Studio will run the application directly from your hard drive.

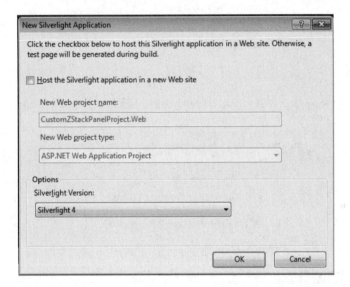

Figure 12-2. Uncheck "Host the Silverlight applciation in a new Web site" check box.

2. Right-click the project in **Solution Explorer** and click **Add ➤ Class,** as I am doing in Figure 12-3.

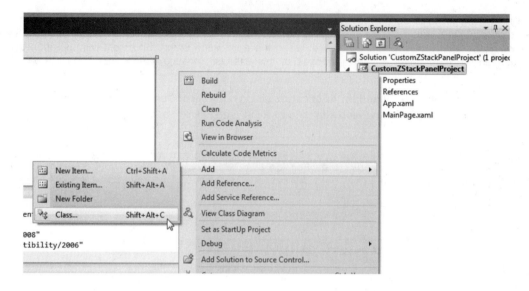

Figure 12-3. Add a new class.

3. In the **Add New Item** dialog box, name the new class ZStackPanel and click **Add**, as shown in Figure 12-4.

Figure 12-4. Name the new class ZStackPanel.

4. When the new class opens, have it extend the Panel class as follows:

```
namespace CustomZStackPanelProject
{
    public class ZStackPanel : Panel
    {

    }
}
```

5. Next we are going to create a private property called rnd. This will allow us to generate random numbers a little later on. It will allow us to randomly rotate every image so it looks as if they were dropped on top of each other, like a pile of cards:

```
namespace CustomZStackPanelProject
{
    public class ZStackPanel : Panel
    {
        private Random rnd = new Random();
    }
}
```

6. We need to have each child item slightly offset and rotated from the one behind it. This way, when they are all stacked on top of each other, they will all be visible. In order to do that, we need two custom DependencyProperty instances for MaxOffset and MaxRotation. We will then have each child slightly offset in the X and/or Y position and rotated with a random number no higher than the MaxOffset for X/Y offset and no higher than the MaxRotation for the angle of rotation. Let's create those DependencyProperty instances now:

```
namespace CustomZStackPanelProject
{
    public class ZStackPanel : Panel
    {
        private Random rnd = new Random();

        #region MaxRotation (DependencyProperty)

        public double MaxRotation
        {
            get { return (double)GetValue(MaxRotationProperty); }
            set { SetValue(MaxRotationProperty, value); }
        }
        public static readonly DependencyProperty MaxRotationProperty =
            DependencyProperty.Register("MaxRotation",
typeof(double),
 typeof(ZStackPanel),
            new PropertyMetadata(0.0, new PropertyChangedCallback
(OnMaxRotationChanged)));

        private static void OnMaxRotationChanged
(DependencyObject d,
```

```
DependencyPropertyChangedEventArgs e)
        {
            ((ZStackPanel)d).OnMaxRotationChanged(e);
        }

        protected virtual void OnMaxRotationChanged
(DependencyPropertyChangedEventArgs e)
        {
        }

        #endregion MaxRotation (DependencyProperty)


        #region MaxOffset (DependencyProperty)

        public double MaxOffset
        {
            get { return (double)GetValue(MaxOffsetProperty); }
            set { SetValue(MaxOffsetProperty, value); }
        }
        public static readonly DependencyProperty MaxOffsetProperty =
            DependencyProperty.Register
("MaxOffset", typeof(double),
typeof(ZStackPanel),
            new PropertyMetadata(0.0, new PropertyChangedCallback
(OnMaxOffsetChanged)));

        private static void OnMaxOffsetChanged(DependencyObject d,
DependencyPropertyChangedEventArgs e)
        {
            ((ZStackPanel)d).OnMaxOffsetChanged(e);
        }

        protected virtual void OnMaxOffsetChanged
(DependencyPropertyChangedEventArgs e)
        {
        }

        #endregion MaxOffset (DependencyProperty)

    }
}
```

7. We need to declare a constructor below the `DependencyProperty` instances that first will run the constructor of the base class (of `Panel`):

```
using System;
using System.Net;
using System.Windows;
using System.Windows.Controls;
using System.Windows.Documents;
```

```
using System.Windows.Ink;
using System.Windows.Input;
using System.Windows.Media;
using System.Windows.Media.Animation;
using System.Windows.Shapes;

namespace CustomZStackPanelProject
{
    public class ZStackPanel : Panel
    {
        private Random rnd = new Random();

        // DependencyProperties not shown

        public ZStackPanel()
            : base()
        {

        }

    }
}
```

8. We need to override two abstract `Panel` classes called `MeasureOverride` and `ArrangeOverride`. These are the two methods that position children in a panel. It is a little out of scope for this book, but basically `MeasureOverride` measures each child and the space available in the panel and then returns how much space and how big each child can be. `ArrangeOverride` then arranges the children in the panel. Let's override those two methods now:

```
namespace CustomZStackPanelProject
{
    public class ZStackPanel : Panel
    {
        private Random rnd = new Random();
// DependencyProperties not shown

public ZStackPanel()
            : base()
        {

        }

        protected override Size MeasureOverride(Size availableSize)
        {

        }

        protected override Size ArrangeOverride(Size finalSize)
```

```
        {

        }

    }
}
```

Starting with the MeasureOverride method, the first thing we need to do is to create a Size variable named resultSize. We need to do this because as you can see from the Method Signature it expects a Size to be returned.

9. Let's create the resultSize variable now:

```
protected override Size MeasureOverride(Size availableSize)
{
    Size resultSize = new Size(0, 0);
}
```

10. We need to do is to cycle through all of the children and measure them. The method then measures the available size of the panel, returns how much space that child will be allocated, and then returns the resultSize variable. Add the following code to measure the children:

```
protected override Size MeasureOverride(Size availableSize)
{
    Size resultSize = new Size(0, 0);
    foreach (UIElement child in Children)
    {
        child.Measure(availableSize);
        resultSize.Width = Math.Max(resultSize.Width,
 child.DesiredSize.Width);
        resultSize.Height = Math.Max(resultSize.Height,
child.DesiredSize.Height);
    }

    resultSize.Width = double.IsPositiveInfinity(availableSize.Width) ?
 resultSize.Width : availableSize.Width;
    resultSize.Height = double.IsPositiveInfinity(availableSize.Height)
 ? resultSize.Height : availableSize.Height;

    return resultSize;

}
```

We can now move on to the ArrangeOverride method. This method is going to cycle through each of the children and center them in the panel by setting each child's X position to be the entire Width of the panel divided by 2 minus the Width of the child divided by 2. Conversely, it will set the Y position of the child to the Height of the panel divided by 2 minus the Height of the child divided by 2. It will then return finalSize.

```
protected override Size ArrangeOverride(Size finalSize)
```

```
{
    foreach (UIElement child in Children)
    {
        double childX = finalSize.Width / 2 - child.DesiredSize.Width
/ 2;
        double childY = finalSize.Height / 2 - child.DesiredSize.Height
/ 2;
        child.Arrange(new Rect(childX, childY,
child.DesiredSize.Width, child.DesiredSize.Height));
    }
return finalSize;

}
```

Now that all the children are centered in the panel, we need to rotate them slightly and offset their and positions. This will make it appear as if the images were all dropped into the container. We can encapsulate that Behavior into its own method called `RotateAndOffsetChild` and call that for each child in the `ArrangeOverride` method, as shown in the following code:

```
protected override Size ArrangeOverride(Size finalSize)
{
    foreach (UIElement child in Children)
    {
        double childX = finalSize.Width / 2 - child.DesiredSize.Width
 / 2;
        double childY = finalSize.Height / 2 - child.DesiredSize.Height
 / 2;
        child.Arrange(new Rect(childX, childY,
child.DesiredSize.Width, child.DesiredSize.Height));
        RotateAndOffsetChild(child);
    }
    return finalSize;

}
        private void RotateAndOffsetChild(UIElement child)
        {
            throw new NotImplementedException();
        }

    }
```

Now, as you probably already ascertained, we are going to rotate each child in the `RotateAndOffsetChild` method. To do this, we need a few variables:

- xOffset: The amount the child will be offset in the X coordinate
- yOffset: The amount the child will be offset in the Y coordinate
- angle: The angle the child will be rotate to

Next we need to create X and Y offset variables as well as the angle. We will use a random number so that each child has slightly different values and thus has a unique position. The following code implements these variables:

```
private void RotateAndOffsetChild(UIElement child)
{

    double xOffset = MaxOffset * (2 * rnd.NextDouble() - 1);
    double yOffset = MaxOffset * (2 * rnd.NextDouble() - 1);
    double angle = MaxRotation * (2 * rnd.NextDouble() - 1);
}
```

Look at what the preceding calculations are doing. The `xOffset` is being set equal to `MaxOffset` multiplied by rnd (a random number) multiplied by 2 minus 1. This calculation will ensure that, at times, we will get negative numbers, and at other times, we will get positive numbers.

> The `Random.NextDouble()` method returns a number greater than or equal to 0 and less than (but not equal to) 1.

Now that we have our numbers, we need to create two transforms, one for the X and Y coordinates and another for the rotation:

```
private void RotateAndOffsetChild(UIElement child)
{
    double randomNumber = rnd.NextDouble();

    double xOffset = MaxOffset * (2 * rnd.NextDouble() - 1);
    double yOffset = MaxOffset * (2 * rnd.NextDouble() - 1);
    double angle = MaxRotation * (2 * rnd.NextDouble() - 1);

    TranslateTransform offsetTF = new TranslateTransform();
    offsetTF.X = xOffset;
    offsetTF.Y = yOffset;

    RotateTransform rotateRT = new RotateTransform();
    rotateRT.Angle = angle;
    rotateRT.CenterX = child.DesiredSize.Width / 2;
    rotateRT.CenterY = child.DesiredSize.Height / 2;
}
```

The last thing we need to do is to create a `TransformGroup` and add the transforms we create to it:

```
private void RotateAndOffsetChild(UIElement child)
{
    double randomNumber = rnd.NextDouble();
```

```
double xOffset = MaxOffset * (2 * rnd.NextDouble() - 1);
double yOffset = MaxOffset * (2 * rnd.NextDouble() - 1);
double angle = MaxRotation * (2 * rnd.NextDouble() - 1);

TranslateTransform offsetTF = new TranslateTransform();
offsetTF.X = xOffset;
offsetTF.Y = yOffset;

RotateTransform rotateRT = new RotateTransform();
rotateRT.Angle = angle;
rotateRT.CenterX = child.DesiredSize.Width / 2;
rotateRT.CenterY = child.DesiredSize.Height / 2;

TransformGroup tfg = new TransformGroup();
tfg.Children.Add(offsetTF);
tfg.Children.Add(rotateRT);
child.RenderTransform = tfg;
}
```

The panel is complete. Now we need to do is implement it, that is, use it in the application. We can start to set this up in Blend. So press Ctrl+Shift+B to compile the application and switch over to Blend. Here are the steps to implement the panel:

1. In Blend open the project.

2. Next, select [UserControl] from the **Objects and Timeline** panel, and in the **Layout** bucket of the **Properties** panel, change the Width to **800** and the Height to **600**, as shown in Figure 12-5.

Figure 12-5. Set the Height and Width of the UserControl to 800×600.

3. Next, click and hold the **Button** tool on the toolbar, and when it appears select **ListBox** (see Figure 12-6).

Figure 12-6. Select the ListBox tool.

4. On the workspace, draw a `ListBox` that is roughly 200 display units wide and 400 display units tall (see Figure 12-7).

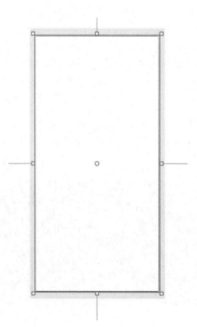

Figure 12-7. Draw a `ListBox` on the workspace.

Next you are going to add images to your project. I suggest you edit the images so they are roughly 200×200 pixels.

5. Right-click the project and click **Add ➤ Existing Item**.

6. Locate the images you would like to use on your hard drive and select them.

7. Your **Projects** panel should look something the one shown in Figure 12-8.

Figure 12-8. You should now have images in your Project panel.

8. Hold down Ctrl and click each image to select them all.

9. Drag the images onto the `ListBox`, and Blend should populate your `ListBox` as shown in Figure 12-9.

Figure 12-9. The images are now in the `ListBox`.

You can also verify that the images are in the ListBox by looking at the **Objects and Timeline** panel (see Figure 12-10).

Figure 12-10. You can see the images are in your ListBox in the Objects and Timeline panel.

As you can see in Figure 12-10, this ListBox is not good for our purposes, because we want to take up as little real estate as possible and not have the user have to use the ListBox's scroll functionality. So, it's now time to use our ZStackPanel:

1. Press Ctrl+Shift+B to compile the application and switch back to Visual Studio.

2. Create a UserControl.Resources node in MainWindow.xaml.

3. In this new node add an ItemsPanelTemplate Resource to describe to the ListBox how to display its items.

4. Inside the ItemsPanelTemplate add the following ZStackPanel (be sure to include the namespace for the ZStackPanel, which is in bold):

> *Step 2 can also be done in Blend visually by right-clicking and left-clicking Edit Additional Templates ➤ Layout of Items.*

```
<UserControl x:Class="CustomZStackPanelProject.Page"
    xmlns="http://schemas.microsoft.com/winfx/2006/xaml/presentation"
    xmlns:x="http://schemas.microsoft.com/winfx/2006/xaml"
    xmlns:CustomZStackPanelProject="clr-namespace:
CustomZStackPanelProject"
```

```
Width="800" Height="600">
<UserControl.Resources>

    <ItemsPanelTemplate
        x:Key="ZItemsPanelTemplate">

        <CustomZStackPanelProject:ZStackPanel
            MaxOffset="20"
            MaxRotation="11" />
    </ItemsPanelTemplate>
</UserControl.Resources>
```

5. Now, all you need to do is to tell your `ListBox` to use your new `ItemsPanelTemplate` named `ZItemsPanelTemplate`:

```
<ListBox
        ItemsPanel="{StaticResource ZItemsPanelTemplate}"
        Margin="218,66,197,-270">
        <Image
            Height="205"
            Width="300"
            Source="Img00.jpg"
            Stretch="Fill" />
        <Image
            Height="205"
            Width="300"
            Source="Img01.jpg"
            Stretch="Fill" />
        <Image
            Height="205"
            Width="300"
            Source="Img02.jpg"
            Stretch="Fill" />
        <Image
            Height="205"
            Width="300"
            Source="Img03.jpg"
            Stretch="Fill" />
        <Image
            Height="205"
            Width="300"
            Source="Img04.jpg"
            Stretch="Fill" />
    </ListBox>
```

In my project, I actually have 15 images. The `ZItemsPanelTemplate` *code has only 5 to save space.*

Now, if you press F5 to compile and run the application, you will see that our `ListBoxItems` all stack on top of each other with a little bit of an (X, Y) offset and at slightly different angles, so we can see that we have more than one image (see Figure 12-11).

Figure 12-11. The `ListBoxItems` all stack on top of each other with different rotation angles as well as X and Y offsets.

At this point, our application is pretty cool, but not very interactive. What we would like to do is move the top item to the bottom of the stack when it's clicked. Let's stop the running application and switch back to Blend to wire this up visually:

1. In Blend, open `MainPage.xaml` and resize your `ListBox` so that it is roughly the same size as your stack of images, as shown in Figure 12-12.

Figure 12-12. Resize your `ListBox` to be about the same size as the collection of images in it.

2. Draw a `Rectangle` that completely covers the `ListBox`, as shown in Figure 12-13.

Figure 12-13. Draw a `Rectangle` that completely covers your `ListBox`.

    3.   In the **Appearance** bucket of the **Properties** panel, set the **Opacity** of the `Rectangle` to **0**.

    4.   Now, give the new `Rectangle` a **Name** of `ImageSelector`.

    5.   Select the `ListBox` and give it a **Name** of `ZStackLB`.

    6.   Press Ctrl+Shift+B to compile the application and switch back to Visual Studio.

Now, we need to go in to `MainPage.xaml.cs` and wire up the selection functionality:

    1.   In `MainPage.xaml.cs`, raise and handle a `MouseLeftButtonDown` event for `ImageSelector`, as shown in the following code:

```
namespace CustomZStackPanelProject
{
    public partial class Page : UserControl
    {
        public Page()
        {
            InitializeComponent();
            ImageSelector.MouseLeftButtonDown += new MouseButtonEventHandler
(ImageSelector_MouseLeftButtonDown);
        }

    void ImageSelector_MouseLeftButtonDown(object sender,
 MouseButtonEventArgs e)
```

```
        {
            throw new NotImplementedException();
        }

    }
}
```

2. Now, all you need to do is to remove the topmost item and add it back to the collection (this will put it at the end). Here is the code:

```
void ImageSelector_MouseLeftButtonDown(object sender, MouseButtonEventArgs e)
{
    // create a generic object and make it equal to the very first item
    // in ZStackLB ListBox.
    object o = ZStackLB.Items.ElementAt(ZStackLB.Items.Count - 1);
     // Make certain the o actually exists and is not null
    if (o != null)
    {
         // Remove o (the first image in the ZStackLB ListBox
        ZStackLB.Items.RemoveAt(ZStackLB.Items.Count - 1);
        // Add o back to the ZStackLB ListBox at the 0 position
        //(the last item in the ListBox)
        ZStackLB.Items.Insert(0, o);
    }
}
```

You can see the result when you click an item in Figure 12-14.

Figure 12-14. The images will now cycle through when clicked.

You can download a copy of my project from the Friends of ED web site or here:

`http://www.windowspresentationfoundation.com/Blend4Book/CustomZStackPanelProject.zip`

If you ever find you need a `ListBox` with three columns you can watch my free Silverlight video tutorial on how to do just that: `http://www.windowspresentationfoundation.com/?p=149`

Summary

In this chapter, you learned that you are not limited by the functionality of the existing panels in Silverlight. You learned that if a particular panel does not fit your needs, you can go ahead and create your own, as long as you extend the `Panel` class to do so. You then learned how to build a custom panel that arranges its children in Z space, rather than using (X, Y) coordinates.

In the next chapter we look at taking your Silverlight applications out of the browser and running them directly on the Desktop. Hold on to your hats!

Chapter 13

Writing a Silverlight 4 Out-Of-Browser Application with Elevated Trust and the New Silverlight 4 COM API

What this chapter covers:

- Creating a Silverlight 4 Out-Of-Browser application
- Setting Elevated Trust on a Silverlight application
- Using the new Silverlight 4 COM API to have a Silverlight application open Microsoft Word, create a new document, and populate it

With Silverlight 4 it is very easy to make a normal online application or an Out-Of-Browser (OOB) application. *Out-Of-Browser applications*, as the name implies, allow your applications to be detached from the browser and run just like any other desktop application. Further, you can make a Silverlight application require Elevated Trust when running outside the browser. When this option is selected, your applications can do some very cool things which Silverlight applications without Elevated Trust cannot do. Here are some special things that Silverlight OOB applications running with Elevated Trust can do:

- *Change the* WindowState*:* You can set the WindowState programmatically to Maximized, Minimized, and so on.
- *Resize the application:* With Silverlight 4 OOB applications you can set the size of the application when it starts or anytime programmatically while the application is running.
- *Access the Clipboard:* This allows you to give users of your applications the ability to copy and paste. This is a new feature to Silverlight 4 but is not limited to OOB applications.
- *Access user folders:* Silverlight can access folders such as My Documents.

- *Use HTML hosting:* Silverlight 4 applications running in Elevated Trust can display HTML via the `WebBrowser` control.
- *Access Toast notification windows:* A Toast window is a small window that pops up from the host application in the Windows system tray.
- *Use a less restricted cross domain policy:* Silverlight 4 applications with Elevated Trust can communicate with services not hosted on the client's machine without the presence of a `ClientAccessPolicy` or `CrossDomain` XML files. Formerly, the absence of either of these files would result in a security exception when the application tried to access services not residing on the same computer or domain.
- *Use COM Interoperability:* This is possibly the coolest feature in Silverlight 4 and one we talk about in greater detail in this chapter. Basically it allows Silverlight OOB applications with Elevated Trust to communicate with any COM-enabled application installed on the end user's machine. This means you can start an instance of another program, say Microsoft Word, and create a new document, or fire up Outlook and allow your users to send an e-mail right from your Silverlight 4 applications.

Creating an Out-Of-Browser Silverlight 4 Application

As you know by now, this is a very hands-on book. So now that you have the basic information on what an OOB Silverlight 4 application can do, let's fire up Blend 4 and Visual Studio 2010 and actually make some of those cool features come to life in a real-world application.

The application we are going to create is one that you can use over and over again when you want to create a new OOB application. This application does some common tasks that are required from all OOB applications—that is, look to see if the application is already installed, and if it isn't then make the install button visible and prompt the user to install the application. Further, it checks for any updates that need to be installed to the application. If updates are in fact required and installed, it prompts the user to close and restart the application to run the most up-to-date version.

1. Fire up Visual Studio 2010 and click **File ➤ New ➤ Project, as** I am doing in Figure 13-1.

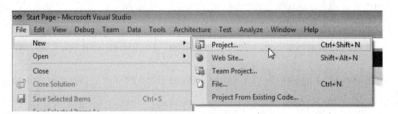

Figure 13-1. Create a new project.

2. Select **Silverlight Application** from the list, name the application `DefaultOutOfBrowserProject`, and make certain your settings match what I have in Figure 13-2.

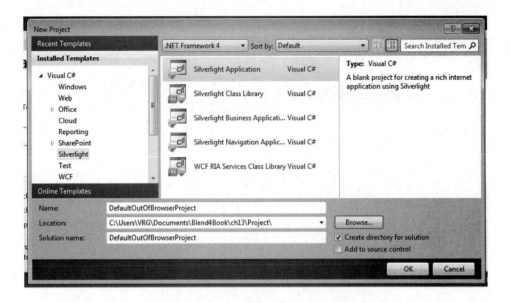

Figure 13-2. Select Silverlight Application and name the project `DefaultOutOfBrowserProject`.

3. Because you don't really need an ASP web site for an OOB application, go ahead and uncheck "**Host the Silverlight application in a new web site**" option in the New Silverlight Application, as I have done in Figure 13-3.

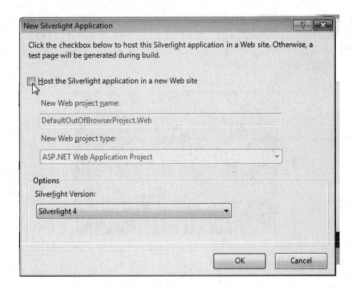

Figure 13-3. Uncheck the option to "Host the Silverlight application in a new Web site."

4. Switch over to Blend and add some visual elements to the application. The fastest way to do this is to right-click `MainPage.xaml` in the **Solution Explorer** and left-click **Open in Expression Blend,** as I am doing in Figure 13-4.

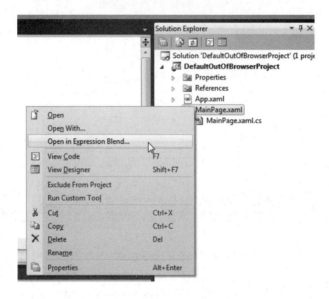

Figure 13-4. Open `MainPage.xaml` in Expression Blend.

Because Visual Studio 2010 makes default Silverlight applications 400×300, click the [UserControl] in Blend's Objects and Timeline panel, as I am doing in Figure 13-5. Move over to the Layout bucket of the Properties panel and change the Width to **800** and the Height to **600**, as I have done in Figure 13-6.

Figure 13-5. Select the [UserControl] in Blend's Objects and Timeline panel.

Figure 13-6. Change the Width and Height properties to 800 and 600 respectively.

The first thing to do is add a background Rectangle that will appear to gray out anything in the application. Then we need to add a default Silverlight Button control on top of that that reads "Install Application." We will then group them both into a container. It is going to be this container that we will programmatically make Collapsed only if the application already has been installed. Let's do that now.

1. Create a Rectangle that is the same size as the [UserControl] (800×600), as I have done in Figure 13-7.

Figure 13-7. Make a Rectangle the same size as the application.

2. Change the Rectangle to have a black Fill and an opacity of 65%, so users can see a little of the application through it when it is visible.

3. Click the Button control from the toolbar and draw a Silverlight Button in the center of the artboard.

4. In the **Properties** panel name the Button InstallBtn.

5. In the **Common Properties** bucket of the **Properties** panel, change the `Button`'s `Content`
    property to *Install Application*, so you have what I have in Figure 13-8.

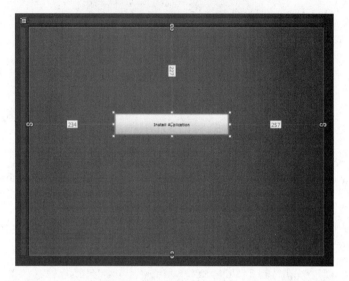

Figure 13-8. Your application should look like this at this stage.

6. Now we need to group the background and `Button` into a `Container` grid. In the **Objects and
    Timeline** panel, Ctrl+click both the `Rectangle` and the Install button.

7. Right-click and left-click **Group Into ➤ Grid, as** I am doing in Figure 13-9.

Figure 13-9. Group the `Rectangle` and `Button` into a Grid.

8. Double-click the newly created Grid in the **Objects and Timeline** panel and name it
   `InstallContainer`, so that your **Objects and Timeline** panel looks like what I have in Figure
   13-10.

Figure 13-10. Your Objects and Timeline panel should now look like this.

Now that you have done this, you can press Ctrl+Shift+B to build the application. Switch back over to
Visual Studio 2010 to set this as an OOB application and wire up the functionality that will determine
whether the `InstallContainer` should be shown or not.

1. Now that you have put in all the install visuals, right-click the Project (not the Solution) in the
   Solution Explorer and left-click **Properties, as** I am doing in Figure 13-11.

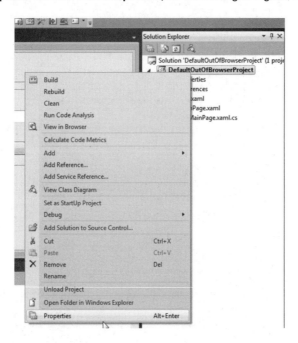

Figure 13-11. Select Properties in Visual Studio 2010's Solution Explorer.

2. Click "**Enable running application out of the browser,**" as I have done in Figure 13-12.

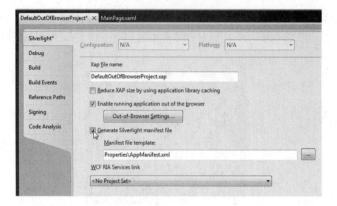

Figure 13-12. Set the application to run out of the browser.

3. Now click the **Out-of-Browser Settings** button, also shown in Figure 13-12.

4. Check "**Require elevated trust when running outside the browser," as** I have done in Figure 13-13, and then click OK.

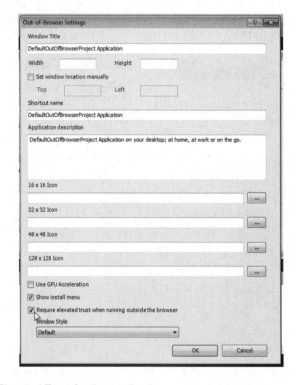

Figure 13-13. Require Elevated Trust for the application.

Now we can go ahead and add the code that will show or hide the `InstallContainer`.

1. Open `MainPage.xaml.cs` and right under the `IntializeComponent();` call type **Loaded +=** and hit the Tab key twice to create a loaded handler. Your code should now look like the following code:

```
namespace DefaultOutOfBrowserProject
{
    public partial class MainPage : UserControl
    {
        public MainPage()
        {
            InitializeComponent();
            Loaded += new RoutedEventHandler(MainPage_Loaded);
        }

        void MainPage_Loaded(object sender, RoutedEventArgs e)
        {
            throw new NotImplementedException();
        }
    }
}
```

When viewing the XAML for a `UserControl`, you can right-click it in Visual Studio 2010 to open its code-behind file (see Figure 13-14).

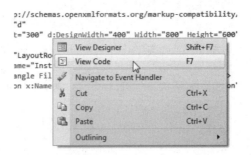

Figure 13-14. Right-click the XAML of a `UserControl` to be taken to its code-behind file.

2. Now you can check to see whether the file is installed, and if it is then you can collapse the `InstallContainer`. See the following code:

```
void MainPage_Loaded(object sender, RoutedEventArgs e)
{
    if (App.Current.InstallState == InstallState.Installed)
    {
        InstallContainer.Visibility = Visibility.Collapsed;
    }
}
```

At this point if you were to run the application, you would in fact see the install button because the application has not yet been installed. But currently if we clicked the install button, nothing would happen. Let's fix that now.

1. Under the code that sets the visibility of the `InstallContainer` type **InstallBtn.Click +=** and press the Tab key twice. This creates the `Click EventHandler` for you. See my code here:

```
void MainPage_Loaded(object sender, RoutedEventArgs e)
{
    if (App.Current.InstallState == InstallState.Installed)
    {
        InstallContainer.Visibility = Visibility.Collapsed;
    }

    InstallBtn.Click += new RoutedEventHandler(InstallBtn_Click);
}

void InstallBtn_Click(object sender, RoutedEventArgs e)
{
    throw new NotImplementedException();
}
```

2. Now erase the default code and put in the code that installs the application, as I do here:

```
void InstallBtn_Click(object sender, RoutedEventArgs e)
{
    App.Current.Install();
}
```

We need to make the application check for updates when it's started. Fortunately for us Microsoft and the Silverlight team have made that quite easy for us. Let's add that now:

1. Under the `InitializeComponent();` call, add a call to the static `CheckAndDownloadAsync()` call, as I do here:

```
public MainPage()
{
    InitializeComponent();
    App.Current.CheckAndDownloadUpdateAsync();
    Loaded += new RoutedEventHandler(MainPage_Loaded);
}
```

2. We need to handle the event that fires once it has completed. To do this type **CheckAndDownloadUpdateCompleted+=** and press the Tab key twice to wire up the event and create the `EventHandler`. See the following code:

```
public MainPage()
{
    InitializeComponent();
    App.Current.CheckAndDownloadUpdateAsync();
```

```
     App.Current.CheckAndDownloadUpdateCompleted += new↵

CheckAndDownloadUpdateCompletedEventHandler(Current_CheckAndDownloadUpdateCompleted)
;
     Loaded += new RoutedEventHandler(MainPage_Loaded);
}

void Current_CheckAndDownloadUpdateCompleted(object sender,↵
 CheckAndDownloadUpdateCompletedEventArgs e)
{
     throw new NotImplementedException();
}
```

3. Delete the default code out of the new `EventHandler` and do a check to see whether any updates were downloaded. If any were, then you need to inform the user via a `MessageBox` to restart their application. See my code here:

```
void Current_CheckAndDownloadUpdateCompleted(object sender,↵
 CheckAndDownloadUpdateCompletedEventArgs e)
{
    if (e.UpdateAvailable)
    {
    MessageBox.Show("An update has been installed.
To see the updates please exit and restart the application.");

    }
}
```

At this point we are ready to press F5 to compile and run the application. The only problem is Visual Studio 2010 will always run the project as if it were already installed, so switch over to Blend and press F5. When it runs click the Install button and install the application, as I am doing in Figure 13-15.

Figure 13-15. Click Install to install the application.

The application will then install and run, and we see ... nothing, because we don't really have anything in our application. So close it and let's move on.

Switch back over to Blend and click **File ➤ Save Copy of Project, as** I do in Figure 13-16. Call this new project COMProject. Anytime you want to create a new OOB application, you can now use this application as your default application so you don't always have to add an install button, check for updates, make the InstallContainer visible, and so forth. It is all done for you! So all you need to do is to save a new copy of this project and use that for your new OOB applications.

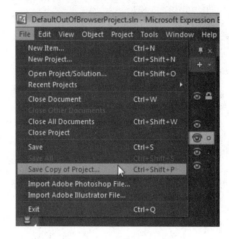

Figure 13-16. Save a copy of your project called ComProject.

Close the DefaultOutOfBrowserProject and open ComProject in both Blend and Visual Studio 2010.

Now you have your default OOB application, which you can use for any OOB applications you build in the future. With the copy of a new project called ComProject, we can go ahead and make a new project that shows how cool the COM API is. In this new project we are going to make an application that has a TextBox in it and a Button that reads LaunchWord. When the user types text in the TextBox and hits the LaunchWord Button, we are going to programmatically open Microsoft Word and create a new document that has the text that the user typed in our application. Pretty cool, huh? Let's do that now.

With the project still open, go to Blend's **Objects and Timeline** panel and click the eyeball icon next to the InstallContainer, as I am doing in Figure 13-17, to make the InstallContainer invisible. This will only make it invisible in design time, since we programmatically handle its visibility when the application is loaded.

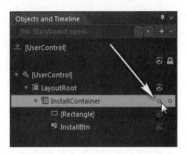

Figure 13-17. Make the `InstallContainer` hidden during design time.

1. Now that we have done that, select the `LayoutRoot` and draw a `TextBox` out on the artboard (about 400 display units wide and 200 tall). Make sure your `TextBox` is above the `InstallContainer` in the **Objects and Timeline** panel.

2. Then draw a `Button` control under it so you have what I have in Figure 13-18.

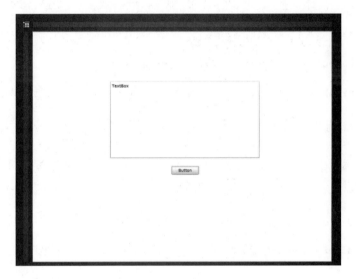

Figure 13-18. Draw a `TextBox` and a `Button` on the artboard.

3. Now name the `Button` `LaunchBtn`.

4. Name the `TextBox` `TextRegion`.

5. Change the `Button`'s `Content` property to `Launch Word`.

6. Remove the default text from the `TextBox`. Your application should look like what I have in Figure 13-19.

Launch Word

Figure 13-19. Your application should now look like this.

Now you are ready to build (press Ctrl+Shift+B) and switch back over to Visual Studio 2010 to code up the functionality that occurs when you click the "Launch Word" Button.

1. In the Loaded EventHandler, raise and handle a Click event for the LaunchBtn, as I do here:

```
void MainPage_Loaded(object sender, RoutedEventArgs e)
{
    if (App.Current.InstallState == InstallState.Installed)
    {
        InstallContainer.Visibility = Visibility.Collapsed;
    }

    InstallBtn.Click += new RoutedEventHandler(InstallBtn_Click);
    LaunchBtn.Click += new RoutedEventHandler(LaunchBtn_Click);
}

void LaunchBtn_Click(object sender, RoutedEventArgs e)
{
    throw new NotImplementedException();
}
```

2. Now all we need to do is add the code that launches Word and creates a new document with the text from the TextRegion TextBox.

```
void LaunchBtn_Click(object sender, RoutedEventArgs e)
{
    dynamic word = AutomationFactory.CreateObject("Word.Application");
    word.Visible = true;
    dynamic doc = word.Documents.Add();
    string insertText = TextRegion.Text;
    dynamic range = doc.Range(0, 0);
    range.Text = insertText;
```

}

3. You may notice errors, and that is because we need to add a reference to `Microsoft.CSharp`. Right-click the `References` folder in Visual Studio 2010's Solution Explorer and left-click **Add Reference** (see Figure 13-20).

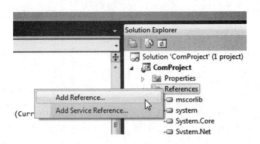

Figure 13-20. Add a reference.

4. Click the Browse button, navigate to `C:\Program Files\Microsoft SDKs\Silverlight\v4.0\Libraries\Client`, and double-click `Microsoft.CSharp.dll`. This should fix the errors you were experiencing.

5. Now press the F6 key to build the application.

6. When the OOB application starts, type some text into the `TextBox` and click the **Launch Word** button.

Notice how Word now opens up for you and displays a document with the text that you added into the `TextBox`. Pretty cool (see Figure 30-21). This should demonstrate to you the real power of the COM API.

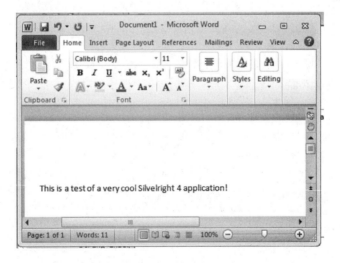

Figure 13-21. Word opens and displays the document.

You can download both projects from the book's page at www.friendsofed.com.

For an extra added lesson in building Out-Of-Browser Silverlight applications, go to http://www.windowspresentationfoundation.com/?p=439 and learn how to build your very own TutorialCam webcam application like I use in my own tutorials. You can watch a video tutorial on how to create your default OOB Silverlight application here: http://www.windowspresentationfoundation.com/?p=265.

Summary

In this chapter, you learned that you can use Silverlight 4 to build applications that can run Out-Of-Browser. You also learned that if you run the application with Elevated Trust you can do quite a bit more with your applications, such as access local user files, access the Clipboard, and more. You also learned how to make a default OOB application that can be used to create more new OOB applications. You then used that application to make an OOB application that used the COM API to launch Microsoft Word and populate it with a new document and text from the application's TextBox.

Chapter 14

Creating a Photobooth Application with the Silverlight 4 Webcam API

What this chapter covers:

- The Webcam API
- Saving images with the `PNGEncoder` class
- Drag and drop Behavior

You will also require the following files available in the book's download package:

- `SaveTheImage.txt`
- `PngEncoder.zip`

With the release of Silverlight 4, it is now easy to incorporate rich content such as webcam video right into your Silverlight applications. Prior to the release of Silverlight 4, doing this was a very difficult task because of the security restrictions in place and wasn't possible at all without circumventing that security via some serious and hacking (bad practice).

With this new API it only takes a few lines of code and your applications are now fully interactive with video taken directly from the webcam. And with the Expression Encoder, the encoding application that ships with Expression Studio, you can do live streaming right from your own computer and have that stream be visible anywhere around the world on any Silverlight client. In this chapter I show you how to use the new webcam API to create an application that makes use of a webcam and displays its stream right in the application. Further, you are going to make it so your application allows you to drag funny little items such as hats on top of the webcam image. Next, you will give your application the ability to take a snapshot of the webcam. Finally, you'll use a handy class developed by Joe Stegman that allows you to actually save the snapshot to your hard drive.

Creating the Application

1. Open Visual Studio 2010 and click **File ➤ New ➤ Project**.

2. When the **New Project** dialog box appears, select **Silverlight Application** for the Template and name the application PhotoboothApp, as I have done in Figure 14-1.

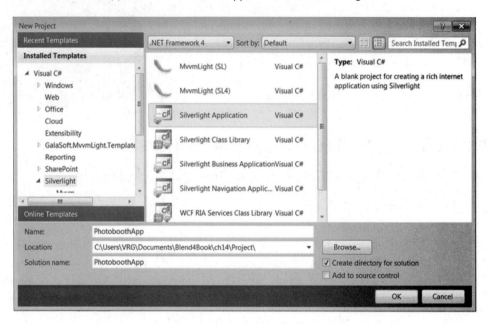

Figure 14-1. The settings for the PhotoboothApp solution.

3. When the New Silverlight Application dialog box appears, uncheck "**Host the Silverlight application in a new Web site,**" **as** I have done in Figure 14-2. This is so Visual Studio 2010 will only create the Silverlight application for you and not the .NET web site.

4. Click OK.

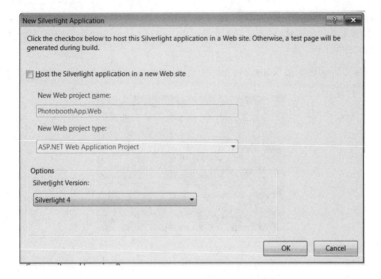

Figure 14-2. Uncheck "Host the Silverlight application in a new Web site."

We are now going to set up our visuals before we start to code against the new Webcam API. We'll do that over in Blend.

Setting Up the Visuals in Expression Blend

1. Go to Visual Studio 2010's **Solution Explorer,** right-click `MainPage.xaml`, and left-click **Open in Expression Blend, as** I am doing in Figure 14-3.

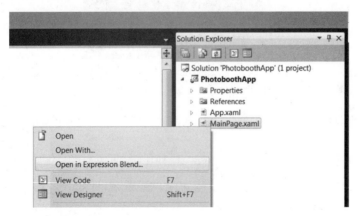

Figure 14-3. Edit the project in Expression Blend.

The first thing that you will notice is the `MainPage.xaml` `UserControl` is quite small. That's because Visual Studio 2010 sets the size of the `MainPage.xaml` `UserControl` to 400×300. To give us some room, let's make that bigger now.

1. In Blend's **Objects and Timeline** panel, click [UserControl], as I have done in Figure 14-4.

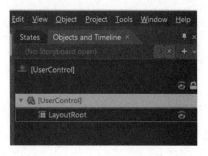

Figure 14-4. Click [UserControl] in Blend's Objects and Timeline panel.

2. In Blend's **Properties** panel find the **Layout** bucket and set the **Width** to 800 and the **Height** to 600, as I have done in Figure 14-5.

Figure 14-5. Set the Width to 800 and the Height to 600.

Next we need to add a `Rectangle` that will serve as the canvas we are going to fill with the image from the webcam.

3. On the artboard draw a `Rectangle` with a `Width` of 300 and a `Height` of 200, as I have done in Figure 14-6.

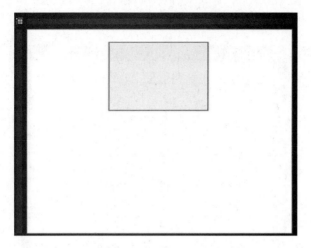

Figure 14-6. Draw a `Rectangle` on the artboard.

    4. In the **Objects and Timeline** panel, double-click this new `Rectangle` and name it `WebcamRectangle`, as I have done in Figure 14-7.

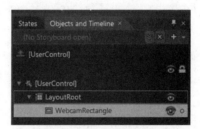

Figure 14-7. Name the new `Rectangle` `WebcamRectangle`.

    5. Click and hold down the Grid tool in the toolbar until you see Canvas appear. When it does, click it to select it, as I am doing in Figure 14-8.

Figure 14-8. Select the Canvas tool from the toolbar.

6. Now draw a Canvas beneath the `Rectangle`, as I have done in Figure 14-9.

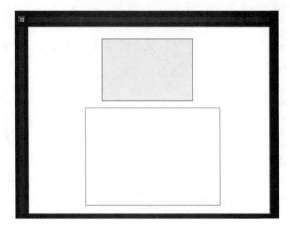

Figure 14-9. Draw a Canvas underneath the `Rectangle`.

This is going to be the holder for the snapshot image we take of the webcam stream. Because we need to write some code to add the snapshot image, we need to name it as well. Do that now.

1. Double-click the new Canvas in the **Objects and Timeline** panel to highlight it.

2. Name it `ImgHolder` so that your **Objects and Timeline** panel looks like what I have in Figure 14-10.

Figure 14-10. Rename the new Canvas to `ImgHolder`.

At this point we have the visuals set up for the webcam stream as well as the snapshot holder. Next we are going to add the items that we are going to be able to drag on top of the stream to make funny pictures. To keep it simple I have decided to add a funny hat and a pair of sunglasses. You can add as many different things as you want. Let's walk through how to do that now.

1. In Expression Blend's toolbar hold down the Pen tool until you see the Pencil tool appear.

2. Select it, as I am doing in Figure 14-11.

Figure 14-11. Select the Pencil tool.

3. Draw a funny hat, as I have done in Figure 14-12.

Figure 14-12. A funny hat created with the Pen tool.

4. Next change the **Fill** of the hat in the **Brushes** bucket of the **Properties** panel, so your panel looks like what I have in Figure 14-13.

Figure 14-13. Change the Fill of the hat.

5. Use the Pencil tool again, and draw a funny pair of sunglasses, as I have done in Figure 14-14.

Figure 14-14. Draw a pair of sunglasses.

6. Change the **Fill** of the sunglasses to black in the **Brushes** bucket of the **Properties** panel.

Before we move ahead with the other visuals, we should make the hat and sunglasses draggable.

Using the MouseDragElementBehavior to make items draggable

At this point we have most of our visuals set up. Before we finish, though, we are going to use the `MouseDragElementBehavior` Behavior to make the hat and sunglasses draggable. Let's do that now!

1. Click the last tool in the toolbar, the Asset Library.

2. Locate the `MouseDragElementBehavior` Behavior (shown in Figure 14-15).

3. Click and drag it over the hat and then let it go to attach it to the hat.

4. Repeat this for the sunglasses.

Figure 14-15. Locate the `MouseDragElementBehavior` Behavior.

Now, if you look at the **Objects and Timeline** panel, you should see the `MouseDragElementBehavior` Behavior under both the hat and the sunglasses (see Figure 14-16).

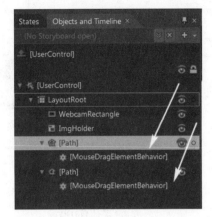

Figure 14-16. *The* `MouseDragElementBehavior` *Behavior under the hat and the sunglasses Paths.*

If you press F5 to compile and run the application, you will see that both the hat and the sunglasses are now draggable (see Figure 14-17).

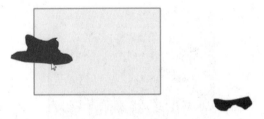

Figure 14-17. *The hat and the sunglasses can now be dragged about the application.*

The last visuals we need to set up are the three buttons that will be in the application. They are:

- Start the webcam
- Take a snapshot
- Save the image

Let's set those up now.

Adding the Buttons

We are going to add three Silverlight default `Buttons` for starting the webcam, taking a snapshot, and saving the image. These will just be basic Blend UI `Buttons`.

1. In the toolbar click the Button tool.

2. Draw three `Buttons` on the artboard, as I have done in Figure 14-18.

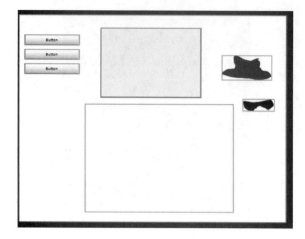

Figure 14-18. Draw three Buttons on the artboard.

3. Name the Buttons StartWebcamBtn, TakeSnapShotBtn, and SaveImgBtn so that your **Objects and Timeline** panel looks like what I have in Figure 14-19.

Figure 14-19. Name the three Buttons.

4. Select the first Button in the **Objects and Timeline** panel, and in the **Common Properties** bucket of the **Properties** panel change the Content property to Start Webcam.

5. Select the second Button in the **Objects and Timeline** panel, and in the **Common Properties** bucket of the **Properties** panel change the Content property to Take Snapshot.

6. Select the third Button in the **Objects and Timeline** panel, and in the **Common Properties** bucket of the **Properties** panel change the **Content** property to Save Image.

Your Buttons should now look like what I have in Figure 14-20.

Figure 14-20. Your Buttons should now look like this.

Now we are complete, and our visuals are all set up. We have a background Rectangle for the webcam stream to show up on. We also have the Canvas that will hold the snapshot. We have the funny hat and sunglasses that can be dragged on top of the webcam stream. And we have the three Buttons to start the webcam, take a snapshot, and save the image. It's time to press Ctrl+Shift+B to build the project and switch back over to Visual Studio 2010 to code up the functionality. If Visual Studio 2010 asks you to reload the project, click **Yes**. Let's add the code that will start the webcam and show it on the Rectangle.

Starting and Displaying the Webcam

Before we can do anything, we need to add a few properties to MainPage.xaml.cs. Go to Visual Studio 2010's Solution Explorer and double-click MainPage.xaml.cs to open it and get started.

1. Above the constructor, add a new CaptureSource that will act as the webcam stream (see my code in bold):

```
namespace PhotoboothApp
{
    public partial class MainPage : UserControl
    {
        CaptureSource CapSrc = new CaptureSource();
        public MainPage()
        {
            InitializeComponent();
        }
    }
}
```

2. Next add a VideoBrush that we will use to brush the webcam stream onto the Rectangle.

```
namespace PhotoboothApp
{
    public partial class MainPage : UserControl
    {
        CaptureSource CapSrc = new CaptureSource();
        VideoBrush MyVideoBrush = new VideoBrush();

        public MainPage()
        {
```

```
                    InitializeComponent();
            }
        }
}
```

3. Finally, add a `WriteableBitmap`:

```
namespace PhotoboothApp
{
    public partial class MainPage : UserControl
    {
        CaptureSource CapSrc = new CaptureSource();
      VideoBrush MyVideoBrush = new VideoBrush();
      WriteableBitmap _bitmap;


        public MainPage()
        {
            InitializeComponent();
        }
    }
}
```

You will have to resolve `WriteableBitmap` *by right-clicking it and left-clicking Resolve ➤ using* `System.Windows.Media.Imaging`.

4. Now we can go under the `InitializeComponent();` call, type **Loaded+=**, hit the Tab key twice to raise the `Loaded` event, and create the `EventHandler`. See my code:

```
public partial class MainPage : UserControl
{
    CaptureSource CapSrc = new CaptureSource();
    VideoBrush MyVideoBrush = new VideoBrush();
    WriteableBitmap _bitmap;
    public MainPage()
    {
    InitializeComponent();
    Loaded += new RoutedEventHandler(MainPage_Loaded);
    }

    void MainPage_Loaded(object sender, RoutedEventArgs e)
    {
        throw new NotImplementedException();
    }
}
```

5. Now we can erase the default `throw new...` code and raise and handle the `Click` event for all three `Buttons`:

```
void MainPage_Loaded(object sender, RoutedEventArgs e)
{
    StartWebcamBtn.Click += new RoutedEventHandler(StartWebcamBtn_Click);
    TakeSnapshotBtn.Click += new RoutedEventHandler(TakeSnapshotBtn_Click);
    SaveImgBtn.Click += new RoutedEventHandler(SaveImgBtn_Click);
}

void SaveImgBtn_Click(object sender, RoutedEventArgs e)
{
    throw new NotImplementedException();
}

void TakeSnapshotBtn_Click(object sender, RoutedEventArgs e)
{
    throw new NotImplementedException();
}

void StartWebcamBtn_Click(object sender, RoutedEventArgs e)
{
    throw new NotImplementedException();
}
```

The first thing we are going to do is work in the `StartWebCamBtn EventHandler`.

1. Check to see if the device has been allowed to start by the user already. If it has not, then request that the user gives us access to the device:

```
void StartWebcamBtn_Click(object sender, RoutedEventArgs e)
{
    if (CaptureDeviceConfiguration.AllowedDeviceAccess ||
CaptureDeviceConfiguration.RequestDeviceAccess())
    {

    }
}
```

2. If the user allows access to the device, we first set the source of `MyVideoBrush` to `CapSrc`:

```
if (CaptureDeviceConfiguration.AllowedDeviceAccess ||
CaptureDeviceConfiguration.RequestDeviceAccess())
{
    MyVideoBrush.SetSource(CapSrc);
}
```

3. Next set the `Fill` of the `Rectangle` to the `VideoBrush`.

```
if (CaptureDeviceConfiguration.AllowedDeviceAccess ||
```

```
CaptureDeviceConfiguration.RequestDeviceAccess())
{
    MyVideoBrush.SetSource(CapSrc);
    WebcamRectangle.Fill = MyVideoBrush;
}
```

4. Next we start CaptureSource:

```
if (CaptureDeviceConfiguration.AllowedDeviceAccess ||
CaptureDeviceConfiguration.RequestDeviceAccess())
{
    MyVideoBrush.SetSource(CapSrc);
    WebcamRectangle.Fill = MyVideoBrush;
    CapSrc.Start();
}
```

Press F5 to run the application and click **Start Webcam**. Notice how you are asked if you will allow Silverlight access to your webcam? Click **Yes**. Your camera starts, and Voilà! Your image appears on the Rectangle! (see Figure 14-21). Cool, eh?!

Figure 14-21. Your webcam stream shows up in your application as the Fill of your Rectangle.

The next thing is have the image appear in the Canvas when the user clicks the **Take Snapshot** Button.

Taking the Snapshot

Now that we have the webcam stream showing up correctly, it's time for us to code up the functionality that allows the user to take a snapshot.

1. Remove the default code from the TakeSnapshot EventHandler.

2. Create a WriteableBitmap using the Rectangle named WebcamContainer (the one that has the CapSrc as its Fill).

```
void TakeSnapshotBtn_Click(object sender, RoutedEventArgs e)
{
    WriteableBitmap snapShot = new WriteableBitmap(WebcamRectangle, null);
}
```

3. Next we need to create a new Image control, and set its Width to 300 and its Source to snapshot:

```
void TakeSnapshotBtn_Click(object sender, RoutedEventArgs e)
{
    WriteableBitmap snapShot = new WriteableBitmap(WebcamRectangle, null);
    Image image = new Image();
    image.Width = 300;
    image.Source = snapShot;
}
```

4. Now we need to check whether ImgHolder has any children such as an existing image. If it does we remove it and simply add image to it:

```
void TakeSnapshotBtn_Click(object sender, RoutedEventArgs e)
{
    WriteableBitmap snapShot = new WriteableBitmap(WebcamRectangle, null);
    Image image = new Image();
    image.Width = 300;
    image.Source = snapShot;
    if (ImgHolder.Children.Count == 1)
    {
        ImgHolder.Children.RemoveAt(0);
    }
    ImgHolder.Children.Add(image);
}
```

Now press F5 to run the application. Start the webcam, pose, and take a snapshot! Voilà! Again! You should now see that we have added a snapshot to our application (see Figure 14-22).

Figure 14-22. You are now able to take snapshots in your application.

Saving the Image

Now we need to be able to save the snapshot. Erase the default code in the `SaveImage` `EventHandler` and let's start doing that.

1.   Add a class created by Joe Stegman called `PngEncoder.cs`. You can download that class here (the URL is case sensitive):

    `http://windowspresentationfoundation.com/Blend4Book/PngEncoder.zip`

2.   Next, unzip the file you just downloaded, right-click the project in Visual Studio 2010's Solution Explorer, and click **Add ➤ Existing Item**, as I am doing in Figure 14-23.

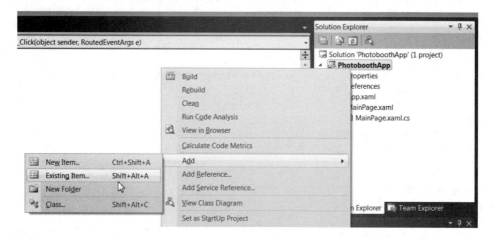

Figure 14-23. Add an Existing Item to the project.

3.   Navigate to where you saved the `PngEncoder.cs` class you downloaded and double-click it to add it to the project.

4.   Next download one more class, also created by Joe, called `EditableImage.cs`:

    `http://windowspresentationfoundation.com/Blend4Book/EditableImage.zip`

5.   Repeat steps 2 and 3 and add `EditableImage.cs` to the project as well.

6.   You need to download a method called `SaveTheImage`. You can find the text for it here (the URL for the download follows the code):

```
private void SaveTheImg()
{
    _bitmap = new WriteableBitmap(ImgHolderParent, null);
    SaveFileDialog sfd = new SaveFileDialog();
    sfd.Filter = "PNG Files (*.png)|*.png|All Files (*.*)|*.*";
    sfd.DefaultExt = ".png";
    sfd.FilterIndex = 1;
```

```
if ((bool)sfd.ShowDialog())
{
    using (Stream fs = sfd.OpenFile())
    {
        int width = _bitmap.PixelWidth;
        int height = _bitmap.PixelHeight;

        EditableImage ei = new EditableImage(width, height);

        for (int i = 0; i < height; i++)
        {
            for (int j = 0; j < width; j++)
            {
                int pixel = _bitmap.Pixels[(i * width) + j];
                ei.SetPixel(j, i,
                            (byte)((pixel >> 16) & 0xFF),
                            (byte)((pixel >> 8) & 0xFF),
                            (byte)(pixel & 0xFF),
                            (byte)((pixel >> 24) & 0xFF)
                );
            }
        }
        Stream png = ei.GetStream();
        int len = (int)png.Length;
        byte[] bytes = new byte[len];
        png.Read(bytes, 0, len);
        fs.Write(bytes, 0, len);
    }
}
}
```

http://windowspresentationfoundation.com/Blend4Book/SaveTheImage.txt

7. Copy the text in the downloaded file and paste it right after your three `EventHandlers`. You need to resolve `Stream` (using `System.IO`) and `EditableImage` (using `SilverlightSamples`). If you don't remember, do this by right-clicking and left-clicking Resolve. You can also click the preceding items and press Ctrl+. (period).

8. Hit Ctrl+Shift+B to build the application.

9. Now all you need to do is to put `SaveTheImg();` in the `Save EventHandler`. See my code:

```
void SaveImgBtn_Click(object sender, RoutedEventArgs e)
{
    SaveTheImg();
}
```

Now press F5 to run the application, start the webcam, take a snapshot, and click the Save Image button. Notice how you get a standard Windows **Save** dialog box with `.png` as the default file type (see Figure 14-23).

Figure 14-24. The Save dialog box.

Go ahead and save your image and then open it up to check it out. Pretty cool again, huh? Now all we have left is to add the dragged items to the image. Let's incorporate that now.

Adding the Draggable Items to the Saved Image

When we save the `Image`, we actually take a snapshot of `ImgHolder` and then use Joe Stegman's `PngEncoder` to write that to a `.png` file. If we were to place the dragged items over the image we are about to save they would never make it into the saved image because they are not inside of `ImgHolder`. What we need to do is to wrap `ImgHolder` into a parent Canvas and then add the draggable items to that parent container. We can then change the name of the container that the `SaveTheImg()` method uses from `ImgHolder` to the name of the new parent container. This way, `ImgHolder` as well as the draggable items will be what is written into the image. Let's do that now.

1. Stop the running application and switch back to Blend, reloading if asked.

2. In the **Objects and Timeline** panel right-click ImgHolder and left-click and click **Group Into ➤ Canvas**, as I am doing in Figure 14-25.

Figure 14-25. Group `ImgHolder` into a Canvas.

   3.   Name the new Canvas `ImgHolderParent`.

   4.   In the **Objects and Timeline** panel, drag both Paths, the hat, and the sunglasses into `ImgHolderParent`, as I am doing in Figure 14-26.

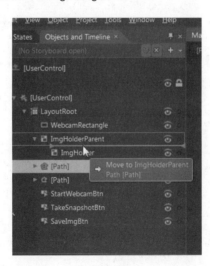

Figure 14-26. Drag both Paths into the new `ImgHolderParent` Canvas.

   5.   Make sure that both Paths are beneath the `ImgHolder` so that when you drag them they're not behind the saved image. You may have to drag them in the **Objects and Timeline** panel to rearrange their order. Your **Objects and Timeline** panel should look like what I have in Figure 14-27.

Figure 14-27. Your Objects and Timeline panel should now look like this.

When I dragged my two Paths for the hat and sunglasses into the new `ImgHolderParent`, they moved off the artboard. You may need to adjust their position once you drag them in your project.

6. Now hit Ctrl+Shift+B to rebuild the application and switch back to Visual Studio 2010, reloading if asked.

7. Go into the `SaveImg()` `EventHandler` and change `ImgHolder` to `ImgHolderParent` (see my code in bold):

```
private void SaveTheImg()
{
    _bitmap = new WriteableBitmap(ImgHolderParent, null);
    SaveFileDialog sfd = new SaveFileDialog();
    sfd.Filter = "PNG Files (*.png)|*.png|All Files (*.*)|*.*";
    sfd.DefaultExt = ".png";
    sfd.FilterIndex = 1;

    if ((bool)sfd.ShowDialog())
    {
        using (Stream fs = sfd.OpenFile())
        {
        int width = _bitmap.PixelWidth;
        int height = _bitmap.PixelHeight;

        EditableImage ei = new EditableImage(width, height);
```

```
    for (int i = 0; i < height; i++)
    {
        for (int j = 0; j < width; j++)
        {
            int pixel = _bitmap.Pixels[(i * width) + j];
            ei.SetPixel(j, i,
                (byte)((pixel >> 16) & 0xFF),
                (byte)((pixel >> 8) & 0xFF),
                    (byte)(pixel & 0xFF),
                (byte)((pixel >> 24) & 0xFF)
            );
        }
    }
    Stream png = ei.GetStream();
    int len = (int)png.Length;
    byte[] bytes = new byte[len];
    png.Read(bytes, 0, len);
    fs.Write(bytes, 0, len);
    }
  }
}
```

Now press F5 to run the application, start the webcam, take a snapshot, drag the hat and sunglasses onto your head in the snapshot—*not* the live video feed—and click the Save the Image button. You will see, as you can in Figure 14-18, that now the image is saved along with the draggable items.

You did it! You have successfully made a fun, interactive, webcam application that allows you to show your webcam stream, take snapshots, drag funny items onto your head, and even save the images. I have seen a ton of Silverlight 4 webcam apps that do a lot with snapshots, but this is the only one that I have seen thus far that actually lets you have a souvenir from playing with the application!

Figure 14-28. The image I saved from my application.

For an extra credit exercise I want you to make it so the video feed is the image that is saved. Also I want you to make it so the image saved contains the hat and glasses over the video feed. Hint, to do this you will need to add the video feed, hat, and glasses to a parent container. You then need to target this new parent container in your SaveTheImage method.

My project can be found at `http://windowspresentationfoundation.com/Blend4Book/Photo` `boothApp.zip`.

To see a video of the preceding exercise, you can go here: `http://www.windowspres` `entationfoundation.com/?p=211.` To see a video tutorial on how to use Joe Stegman's PNGEncoder go here: `http://www.windowspresentationfoundation.com/?p=406.`

Summary

In this chapter you learned about the new and very cool Webcam API. This allows you to view your webcam stream right inside your Silverlight 4 applications. You learned how to use the webcam API as well as how to use the `MouseElementDragBehavior` Behavior. You also learned how to take a snapshot from your webcam stream. You even learned how to import Joe Stegman's `PngEncoder` classes to save a `.png` from your Silverlight 4 applications. In the next chapter you learn all about Sketchflow Prototyping.

Chapter 15

MVVM: Model-View-ViewModel

Written by Bill Moore

What this chapter covers:

- MVVM Features in Silverlight 4
- Create your first MVVM application
- Project creation, structure, and the model
- The ViewModel
- MVVM and Blend
- MVVM Toolkits for Silverlight

The goal for this chapter is to provide an overview of MVVM and what new features in Blend 4 have been added to support developing applications using this software pattern. I first take a brief look at what a software pattern is and why it is useful. I then create a small sample application, leveraging the new project template and further clarifying the MVVM concept.

Overview

A *design pattern* refers to a reusable solution to a software design problem. Patterns have been used successfully in various industries for years. Applied to software, they enable us to apply tested development techniques to solve various problems that we encounter in software development. MVVM (which stands for Model-View-ViewModel) is one of those patterns; it separates what we see, the View, from how we get the data, our Model. The ViewModel is the glue that ties it all together.

History of MVVM

John Gossman, architect for Silverlight and WPF, came up with the MVVM pattern in 2005 as a way to leverage the Presentation Model (PM) pattern and apply it to the features in both WPF and Silverlight to simplify the creation of UIs. MVVM allows us to apply some basic UI patterns and take advantage of the great binding system in WPF and Silverlight. Microsoft is even using this pattern internally: Blend was created using MVVM, and the new version of Visual Studio. This separation allows for a much smoother workflow between designers and developers. The tooling coming out of Microsoft is starting to reflect this trend.

Read more on the Presentation Model at `http://martinfowler.com/eaaDev/PresentationModel.html`.

There are several benefits to using the MVVM development pattern:

Independent development: Development of the View and the Model can be done independently and tied together with the ViewModel at a later time.

Easier testing: Automated testing of the UI has always been rather difficult to perform and get right. Testing a ViewModel, which should contain all the interactions for a View, is easier because you are not dealing with any UI components.

Multiple UIs: You can create multiple Views that take advantage of the same ViewModel for displaying information in different ways or for different users.

Separation of responsibility: Everything is broken out and clearly defined. The View contains the Visuals for the application and consumes the ViewModel. The ViewModel glues the view and Model together. The Model contains all the interaction to retrieve and save data for the application.

Data Binding, DataTemplates, and Commanding

Data Binding allows us to bind properties from the ViewModel to our View. DataTemplates can be used to specify how items in a list should be viewed. Commanding can be used to wire up actions from your View to your ViewModel.

Blend 4 adds some great new features to support MVVM. These include a project specifically for creating an MVVM-type application (Figure 15-1).

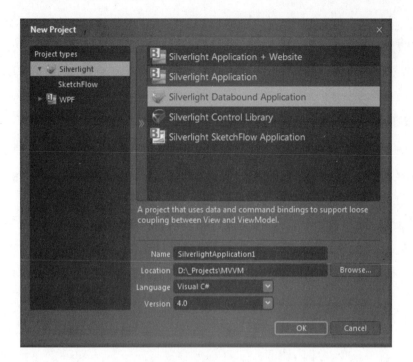

Figure 15-1. New project type in Blend supporting MVVM.

Model

What is the Model part? The *Model* represents the data that an application will use to populate the various views. It has the responsibility of getting the data from a web service, file system, or database. The Model also has the responsibility of presenting the data in a manner that is easily used by the ViewModel.

View

The *View* represents the UI portion of the pattern. The View binds to a ViewModel and displays the information for the user either to view or to edit. It represents the visual side of the Model. It defines all of your visual elements and bindings needed to tie our View and ViewModels together. You can also store any needed storyboards or animations in your View. It is common practice to set the DataContext of the View equal to an instance of your ViewModel. This can be done as a resource in XAML, or as a variable created in the code-behind. I have found it beneficial to have a 1:1 correspondence of View to ViewModel to begin with. If at a later date you need to change the visuals of your ViewModel, you can create a new View and take advantage of your existing ViewModel.

ViewModel

Finally, what is the *ViewModel*? The ViewModel glues everything together. The View consumes the ViewModel for Data Binding and command execution (event execution from the UI). The ViewModel also pushes data back to the Model for CRUD (Create, Read, Update, Delete) operations. The Model for this sample application will be created with sample data. The binding syntax in Silverlight allows us to tie the View and ViewModel together so that updates to the View are pushed to the Model without any extra coding we do this using two way bindings.

MVVM Features in Silverlight 4

One of the major new features in Silverlight 4 for MVVM is improved support for Commanding.

The interface for Commanding, ICommand, was first presented in Silverlight 3, but lacked any implementation out of the box. ICommand is found in the `System.Windows.Input` namespace. In Silverlight 4, a `command` property was added to `ButtonBase` and `Hyperlink` to enable you to hook your buttons up to your ViewModel. Here is what ICommand Interfaces look like:

```
Public interface ICommand
    {
        event EventHandler CanExecuteChanged;
        bool CanExecute(object parameter);
        void Execute(object parameter);
    }
```

Creating Your First MVVM Application in Blend 4

We are going to apply MVVM and the new template in Blend 4 to create our portion of the MVVM Masters Tracker application. Our project will display a list of users on one side and detailed information about each MVVM master on the other side. I cover the various aspects of the project template and create a working implementation of MVVM. I will point out the various pieces of MVVM as we progress and provide some more detailed explanation as we move forward. First let's go over the project template.

1. Open Blend 4.

2. Click **File ➤ New Project (Figure 15-2).**

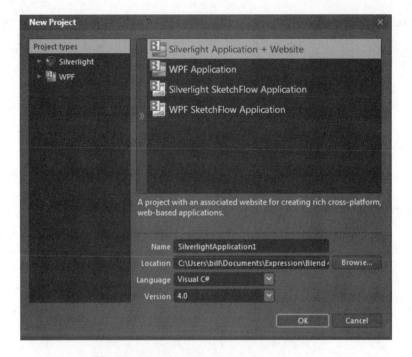

Figure 15-2. The New Project dialog box.

3. Select **Silverlight** as the Project type (Figure 15-3).

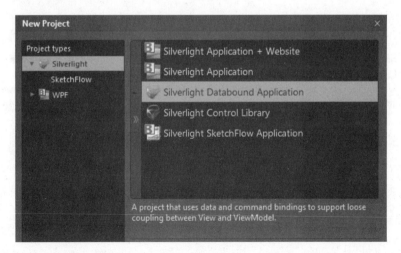

Figure 15-3. Select Silverlight as the project type.

4. Select **Silverlight Databound Application.** You can accept the default name for the application or name the Application MvvmApplication1, as I have.

5. Press **OK** to continue.

The solution should look like Figure 15-4:

Figure 15-4. Project structure.

Overview of the MVVM Template Project

The MVVM project includes the following examples files: `MainViewModelSampleData.xaml`, `MainViewModel.cs`, and `MainView.xaml`. `MainViewModelSampleData` contains sample data consumed by the `MainViewModel` and is presented to the `MainView` for display. These files are samples to get you started on your first MVVM application and are a good reference for understanding MVVM in general.

The first directory of note is the `SampleData` directory. This directory should contain any sample data that you create for the project. The template used to create this project contains one item called `MainViewModelSampleData.xaml`. This file contains the sample data used by the `MainView.xaml`.

Next is the `ViewModels` directory. Place any new ViewModels you create in here. This directory contains one sample file called `MainViewModel.cs`. This ViewModel will be bound to the `MainView`. Remember the ViewModel contains the information from the Model in a form that the View can bind to.

The final folder of interest is called `Views`. This folder contains `MainView.xaml`. This is the view that the user interacts with to view and manipulate information in our application. `MainPage.xaml` is the container application which contains our navigation and content area where the views will be loaded. `App.xaml` contains application level resources and app startup and shutdown events.

First I address the plumbing pieces of the application. We are going to use a combination of `SampleData` for design time support, and static data for display when we run the application. We will approach our MVVM application in the following order: create the `User` class, set up the Model, set up the ViewModel, set up the `SampleData`, and finally set up the View.

First up is the `User` class. This class will contain properties for the information we want to display, and implement `INotifyPropertyChanged`. `INotifyPropertyChanged` is an important interface that allows a class or object to participate in TwoWay Binding. *TwoWay Binding* means if we change the data displayed in the UI or the `User` object via some other means, it will update in both places. This saves a lot of plumbing code to keep the two values in sync.

More information on `INotifyPropertyChanged` can be found here:

```
http://msdn.microsoft.com/en-
us/library/system.componentmodel.inotifypropertychanged.aspx
```

Creating Supporting Objects

1. Right-click the project and select **Add New Folder** (Figure 15-5). Name the folder `BusinessObjects`.

Figure 15-5. Add New Folder.

2. Right-click the `BusinessObjects` folder and again add a new class item. Name it `User` (Figure 15-6).

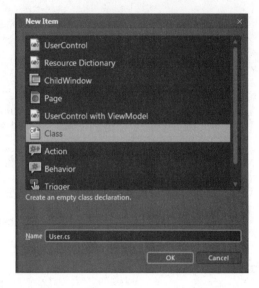

Figure 15-6. Add new class the name is `User`.

3. The `User.cs` file should open automatically; if it doesn't, double-click the file to open it.

4. Following is the code for the `User` object. Here we can see an implementation of the `INotifyPropertyChanged` interface. By implementing the interface we agree to provide code that implements the event.

```
public event  PropertyChangedEventHandler PropertyChanged;
```

What this event does is tell the binding system where to say, "Hey, notify me if you change any part of your object." We do this in the `NotifyPropertyChanged` event where we first check to see if we have any subscribers to be notified and then fire off the `EventHandler`.

```
        if (PropertyChanged != null)
        {
            PropertyChanged(this, new PropertyChangedEventArgs(info));
        }
```

Notice anytime we set a property we call our `NotifyPropertyChanged` event. Now anytime the properties of our object are changed, the UI will automatically update. We also need to add the following properties to our object: `Name`, `Active`, and `Birthday`.

Here is a complete listing of the code:

```
public class User : INotifyPropertyChanged
        {
            public User()
            {
```

```
            // Insert code required on object creation below this point.
        }
    private string _Name;
    public string Name
    {
        get { return _Name; }
        set
        {
            _Name = value;
            NotifyPropertyChanged("Name");
        }
    }
    private bool _Active;
    public bool Active
    {
        get { return _Active; }
        set
        {
            _Active = value;
            NotifyPropertyChanged("Active");
        }
    }
    private string _Birthday;
    public string Birthday
    {
        get { return _Birthday; }
        set
        {
            _Birthday = value;
            NotifyPropertyChanged("Birthday");
        }
    }


    public event PropertyChangedEventHandler PropertyChanged;
    private void NotifyPropertyChanged(String info)
    {
        if (PropertyChanged != null)
        {
            PropertyChanged(this, new PropertyChangedEventArgs(info));
        }
    }
    }
}
```

Add another new folder called Model. We will use this folder to supply sample data at runtime.

We can simulate getting data from some type of service by populating the model with some static data. We'll create a model class that will return an ObservableCollection of User objects.

What is an `ObservableCollection`? It is a list that implements the `INotifyPropertyChanged` under the hood. What does this do? Well, put simply it allows the collection to notify the UI anytime there are changes so that the UI can update the visual elements to reflect those changes. So anytime our list changes the UI will re-bind all the items in the list to our ItemsControl or ListBox.

> *You have to set the bindings to TwoWay if you want to receive updates from the source to the binding target.*

5. Right-click the `Model` folder and add a new Class Item (choose Add New Item ➤ TRA Class). Name the class `UserModel`. The `UserModel` class will provide some static data for runtime. The class is listed here:

```csharp
using System.Collections.ObjectModel;

    public class UserModel
      {
    public UserModel()
          {
                // Insert code required on object creation below this point.
          }
          public static ObservableCollection<User> GetUserList()
          {
List<User> _Users = new List<User>();
_Users.Add(new User() { Name = "Bill Moore", Birthday = "06/22/1978", Active = true
 });
_Users.Add(new User() { Name = "Victor Gad", Birthday = "10/22/1999", Active = true
 });
_Users.Add(new User() { Name = "Paul Gebo", Birthday = "08/15/1935", Active = true
 });
_Users.Add(new User() { Name = "Jason Rain", Birthday = "02/10/1979", Active = true
 });
_Users.Add(new User() { Name = "Thomas Train", Birthday = "05/19/1967", Active =
 true });
return _Users;
          }
      }
```

Setting Up the ViewModel

Open up the `MainViewModel.cs` by doubleclicking the file so we can make the modification to support our application. We need to discuss some of the important aspects of this code file. Listed here is the file in its unmodified state:

```csharp
using System;
using System.ComponentModel;
```

```
namespace MvvmApplication1
{
        public class MainViewModel : INotifyPropertyChanged
        {
            public MainViewModel()
            {
                // Insert code required on object creation below this point.
            }

            private string viewModelProperty = "Runtime Property Value";
/// <summary>
/// Sample ViewModel property; this property is used in the view to display its↵
 value using a Binding.
/// </summary>
/// <returns></returns>
            public string ViewModelProperty
            {
                get
                {
                    return this.viewModelProperty;
                }
                set
                {
                    this.viewModelProperty = value;
                    this.NotifyPropertyChanged("ViewModelProperty");
                }
            }
            /// <summary>
/// Sample ViewModel method; this method is invoked by a Behavior that is↵
 associated with it in the View.
/// </summary>
            public void ViewModelMethod()
            {
if(!this.ViewModelProperty.EndsWith("Updated Value", StringComparison.Ordinal))
                {
                    this.ViewModelProperty = this.ViewModelProperty + " -↵
 Updated Value";
                }
            }
            #region INotifyPropertyChanged
            public event PropertyChangedEventHandler PropertyChanged;
            private void NotifyPropertyChanged(String info)
            {
                if (PropertyChanged != null)
                {
                    PropertyChanged(this, new PropertyChangedEventArgs(info));
                }
            }
```

```
        #endregion
    }
}
```

We want to modify the code so it looks like the class that follows. To accomplish this, all we need to do is remove some of the sample code and add a Collection of Users. We modified the constructor to supply data when you run the application.

```
public class MainViewModel : INotifyPropertyChanged
    {
        private List<User> _Users = new List<User>();
        public List<User> Users
        {
            get { return _Users; }
            set
            {
                _Users = value;
            }
        }
        public MainViewModel()
        {
            // Insert code required on object creation below this point.
            _Users = UserModel.GetUserList();
        }
}

        #region INotifyPropertyChanged
        public event PropertyChangedEventHandler PropertyChanged;
        private void NotifyPropertyChanged(String info)
        {
            if (PropertyChanged != null)
            {
                PropertyChanged(this, new PropertyChangedEventArgs(info));
            }
        }
    }
    #endregion
}
```

Setting Up the Sample Data Source

1. Double-click MainView.xaml and then select the **Data** tab. By default, it is next to the **Properties** and **Resources** tabs on the right-hand side (Figure 15-7).

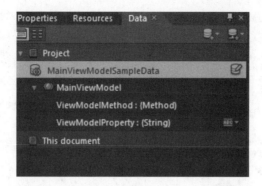

Figure 15-7. The Data tab.

2. Right-click the `MainViewModelSampleData` Source and select "**Delete data source.**"

3. Make sure your project builds by pressing Ctrl+Shift+B.

4. Select Project and click the Create Sample Data button.

5. Select Create Sample Data from Class (Figure 15-8).

Figure 15-8. Select project ➤ Create Sample Data button ➤   Create Sample Data from Class.

6. In the dialog box for **Data Source Name**, type **MainViewModelSampleData**. In the **Select Class** search box, type **MainViewModel**. Select the `MainViewModel` class under `MVVMApplication1` (Figure 15-9). Click **OK**.

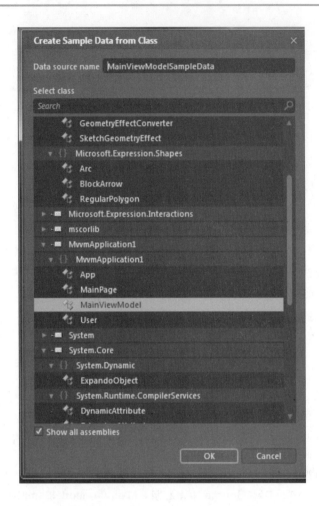

Figure 15-9. Select the `MainViewModel`.

Now the Data tab should look like Figure 15-10.

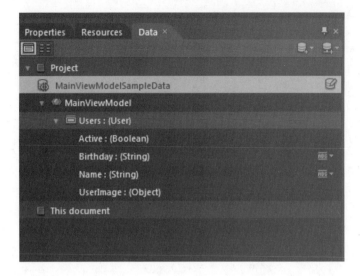

Figure 15-10. The Data tab.

   7.   Select the icon next to Birthday and change the **Format** to Date (Figure 15-11).

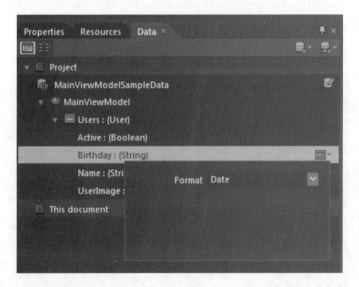

Figure 15-11. Set the Birthday Format to Date.

   8.   Set the **Format** for Name to Name (Figure 15-12).

Figure 15-12. Set the Format for Name to Name.

Setting Up the View

Now we need to setup our View. We are going to have a little fun with this View and use the `pathlistbox`.

1. Delete the `TextBlock` and `Button` from the `LayoutRoot`.

2. Divide the Grid into two `Columns` (see Figure 15-13).

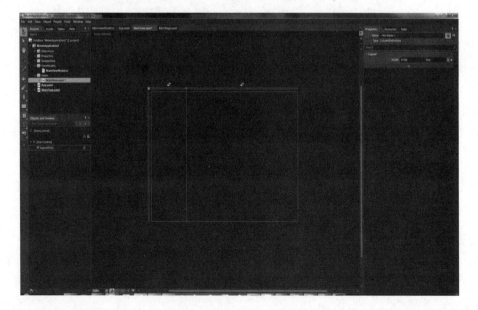

Figure 15-13. Divide the Grid into two `Columns`.

3. Let's use the `PathListBox`. Create a Path in the first `Column` using the Pen or Shape tool. It can be any type of Path that you want. See Figure 15-14.

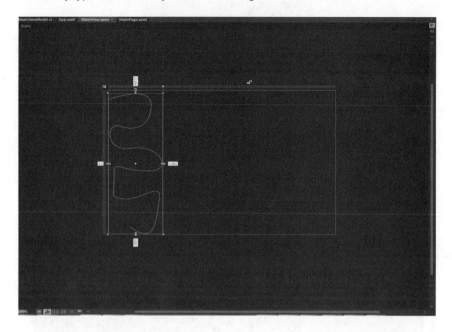

Figure 15-14. Add a Path to the first `Column`.

4. Set the Path opacity to 0%. Add a `PathListBox` (Figure 15-15). It doesn't matter where you place it. You can place it in the second `Column` near the bottom so it's out of the way.

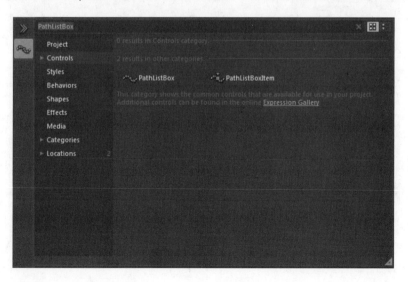

Figure 15-15. Selecting the `PathListBox`.

357

5. Set the Foreground color for the `PathListBox` to black (Figure 15-16).

Figure 15-16. Make the foreground black.

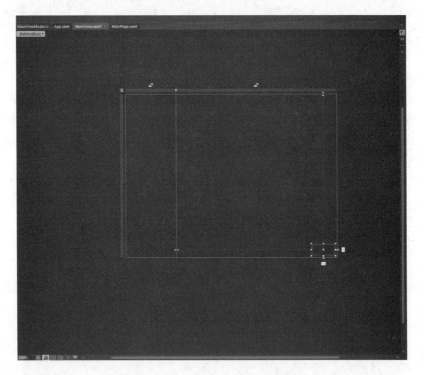

Figure 15-17. Placing the `PathListBox`.

Remember, the location of the `PathListBox` doesn't matter. The items in the `ListBox` will be rendered along the Path that we select in next step.

6. Assign the Path created to the `PathListBox` using the Layout Paths property panel (Figure 15-18).

Figure 15-18. Using the `LayoutPaths` panel.

7. Select the circle reticule. Then select the Path we created in the **Object and Timelines** panel (Figure 15-19).

Figure 15-19. Select the path as the Layout Path for the `PathListBox`.

8. Rename the `PathListBox` to `UserList`.

9. Switch to the Data tab. Select the `MainViewModel` and drag it over to the `LayoutRoot`. This will bind the `DataContext` of `LayoutRoot` to the `MainViewModel` (Figure 15-20).

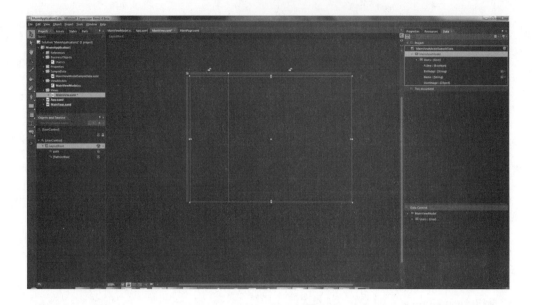

Figure 15-20. Bind the `DataContext` of `LayoutRoot` to the `MainViewModel`.

10. Using the Data Context window, select the `User`'s chevron. Drag Name onto the `PathListBox` (`Figure 15-21`). Adjust the Grid `Column` to fit the content. You may also want to set the `Capacity` on the `PathListBox` to 8 instead of the default 10.

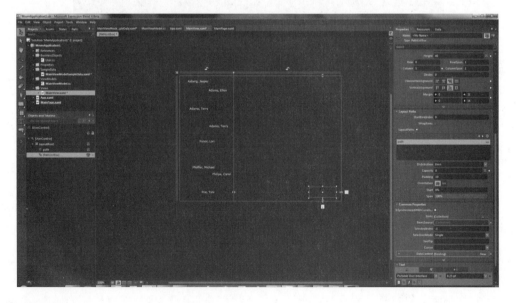

Figure 15-21. Binding the `PathListBox` to Name.

11. Drag a new Canvas onto the second `Column` (`Figure 15-22`). Name it `detailsCanvas`.

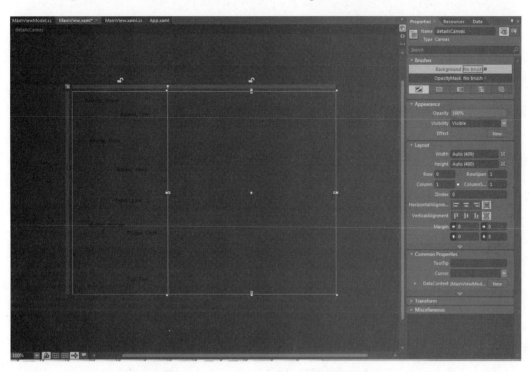

Figure 15-22. Add another Canvas control to the second `Column`.

12. We need to add another property to our `MainViewModel` that will hold the `SelectedUser` from the `PathListBox`. Notice the call to `NotifyPropertyChanged`. This allows the binding system to automatically update our fields every time the `SelectedUser` property is changed. Add the code just below the class declaration.

```
public partial class MainView : UserControl
{
        private User _selectedUser;
        public User SelectedUser
        {
                get {return _selectedUser;}
                set {_selectedUser = value;
                        NotifyPropertyChanged("SelectedUser");
                }
        }

        public MainView()
        {
                // Required to initialize variables
```

```
                    InitializeComponent();
         }
```

13. We need to create a ViewModel that will be used by our View. Add this code right under the class declaration.

```
MainViewModel _viewmodel = new MainViewModel();
```

Here is the new code in context:

```
public partial class MainView : UserControl
{
        MainViewModel _viewmodel = new MainViewModel();

        private User _selectedUser;
        public User SelectedUser
        {
                get {return _selectedUser;}
                set {_selectedUser = value;
                        NotifyPropertyChanged("SelectedUser");
                }
        }


        public MainView()
        {
                // Required to initialize variables
                InitializeComponent();
        }
```

14. Click the `MainView.xaml` tab. Then select `LayoutRoot` in the **Objects and Timeline** panel. Click the **Advanced Options** button next to `DataContext`. Then go to **Reset**. This will remove the `DataContext` for `LayoutRoot`. We are setting the `DataContext` in the code.

We need to wire up some events in our `MainView`. To do this we will need to open up the `MainView.xaml.cs` file. Find this file in the **Project** panel and double-click to open it. We will add the following line at the bottom of the constructor. This will allow us to handle the event when someone selects a `User` from our list.

```
UserList.SelectionChanged += new SelectionChangedEventHandler↵
(UserList_SelectionChanged);
```

15. The new constructor for `MainView.xaml.cs` should look like the one here.

```
        public MainView()
        {
                // Required to initialize variables
        InitializeComponent();
        UserList.SelectionChanged += new
```

```
SelectionChangedEventHandler(UserList_SelectionChanged);
}
```

16. Set the `DataContext` to the instance of our ViewModel we just created. We will add this line to the bottom of our constructor. Setting the `DataContext` tells our View where to pull the data from. All the bindings we set up in the View are properties or collections of our ViewModel. Once we set the `DataContext` to an instance of our ViewModel, we will see our user data appear if our bindings are correct.

```
this.DataContext = _viewmodel;
```

The constructor should look like this now.

```
public MainView()
{
        // Required to initialize variables
InitializeComponent();
UserList.SelectionChanged += new
SelectionChangedEventHandler(UserList_SelectionChanged);
this.DataContext = _viewmodel;
}
```

17. When the user selects an item from our `PathListBox` we need to update the Selected User field in our ViewModel. The code that follows first checks to see if we have something selected. The code should always have something selected, but we want to err on the side of caution. It then sets the `SelectedUser` property in our ViewModel to the currently selected item.

```
private void UserList_SelectionChanged(object sender,Controls↵
.SelectionChangedEventArgs e)
{
        // TODO: Add event handler implementation here.
        if (UserList.SelectedItem != null)
        {
        _model.SelectedUser = UserList.SelectedItem as User;
        }

    }
```

18. Select `detailsCanvas` in the **Objects and Timeline** panel. Find the `DataContext` property and click the **Advanced Options** button. Then select the DataContext tab.

19. Click the dropdown for `MainViewModel`. Then pick the `SelectedUsers` property. See Figure 15-23.

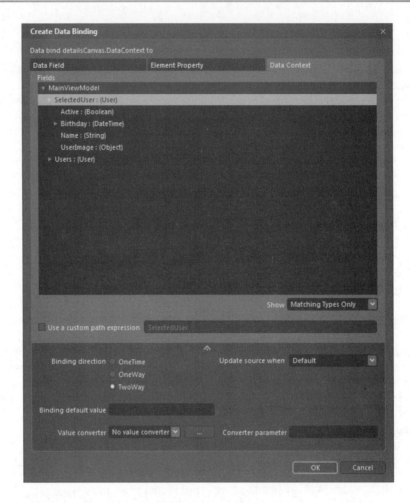

Figure 15-23. Set the `DataContext` of the Canvas to `SelectedUser`.

20. Add a `CheckBox` for `Active`. Name it `chkActive` and for its `Content` property set it to `Active`. The `IsChecked` property should be bound to the `Active` field of our `User` object. See Figure 15-24.

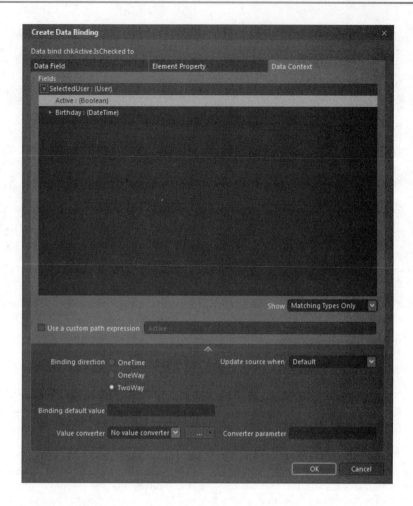

Figure 15-24. `IsChecked` should be bound to the `Active` property of `SelectedUser`.

21. Add a `TextBlock` beneath `Active` and set its `Content` to `Name`. Add a `TextBox` and bind the `Text` property to the `Name` field of our `SelectedUser`.

22. Add another `TextBlock` and set its `Content` to `Birthday`. Add a `DatePicker` next to it and bind the `SelectedDate` to the `Birthday` field of the `SelectedUser`. See Figure 15-25.

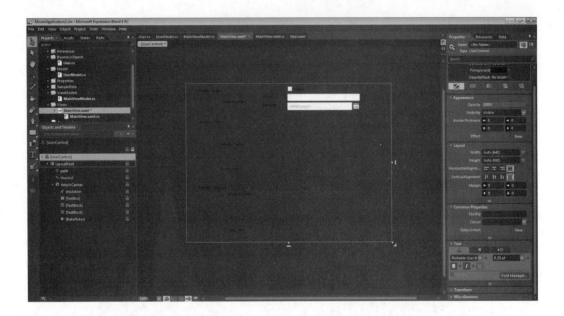

Figure 15-25. The final look for our View.

Assuming you have done everything correctly, when you run the application you should see a list of Users, and as you select the Users the detail form will populate.

This sample shows how to create a basic application and how to apply the MVVM pattern. We created a list of Users in our Sample Model class. We then took that list into our ViewModel and bound to it in our View.

One question that may come up is: what use is the ViewModel? It looks like it just passes the data along. This is true in this simple situation, but in more complicated projects the ViewModel may combine multiple Models together and expose them to a View. Every piece of the pattern plays an important role.

MVVM Toolkits and Frameworks for Silverlight

Let's talk about some of the MVVM toolkits, and new technologies in .NET 4.0 that can be used in conjunction with the MVVM pattern for even more extensibility. Following is a list of MVVM toolkits and tools that support and provide functionality for using MVVM in your application. MEF is mentioned in this list for its composition capabilities. With MEF, new in .NET 4.0, you can have MEF supply your Views at runtime. The tool with the best support for Blend is the MVVM Light Toolkit. More information can be found with the links provided.

- *MVVM Light Toolkit:* This open source project provides some features to help designers adopt MVVM. The toolkit includes a Messenger class, Commanding implementation, and many more features.

    Also as of the writing this is the most Blend-friendly MVVM toolkit.

http:// mvvmlight.codeplex.com

- *Caliburn Micro:* Another open source project. This one was born from a talk at MIX called "Build Your Own MVVM Framework." Extremely lightweight with some great features, including automatically wiring up your View and ViewModels. It also includes automatic event wiring.

http://caliburnmicro.codeplex.com

- *MEF:* This stands for *Management Extensibility Framework.* This framework allows you to add extensibility and plug-in support to your application.

http://msdn.microsoft.com/en-us/library/dd460648.aspx

Summary

MVVM is great once you wrap your head around it. You can create different views based on customer demand while leveraging your existing ViewModels. It lets you take advantage of binding and helps you separate out the various pieces of your application.

Chapter 16

SketchFlow Prototyping

What this chapter covers:

- Creating a SketchFlow prototype

A very innovative feature to Blend and Silverlight 4 is SketchFlow prototyping. There are three major goals of SketchFlow prototyping:

- Quickly experimenting with a dynamic UI
- Communicating design intent
- Delivering compelling proposals to clients quickly and cost-effectively

SketchFlow prototyping is a way for you to create an interactive version of an application that is meant to demonstrate the intended interaction, design intent, and screenflow. This SketchFlow prototype can then be delivered to the client for immediate feedback that can be integrated directly into the prototype and seen by the developer. This prototype can be made very quickly and easily in Blend 4 and thus is cost-effective. This prototype is then used by the designers and developers as a roadmap for the application. Further, assets and/or functionality created in the prototype can be used in the actual application. To better illustrate what SketchFlow prototyping is, I lead you through an exercise that will show you how to build an application prototype. With that, let's fire up Blend 4 and create a new SketchFlow prototype for a web application for a shopping web site.

Create the Project

1. Open Blend.

2. Click **File ➤ New Project.**

3. Select **Silverlight SketchFlow Application.**

- Name the project ShoppingSketchflow, as I have done in Figure 16-1.

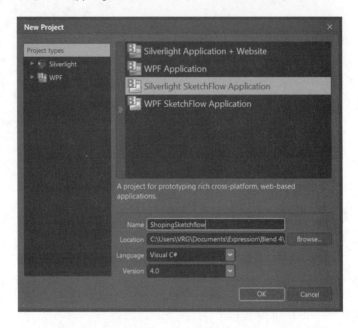

Figure 16-1. Create a new SketchFlow application in Blend.

Notice at the bottom of Blend next to the **Results** panel you see a new panel called **SketchFlow Map** (see Figure 16-2). If you don't see this panel, you can click **Window ➤ SketchFlow Map**. This panel is a visual representation of your SketchFlow application and shows you how a user would work their way through your application. When you add a new Screen (we will do this soon), you will see a new blue tile appear that represents your new Screen.

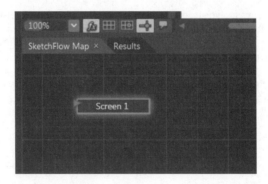

Figure 16-2. The SketchFlow Map.

Setting Up the SketchFlow Structure

1. Double-click the `Screen1` tile in the SketchFlow Map and rename it `Homepage`. You will see that `Screen1` will be renamed in your **Project** panel as well.

2. Hold your mouse cursor over `Homepage` in **SketchFlow Map** until you see a drawer slide out. When it does, place your mouse cursor over the farthest left icon. This icon is the "Create a connected screen" icon shown in Figure 16-3. Click and drag this to create a new Screen connected to the `Homepage`.

Figure 16-3. The "Create a new screen" icon.

3. Once you create a new Screen (see Figure 16-4), you can name it `ShopForBooks`.

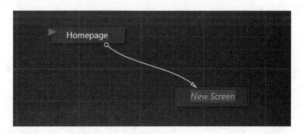

Figure 16-4. Drag out a new Screen.

4. Repeat this and name the new Screen `ShopForMusic`.

5. Repeat this and name the new Screen `ShopForMovies` so that your SketchFlow Map looks like what I have in Figure 16-5.

Figure 16-5. You should now have for Screens in your SketchFlow application.

    6.   Now draw a new Screen from `ShopForMovies` called `CheckOut`.

    7.   Hold your mouse over `ShopForMusic` until the drawer slides out and place your mouse cursor over the icon that is second from the left. This is the "Connect an existing screen" icon shown in Figure 16-6. Drag this to the `Checkout` Screen so that it too is now connected to `Checkout`.

Figure 16-6. The "Connect to an existing screen" icon.

    8.   Repeat the last step so that `ShopForBooks`, `ShopForMovies`, and `ShopForMusic` are all connected to `Checkout`, as in Figure 16-7.

Figure 16-7. Your SketchFlow Map should now look like this.

Adding the Visuals

Now that we have the structure of the SketchFlow down, it is time to start adding some visuals. SketchFlow applications are meant to be design-less, but we still need something to convey the idea of what the final application will do. For this reason, we keep our visuals very simple and without final design. We are going to start off with a `TextBlock` on each page saying what that page is. We are going to use a `BasicTextBlock-Sketch` Style for our `TextBlock`. Double-click the `Homepage` Screen to start editing it and you can then click the Asset Library and type **Sketch** to find the `BasicTextBlock-Sketch` Style, as I am doing in Figure 16-8.

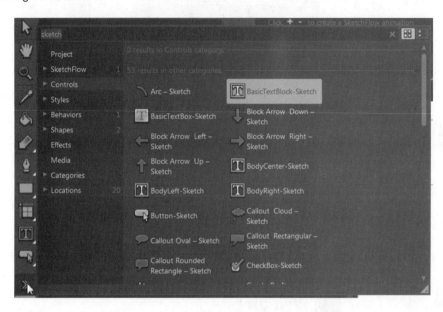

Figure 16-8. Locate the `BasicTextBlock-Sketch` Style in the Asset Library.

1. With this new Style selected, draw a `TextBlock` out on the `Homepage` Screen, as I have done in Figure 16-9.

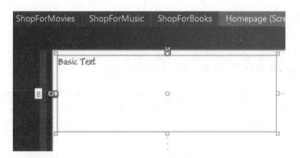

Figure 16-9. Draw a `TextBlock` out on the `Homepage` screen.

You can easily navigate to any of the screens by double-clicking it in the SketchFlow Map.

2. Change the Text to read *Welcome*.

3. With the `TextBlock` still selected, go to the **Text** bucket of the **Properties** panel and change the font size to 36, as I am doing in Figure 16-10.

Figure 16-10. Change the font size to 36.

You should now have something like I have in Figure 16-11.

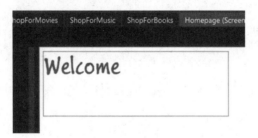

Figure 16-11. Your `Homepage` should now look like this.

4. Now with the `TextBlock` still selected press Control+C to copy it and paste in a `TextBlock` for each page and change the text to the corresponding page. For example, the `ShopForBooks` `TextBlock` should read *Shop for Books*, and so on.

5. Now go to the `Homepage` and add suitable images (I found mine on the internet) for a book, a musical note, and a movie camera to give the idea that the `Homepage` will have visual indicators of what can be found inside this site. You can see my homepage in Figure 16-12.

You can easily right-click an image in your web browser and left-click copy and switch over to Blend and hit Control+V to paste that image right onto the artboard.

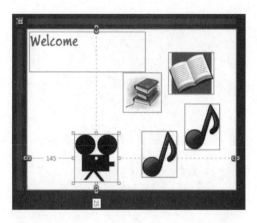

Figure 16-12. Copy images from the Internet into your `Homepage` Screen.

> To find images like I have in Figure 16-11, Google **movie camera** and then click the Images link. This lets you to find a large variety of different iconography to use in your SketchFlow application. Remember that this is just a mock-up, so none of the art will be final.

6. Now Copy and paste the movie camera in the `ShopForMovies` Screen.

7. Copy and paste the musical note image into the `ShopForMusic` screen.

8. Copy and paste the books image into the `ShopForBooks` screen.

Now that you have set up the visuals for all of your Screens, you can move on and make a navigation Component Screen.

Creating a Navigation Component Screen

Now that we have all the Screens set up, and they all have some visuals, we need a way for users of your SketchFlow application to get from one Screen to the next. We can do this quickly and easily by adding a Component Screen. Let's do that now.

1. Click the Asset Library and type **Sketch** again (if it's not still there from the last time) and locate the `Button-Sketch`, as I am doing in Figure 16-13.

Figure 16-13. Locate the `Button-Sketch` in the Asset Library.

2. On the `Homepage` draw a `Button` for each page and label it, as I have done in Figure 16-14.

Figure 16-14. Draw `Buttons` for each of the Screens in the SketchFlow application.

3. Hold down Control and click each of the `Buttons` so they are all selected.

4. Right-click and left-click **Make Into Component Screen**, as I am doing in Figure 16-15.

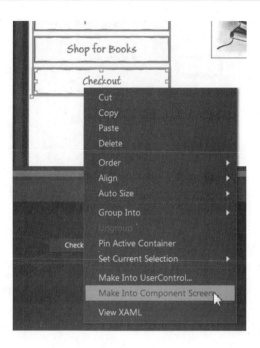

Figure 16-15. Turn the `Buttons` into a Component Screen.

    5. When the **Make Into Component Screen** dialog box appears, name it `Nav` and click **OK**, as I am doing in Figure 16-16.

Figure 16-16. Name the Component Screen `Nav`.

    6. When Blend creates the `Nav` Component Screen for you, right-click `Homepage` and click **Navigate To ➤ Homepage**, as I am doing in Figure 16-17.

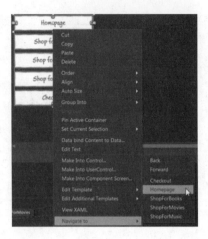

Figure 16-17. Make the `Homepage Button` navigate to the Homepage Screen.

7. Repeat this for each button—for example, the `ShopForMusic Button` should navigate to the `ShopForMusic` Screen, and so on.

Connecting to the Nav Component Screen

If you look at your Navigation Map you will see there is now a green tile for `Nav`. It is green to represent the fact that it is a Component Screen and not a regular screen, which is blue. You can see that the Component Screen has blue arrows, meaning that you can get to any of the Screens from the Component Screen—but notice that only one screen, the `Homepage` Screen, has a green line coming from the Component Screen. This is because all the other Screens don't have the `Nav` Component Screen on them. We need to change this now:

Hold your mouse cursor over the `Nav` Component Screen until its drawer slides out and place ther cursor over the third icon from the left (shown in Figure 16-18). This is the "Insert a Component screen" icon. Click and draw a connection to each of the existing screens (except the `Homepage` Screen, which is already connected).

Figure 16-18. The "Insert a Component screen" icon.

Your SketchFlow Map should now look like what I have in Figure 16-19.

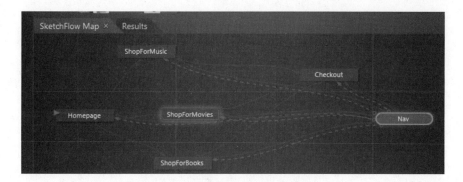

Figure 16-19. Your `Nav` Component Screen should now have green lines to each of the Screens.

If you look at each of the pages you will see they do in fact have the `Nav` Component Screen on them. They need to be positioned so that they are directly under the `TextBlock` for the page. Adjust each page's `Nav` Component Screen now. Once you have done that, press F5 to compile and run the application and use the navigation Component Screen to move around the different pages. Pretty cool!

Adding Some Interaction to the Pages

We now have the start of an interactive SketchFlow application. Next we need to add some content to one of the pages. I figure we will start with the `ShopForMusic` page. On this page we are going to add a mock-up song that shoppers can purchase. When they do purchase the song, we are going to use the Visual State Manager to show a dialog box that thanks the shopper for purchasing the song. They then have the option of going to the `Checkout` page or to continue shopping. Let's add that functionality now:

1. Go to the `ShopForMusic` page by double-clicking it in the SketchFlow Map.

2. Add another note image (I found mine on the Internet) .

3. Add some Sketch `TextBlocks` for a fake song and a fake artist.

4. Add a fake price `TextBlock`.

5. Add a Sketch `Button` that reads *Buy Now*, as I have done in Figure 16-20.

Figure 16-20. Add a fake song to the `ShopForMusic` page.

6. Next draw a `Rectangle` out for what is to be the background for the dialog box.

7. Add text that thanks the shopper for the purchase and a couple of `Buttons` that give them the option to continue shopping or to check out, as I have done in Figure 16-21.

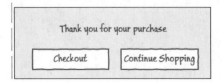

Figure 16-21. Add a fake dialog box to the `ShopForMusic` Screen.

8. Press and hold Control and click all the elements that make up the fake dialog box in the **Objects and Timeline** panel, as I have done in Figure 16-22.

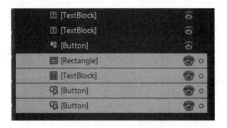

Figure 16-22. Select the objects that make up the fake dialog box in the Objects and Timeline panel.

9. Next right-click the objects in the **Objects and Timeline** panel and left-click **Group Into ➤ Grid**, as I am doing in Figure 16-23.

Figure 16-23. Group the dialog box objects into a Grid.

10. Rename the dialog box Grid `DialogBox`.

11. With the `DialogBox` Grid still selected, change the Opacity to 0% in the **Appearance** bucket of the **Properties** panel, as I have done in Figure 16-24. Then in the Common Properties bucket uncheck `IsHitTestVisible`. This will make the dialog box invisible and not able to be clicked. This is the default state of the dialog box.

> In addition to giving the `DialogBox` Grid an Opacity of 0% we also set its `IsHitTestVisible` property to false. We do this so that when the `DialogBox` is not showing it doesn't interfere with other objects in the application.

Figure 16-24. Change the Opacity of the `DialogBox` Grid to 0%.

Adding the Visual State Group

Now that the fake dialog box is no longer visible or hittest visible, we can go ahead and add the Visual State Group to make it visible and able to be clicked when the user clicks the Buy Now `Button`; this is common functionality in many shopping applications.

1. In the **States** panel click the "Add state group" button, as I am doing in Figure 16-25.

Figure 16-25. Add a new State Group.

2. Name the new Visual State Group `ShowHideDialogBox` and give it a default transition time of 0.2 seconds.

3. Click the "Add state" icon, as I am doing in Figure 16-26.

Figure 16-26. Add a visual State.

4. Name the new State `HideDialog`.

5. Add another State called `ShowDialog`.

6. Set the Opacity on the `DialogBox` Grid to 100% in the **Appearance** bucket of the **Properties** panel and check the `IsHitTestVisible` property in the Common Properties bucket. This will allow the `DialogBox` to be clicked once again.

7. Click on the Base State so that you are no longer recording any Visual States, as I have done in Figure 16-27.

Figure 16-27. Click the Base State to stop recording.

Hooking the Visual States Up

Now we have the Visual States we need to actually hook them up to do something. Specifically, we want the Buy Now buttons to activate the `ShowDialog` state so that the `DialogBox` will appear and be able to be clicked.

1. Right-click the Buy Now `Button` and left-click **Activate State ➤ ShopForMusic / ShowDialog**, as I am doing in Figure 16-28.

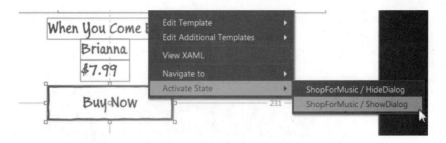

Figure 16-28. Hook the Buy Now `Button` up to the `ShowDialog` State.

2. Change the Opacity of the `DialogBox` Grid to 100% so we can see it to work on it. We will change its default state back to 0% Opacity before we run the application.

At this point we have the `DialogBox` Grid appearing when we click the Buy Now `Button`. We also need to make the `DialogBox` disappear when the user clicks the Continue Shopping `Button` in the `DialogBox` or navigate to the `Checkout` Screen if the user clicks the Checkout `Button` also contained in the `DialogBox` Grid. Let's do that now!

1. Right-click the Checkout `Button` and left-click on **Navigate to ➤ Checkout**, as I am doing in Figure 16-29.

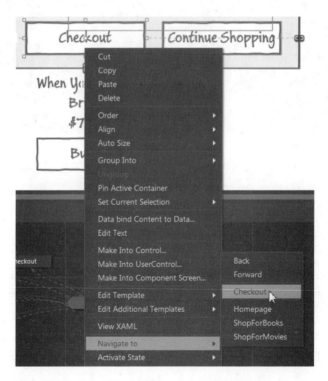

Figure 16-29. Have the Checkout `Button` navigate to the Checkout Screen.

2. Right-click the Continue Shopping `Button` and left-click on **Activate State ➤ ShopForMusic / HideDialog**, as I am doing in Figure 16-30. This will make the `DialogBox` Grid disappear when the user clicks Continue Shopping.

Figure 16-30. Have the Continue Shopping `Button` activate the `HideDialog` State.

3. Change the `DialogBox` Grid Opacity back to 0%.

Now press F5 to run the application and navigate to the Shop for Music page and click the Buy Now `Button`. Notice how your dialog box appears. If you click Continue Shopping it will just disappear but if you click Checkout it will actually navigate to the Checkout Screen. Pretty cool, huh? So, now you have an interactive SketchFlow application that has different screens and even a partially functional Shop for Music Screen. I challenge you to go ahead and add a fake Movie to the Shop for Movies page, and a fake Book to the Shop for Books page. And then add an interactive dialog box like we added to the Shop for Music Screen.

The SketchFlow Player and Feedback

The SketchFlow Player shown in Figure 16-31 is what the users see when they run your SketchFlow application. It is here that they can navigate the different Screens. They can also make annotations to give you, the developer, feedback on the application. To show you better, let's add some annotations that we can then load up and view as the developer.

Figure 16-31. The SketchFlow Player in the browser.

1. Press F5 to run the application.

2. Click the `ShopForMovies` Screen, as I am doing in Figure 16-32.

Figure 16-32. Click the `ShopForMovies` Screen.

3. Click the Enable Ink Feedback icon, as I am doing in Figure 16-33.

Figure 16-33. Click the Enable Link Feedback icon.

4. Draw a circle with an X, as I have done in Figure 16-34.

Figure 16-34. Draw a circle with an X.

5. Click the feedback area and type a message to the developer, as I have done in Figure 16-35.

Figure 16-35. Type a message to the developer.

6. Click the Feedback Options icon and click **Export Feedback**, as I am doing in Figure 16-36.

Figure 16-36. Export the Feedback.

7. Enter your name in the Feedback Author Information dialog box, as I have done in Figure 16-37 and click **OK**.

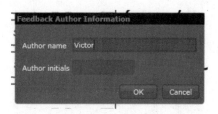

Figure 16-37. Enter your name in the Feedback dialog box.

8. Give the Feedback a name of `MyFeedBack`, as I have done in Figure 16-38, and click OK.

Figure 16-38. Give the Feedback a name of `MyFeedback`.

9. Switch back to Blend and click **Window ➤ SketchFlow** Feedback, as I am doing in Figure 16-39.

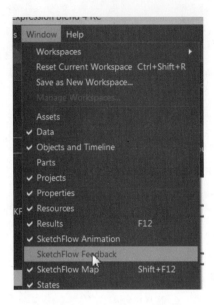

Figure 16-39. Show the SketchFlow Feedback.

> **10.** When the **SketchFlow Feedback** panel appears, click the Add Feedback icon, as I am doing in Figure 16-40.

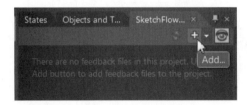

Figure 16-40. Add Feedback.

> **11.** You can then see the Feedback that you entered when you were viewing the site in the browser (see Figure 16-41).

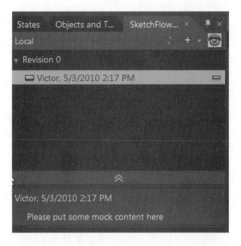

Figure 16-41. You can see the feedback you entered earlier in the browser.

Moreover, the developer can see the ink revisions made by the client (see Figure 16-42).

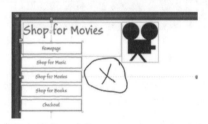

Figure 16-42. The developer can see the ink notations from the client right in Blend.

As you can see, this is a feature that will quickly help the client and the developer communicate changes that should be made to the SketchFlow application.

Word Documentation

Once your SketchFlow is complete, and all the Screens are signed off on, then it is time to build the real application. SketchFlow has a very handy feature whereby you can create a document that will serve as the development guide to the team that is going to build the real application. Let's go ahead and create the documentation for our SketchFlow application.

1. Go to **File ➤ Export to Microsoft Word**, as I am doing in Figure 16-43.

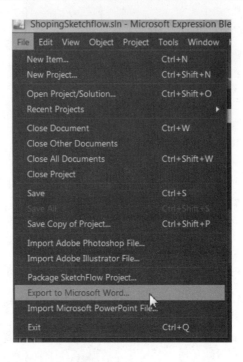

Figure 16-43. Export the SketchFlow application to Word.

2. When the **Export to Word** dialog box appears, check "**Include feedback**" and "**Open document when complete**," as I have done in Figure 16-44, and click **OK**.

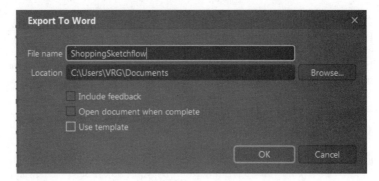

Figure 16-44. These are the settings for your Export to Word dialog box.

When the Word document opens (see Figure 16-45) you will see that there is a very thorough document that tells you about all of the different Screens, the Visual States, a SketchFlow Map, and even the Feedback we entered earlier. This is not exactly as complete as a wireframe document that is given to developers before they are about to build a piece of software, but it is an amazingly wonderful start.

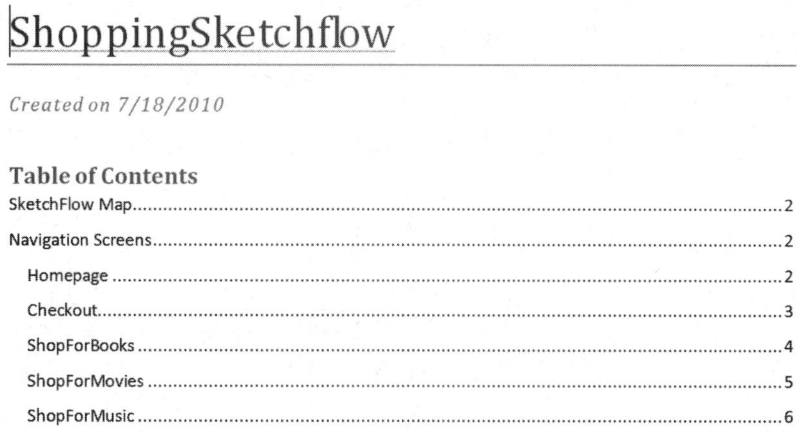

ShoppingSketchflow

Created on 7/18/2010

Table of Contents

SketchFlow Map..2

Navigation Screens....................................2

Homepage..2

Checkout..3

ShopForBooks..4

ShopForMovies...5

ShopForMusic..6

Figure 16-45. The SketchFlow Word document,

My project can be found on the download page on the Friends of ED web site, and here: `http://windowspresentationfoundation.com/Blend4Book/ShopingSketchflow.zip`

My SketchFlow Word document, from Figure 16-45, can be found here: `http://windowspresentationfoundation.com/Blend4Book/ShopingSketchflow.doc`. To watch a video tutorial on how to create a Sketchflow Prototype application navigate to: `http://www.windowspresentationfoundation.com/?p=116`.

Summary

In this chapter you learned about SketchFlow Prototyping and why it is used. You then made your own SketchFlow application complete with different Screens, a Component Screen, and even a Visual State Group to show and hide a fake dialog box. You then learned how easy it is to give feedback as a client and then load that feedback right into Blend as a developer. Finally, you learned how to easily create a Word document from your SketchFlow application that can be used as the basis for wireframes to help developers actually develop your SketchFlow into a real piece of software. In the next chapter I talk about some of the new features in Silverlight 4 that I haven't covered yet.

Chapter 17

New Features of Silverlight 4

What this chapter covers:

- Mouse wheel Support and right-click handling
- The Printing API
- ICommand support
- `RichTextArea`
- Clipboard API
- Network authentication
- Improved Data Binding
- `ViewBox`
- Keyboard access in Full-screen mode
- Google Chrome support
- Right-to-left support
- Managed Extensibility Framework
- Offline DRM
- Fluid UI support
- Cross-Domain networking made easier
- Text trimming

In this book I have thus far covered many new features of Silverlight 4. Some of the features we have covered up until now are the COM API, Out-Of-Browser Experience, and the Webcam API, among others. However, this is just a fraction of the numerous new features of Silverlight 4. For this reason I wanted to dedicate a chapter to at least mention *all* of the new features of Silverlight 4. In this chapter I talk about all the new features of Silverlight 4 that I haven't mentioned yet. I go over some of these features in depth, while just touching upon other, less important features. Let's start off with the newly added mouse wheel and right-click support.

Right-click and Mouse Wheel Support

In the last version of Silverlight you had to depend on helper classes to allow the user to make use of the mouse wheel for things like deep zoom or scrolling. In Silverlight 4 the APIs for this are built in, so you no longer have to rely on any external reference assemblies. Further, if you have `ItemControls` such as `ListBoxes`, you don't have to write any code to get scrolling to work, as native support for scrolling is built right in to the controls for you.

Similarly, there was no support for right-clicking in Silverlight 3. Therefore doing things like having right-click context menus was impossible. Now you can raise and handle a right-click event just like any other mouse event, such as `MouseLeftButtonDown`. Following is an example of how you would handle and raise a right-click event on a `Rectangle` named `SimpleRectangle`:

```
public MainPage()
{
    // Required to initialize variables
    InitializeComponent();
    SimpleRectangle.MouseRightButtonDown
        += new MouseButtonEventHandler(SimpleRectangle_MouseRightButtonDown);
}

void SimpleRectangle_MouseRightButtonDown(object sender, MouseButtonEventArgs e)
{
        // do something here
}
```

> To disable the default Silverlight context menu you can replace my `// do something here` code above with `e.Handled = true;`.

Further, just like the mouse events, you have access to both `MouseRightButtonDown` as well as `MouseRightButtonUp`.

The Printing API

In Silverlight 4 you can now easily print all, or just parts of your applications. To show you how to do this, let's go into Blend and create a new Silverlight application called `PrintingTest`. You can see my settings in Figure 17-1.

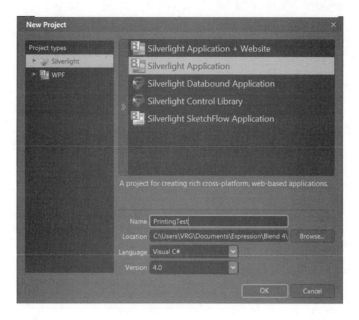

Figure 17-1. Create a new application in Blend 4.

Now that we have our project created, we need to add some visuals so we have something to print. I think an image would be the quickest solution. Let's add an image now.

1. Right-click on the `PrintingTest` folder in Blend's **Projects** panel and left-click **Add Existing Item**, as I am doing in Figure 17-2.

Figure 17-2. Add an Existing Item to the project.

2. Navigate to an image on your hard drive and double-click it.

3. When the image appears in the **Projects** panel, drag it onto the artboard, as I have done in Figure 17-3.

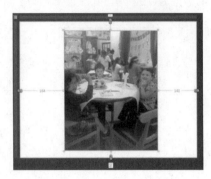

Figure 17-3. Drag the image to the artboard.

Now that we have some visuals to print, we can press Control+Shift+B to build the application and then switch over to Visual Studio 2010 to add the code that will allow us to print our main `LayoutRoot` Grid (which contains the image we just added).

In Visual Studio 2010, right under the `InitializeComponent();` call, we are going to raise and handle a `MouseLeftButtonDown` event on this, the entire application. To do that:

1. Place your mouse cursor after the `IntializeComponent();` call, add another line, type **this.MouseLeftButtonDown** and type **+=** and press the Tab key twice. This should give you what I have here:

```
public MainPage()
{
        // Required to initialize variables
        InitializeComponent();
    this.MouseLeftButtonDown +=
new MouseButtonEventHandler(MainPage_MouseLeftButtonDown);
}

void MainPage_MouseLeftButtonDown(object sender, MouseButtonEventArgs e)
{
    throw new NotImplementedException();
}
```

2. Now erase the default code and create the new `PrintDocument`, as I have done below:

```
void MainPage_MouseLeftButtonDown(object sender, MouseButtonEventArgs e)
{
    PrintDocument printDoc = new PrintDocument();


}
```

3. Next you need to tell the printing API what you want to print. In this case we specify the `LayoutRoot` Grid:

```
void MainPage_MouseLeftButtonDown(object sender, MouseButtonEventArgs e)
{
    PrintDocument printDoc = new PrintDocument();
    printDoc.PrintPage += (s, args) =>
    {
        args.PageVisual = LayoutRoot;
    };

}
```

4. The last thing you need to do is to tell `printDoc` to print, as I have done here:

```
void MainPage_MouseLeftButtonDown(object sender, MouseButtonEventArgs e)
{
    PrintDocument printDoc = new PrintDocument();
    printDoc.PrintPage += (s, args) =>
    {
        args.PageVisual = LayoutRoot;
    };

    printDoc.Print("MyPrintJob");

}
```

That's all there is to it! Press F5 to run the application and click anywhere on the page when it loads in the browser. Notice that your Print dialog box appears. Go ahead and print the document, and you will see the image we added as a nice printed page! As you can imagine, the print API has endless possibilities for Silverlight applications, from images to business applications. In fact, I think it would be a good idea to go back to the PhotoBooth application we made back in Chapter 14 and add an option to be able to print your creations out. Consider that a challenge.

ICommand Support

The `ButtonBase` and `Hyperlink Buttons` now support ICommand infrastructures. This allows `Buttons` to bind to commands rather than execute `EventHandlers` in their code-behind files directly. This makes for easier unit testing, as your tests don't require a rendered UI to make sure your code executes correctly. Further, this support allows for implementation of popular development patterns such as the very popular Model-View-ViewModel pattern we saw in Chapter 15, where the code is executed in ViewModels rather than the Views which contain the UI.

Addition of the RichTextArea Control

The `RichTextArea` control is something I like to refer to as a `TextBlock` on steroids. That is, it is a text area that allows to you include formatted `Text` (bold, italics, underline, and more) along with other UI elements such as `Buttons`, `Images`, and so forth. This would be a control that is great for implementing a newspaper-style application. You can see an example of a `RichTextArea` in Figure 17-4.

Figure 17-4. A `RichTextArea` control.

Clipboard API

In Silverlight 4 you have access to the Clipboard. Prior to Silverlight 4 this was difficult and only possible in Internet Explorer. Following is an example of how you can add text to the machine's Clipboard memory:

```
Clipboard.SetText("Foundation Blend 4 with Silverlight 4");
```

Network Authentication

There are times when you may want your Silverlight applications to interact with web services, such as the Twitter or Facebook APIs. In order to do this, you need to be able to authenticate the user via a username and password. More often than not, the username and password will be different from the credentials of the person logged into that machine. For this reason, Microsoft makes this type of authentication possible and even easy. The following code is an example of how you would programmatically log a user into a web service:

```
void AutheicateMe(object sender, MouseButtonEventArgs e)
{
    WebRequest.RegisterPrefix("http://",
 System.Net.Browser.WebRequestCreator.ClientHttp);
    WebClient SocialNetworkService = new WebClient();
    SocialNetworkService.Credentials = new NetworkCredential("Myusername",
 "Mypassword");
    SocialNetworkService.UseDefaultCredentials = false;
    SocialNetworkService.DownloadStringCompleted += new
 DownloadStringCompletedEventHandler(SocialNetworkService_DownloadStringCompleted);
    SocialNetworkService.DownloadStringAsync(new
 Uri("http://somesocialnetworkingservice.com/authenticatedservice"));
}

void SocialNetworkService_DownloadStringCompleted(object sender,
 DownloadStringCompletedEventArgs e)
{}
```

Improved Data Binding

Data Binding is the concept of binding a reference to something that is larger or used often in computer programming. Data Binding is a very important concept to Windows Presentation Foundation and now in Silverlight. Microsoft has made some significant improvements for Data Binding in Silverlight 4. I talk quickly about some of those here:

> StringFormat: In Data Binding you can now specify how you would like your String formatted. For example, you can now specify a Data format when binding to a TimeDate object:

```
<TextBox Text="{Binding Path=BirthDay, Mode=OneWay, StringFormat='MM-dd-yyyy'}"/>
```

> FallbackValue: When the object you are binding to is broken, you can now specify a FallbackValue that will appear in this case:

```
<TextBox Text="{Binding Path=ABrokenBindingObject, Mode=OneWay,
FallbackValue=BrokenBinding}" />
```

> TargetNullValue: In instances when the object you are binding to is null, you can now provide a value that will appear in this situation:

```
<TextBox Text="{Binding Path=NullValueObject, Mode=OneWay, TargetNullValue=0}" />
```

> DependencyObject Binding: You can now bind properties of DependencyObjects such as the RenderTransform of a Rectangle. Previously, it was only possible to bind values of FrameworkElements.

Addition of ViewBox

The ViewBox control is a container that can contain one, and only one, child. The difference is that when the ViewBox is scaled it scales its children with it. This makes this a unique content control and one that has been around in WPF for quite some time now. Silverlight developers have long requested this be added to the Silverlight Framework because of its unique abilities. Prior to Silverlight 4 developers had to download and install the Silverlight Toolkit to make use of this control. Now, it is simply available when you install Silverlight 4.

Keyboard Access in Full-screen Mode

Prior to Silverlight 4, users of your applications only had access to a limited set of keys on the keyboard. Now any Silverlight Out-Of-Browser (OOB) application with elevated trust has access to the full keyboard in Full-screen mode. This allows the users to make use of controls such as the TextBox for entering information (text) into your Silverlight applications.

Google Chrome Support

This is the first release of Silverlight to officially support the Google Chrome Browser. Past versions of Silverlight have tended to work in Google Chrome, but now Microsoft has added the Chrome browser to its testing cycle as well as its support matrix.

Right-to-Left Support

Silverlight 4 controls now have a FlowDirection attribute that allows you to specify which way the content of that control is laid out: right-to-left or left-to-right. Consider the following ListBox code:

```
<ListBox
    Background="Pink"
    Width="400">

    <ListBoxItem
        Content="هذا لقرارة شكرا! رسائل اعي جديدة! الأمازونترك استعراض كبري على
الكتاب!" />

    <ListBoxItem
        Content="ترك استعراض كبري على رسائل اعي جديدة! شكرا لقرارة هذا! الأمازون
الكتاب!" />
    <ListBoxItem
        Content="ترك استعراض كبري على اعي جديدة! شكرا لقرارة هذا! الأمازون رسلرلئا
الكتاب!" />
</ListBox>
```

The preceding code is a ListBox with ListBoxItems that have Arabic text in them. If I were to run this application and look at the ListBox, it would look like what I have in Figure 17-5.

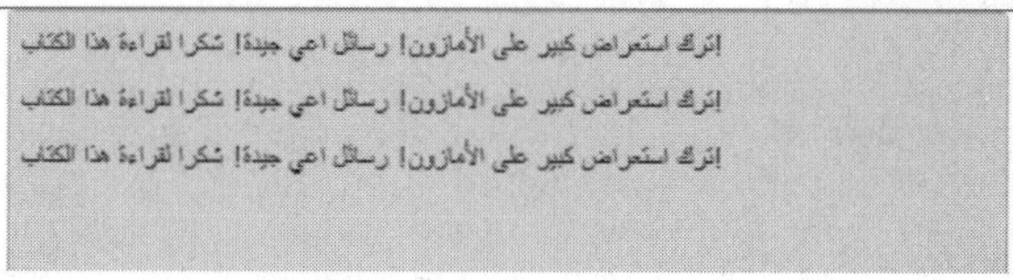

Figure 17-5. A ListBox with the default left-to-right flow direction.

This ListBox would look strange to an Arabic speaker because Arabic is read from the right to the left, whereas this ListBox is laid out from left to right. But what if we were to change the FlowDirection of this ListBox to read like what I have here?

```
<ListBox
    Background="Pink"
    FlowDirection="RightToLeft"
    Width="400">

    <ListBoxItem
        Content="ترك استعراض كبير على الأمازون! رسائل اعي جيدة! شكرا لقراءة هذا
الكتاب!" />

    <ListBoxItem
        Content="ترك استعراض كبير على الأمازون! رسائل اعي جيدة! شكرا لقراءة هذا
الكتاب!" />
    <ListBoxItem
        Content="ترك استعراض كبير على الأمازون! سرلئاي اعي جيدة! شكرا لقراءة هذا
الكتاب!" />
</ListBox>
```

It would look like what you see in Figure 17-6 with the words reading right-to-left.

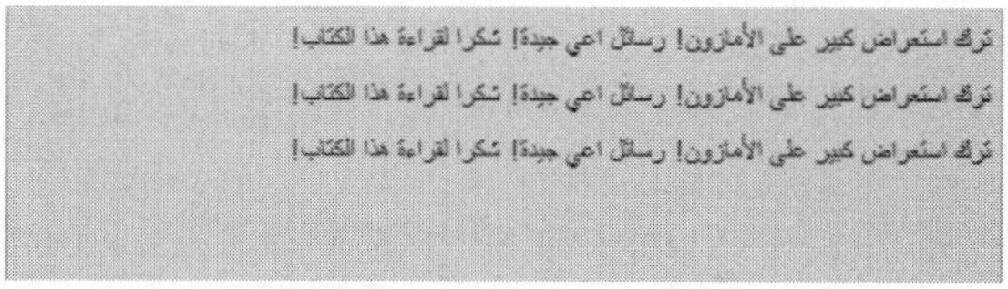

Figure 17-6. The FlowDirection of a ListBox set to right-to-left.

Further, this attribute can be passed down or inherited to child objects.

Managed Extensibility Framework (MEF)

Silverlight 4 has support for the Managed Extensibility Framework, more commonly referred to as MEF. The Managed Extensibility Framework is a library for Silverlight that allows you to build lightweight, reusable, modular applications that can be extended and reused. For the purposes of this book, MEF is quite out of scope, but I encourage you to watch Glen Block's session on MEF at the Professional Developer's Conference (PDC09): http://microsoftpdc.com/Sessions/FT24.

Offline Digital Rights Management (DRM)

PlayReady is a platform developed by Microsoft to provide digital rights management for mobile devices. Silverlight 2.0, since its release in October 2008, has supported content restricted or protected by PlayReady. Until the release of Silverlight 4, PlayReady only supported Silverlight on connected playback with streaming or progressive-downloaded content. Now, however, the PlayReady protection is available offline in order to support three key business models of consumer content: Purchase, Rental, and Subscription.

Fluid UI Support in Items Controls

Microsoft has added new States to `ItemsControl` for a more fluid User Experience (UX). These new States are `BeforeLoaded`, `Loaded`, and `Unloaded`. This allows the developer or designer to add animated transitions between States and thus appear to be more fluid, as opposed to snappy or choppy.

Cross-Domain Networking Made Easier

Some services require a Cross-Domain policy file commonly named `crossdomain.xml` or `clientaccesspolicy.xml`, which are required to use services across domains. Microsoft has loosened the restrictions on this requirement, so that now in Silverlight 4 if you have a trusted application these cross-domain files are no longer required.

TextTrimming

In Silverlight 4 the `TextBlock` now has a `TextTrimming` property that, like WPF, allows you to use the `WordEllipsis` trimming option. This add an `Ellipsis` when the length of the `Text` value exceeds the size of the width of the `TextBlock`. For example, a `TextBlock` with a `Width` value of 100 and a `Text` value of *Peter Piper picked a peck of pickled peppers* would look like what you see in Figure 17-7:

Peter Piper...

Figure 17-7. A `TextBlock` with `WordEllipsis` `TextTrimming`.

The code for the `TextBlock` in Figure 17-7 follows. Notice the `WordEllipsis` value for the `TextTrimming` property.

```
<TextBlock
    HorizontalAlignment="Left"
    VerticalAlignment="Top"
    Width="100"
    TextTrimming="WordEllipsis"
    Margin="8,139,0,0"><Span
        FontSize="12"
        FontFamily="Arial"><Run
            Text="Peter Piper picked a peck of pickled peppers"
/></Span></TextBlock>
```

Summary

The advancements in Silverlight 4 have come a long way from Silverlight 3, and they are quickly making Silverlight the choice for developers, designers, and businesses wanting to develop or run Rich Internet Applications (RIAs). With new APIs like the Webcam, Printing, and MouseHandling, performing complex tasks in Silverlight is easier than ever before. Further, new controls such as the `RichTextArea` and `ViewBox` make pulling off complex user interfaces faster than in other versions of Silverlight. Finally, with all these advancements, including those added to Data Binding, Item Controls, and the addition of support for Managed Extensibility Framework and ICommand, the Silverlight platform is making development of complex, data-rich business applications faster and more fun than ever before.

Index

B

N

You Need the Companion eBook

Your purchase of this book entitles you to buy the companion PDF-version eBook for only $10. Take the weightless companion with you anywhere.

We believe this Apress title will prove so indispensable that you'll want to carry it with you everywhere, which is why we are offering the companion eBook (in PDF format) for $10 to customers who purchase this book now. Convenient and fully searchable, the PDF version of any content-rich, page-heavy Apress book makes a valuable addition to your programming library. You can easily find and copy code—or perform examples by quickly toggling between instructions and the application. Even simultaneously tackling a donut, diet soda, and complex code becomes simplified with hands-free eBooks!

Once you purchase your book, getting the $10 companion eBook is simple:

❶ Visit **www.apress.com/promo/tendollars/**.

❷ Complete a basic registration form to receive a randomly generated question about this title.

❸ Answer the question correctly in 60 seconds, and you will receive a promotional code to redeem for the $10.00 eBook.

233 Spring Street, New York, NY 10013

Offer valid through 2/11.